MW01244710

BEHIND THE
BLUE-STAR BANNER
A Memoir from the Home Front

Michelle S. Cuthrell

Published in Beaverton, Oregon, by Good Catch Publishing.
www.goodcatchpublishing.com
V1.1

Printed in the United States of America

Table of Contents

DEDICATION

I dedicate this book to my incredible husband,
Captain Matthew Cuthrell,
whose unconditional love, support and encouragement
inspire me to serve as an Army wife;
to now-deceased CPL Jeremy Loveless, whose selfless service and
sacrifice remind me why I serve as an Army wife;
to all the incredible wives of the 2-1 Infantry Battalion of the
172nd Stryker Brigade Combat Team in Fort Wainwright, Alaska,
who modeled for me how to serve as an Army wife;
to my amazing family at Friends Community Church
and in Fairbanks, Alaska,
who provided the encouragement to serve as an Army wife;
to my incredible real-life family, who raised me with the positive
attitude required to serve as an Army wife;
and to Christ, who, through thick and thin, provided the strength
to serve proudly.

INTRODUCTION

I wasn't commissioned, and I didn't enlist, but on May 22, 2004, I joined the Army. My uniform was my white wedding dress, my oath of office, my wedding vows. And though I'd heard an awful lot about becoming an Army wife before I walked down that aisle, when I said "I do," I really had no idea just how much I would be "doing."

Three days before we were married, I got my first clue.

That's when my soon-to-be husband received his very first set of orders as a commissioned officer in the United States Army. He had graduated two weeks earlier from the University of Dayton in Dayton, Ohio, and we had been eagerly awaiting the announcement of our very first duty station.

In the real world, most couples figure out where they're going to live and work, and then get married. Some even start making moving arrangements before the big wedding day. But with the Army, it's never quite that simple. Not only do you have to wait on the Army to figure out when you can move and where you're going to live, but you have to work around the entire system just to plan your own wedding.

When Matt and I got engaged, we were told we had two solid weeks where we could be pretty sure Matt would be available to attend our wedding. After that, all bets were off. So even though I had a semester left to finish my journalism degree at Ithaca College, we decided to get married two weeks after he graduated and just endure the whole long-distance relationship for six months until I could move wherever it was the Army was shipping my husband. After all, it was kind of important to me that the groom show up on the big day.

After many long nights and lots of frustrated tears, we'd finally ironed out the wedding details, but three days before that Cinderella event, we still had no idea about all our other life details — like where we were going to live for the next three or four years of our lives.

The wedding date was nearing, and I was starting to get nervous. We had the wedding planned, the reception booked, all we needed to know was where the heck to send all the wedding gifts once we returned from the honeymoon.

BEHIND THE BLUE-STAR BANNER

Growing up in the suburbs of Dayton, Ohio, in a development across from Fulmer's strawberry field and just behind what used to be an old pear orchard, I'd led a pretty sheltered Midwestern life. Yes, I'd attended college in the state of New York, and yes, I'd spent a semester abroad in Singapore. I'd definitely accumulated some world-class cultural experiences under my belt. But at heart, I was still a hometown country fruit farm girl to the core, and the idea of moving to any city the Army happened to pick out scared me just a bit. At least before, I had the comfort of college campuses to keep me safe. But now I was about to enter the real world, and I didn't know what I thought about living in places like Fort Polk, Louisiana, or Landstuhl, Germany.

As we walked hand in hand into the University of Dayton ROTC office, I started to shake. The Army wouldn't really send us somewhere crazy, would they? We were just hometown Ohio kids starting our lives together — they wouldn't move us any farther than driving distance from the family we'd been surrounded by our entire lives — or would they?

As Matt picked up his very first set of orders, I closed my eyes and clenched my fists and prayed a quick prayer that we'd be living somewhere calm, somewhere normal, somewhere I could at least bathe in the sun on long, lonely days away from family.

"Arkansas?" he questioned as he stared curiously at the packet of orders in his hands, looking desperately disappointed.

For a moment, I thought, *Arkansas, what a great choice! It's warm, it's in the South, it's within driving distance of our parents. That's not so bad!*

But my sunbathing dreams were shattered when the secretary giggled, took the orders from my husband's hand and pointed out that we were being sent to the state with the abbreviation AK — for Alaska.

Goodbye sunshine, hello Last Frontier. Not exactly the close-to-home, familiar culture, sunshine paradise I had hoped for.

But with an impending wedding and nearly 400 guests coming into town for our big day, I also didn't have much time to analyze it, either.

So one week after we said "I do," I had a whole lot of other "doing" to do — winterizing Matt's truck, packing for frozen tundra climates and all the other normal tasks any couple completes the day they return from a honeymoon in the tropics. And we only

INTRODUCTION

had one day to do it in before I had to be in Washington, D.C. for a summer journalism internship and then my new husband had to head to San Antonio for his Officer Basic Course, and from there on to Fairbanks to report to his first duty station. We were already starting our rushed and down-to-the-last-minute new life together, just the three of us: Army, husband and wife.

For being the most famous bureaucracy on the face of the planet, the Army sure didn't take long to put the paperwork through on that motion. I went from "Michelle" to "military dependent" in less than a week.

At first, it was kind of exciting.

Upon marriage, the Army issues you a military identification card to make you feel like part of this special club or this secret society — the kind for "members only." They invite you to spouses' clubs and hold craft fairs on post, plan company picnics and create clandestine social affairs for the whole family. Then they seduce you with visions of men in uniform and military balls, and somehow forget to mention the ticket to those fancy formals is the invasion of something that must be so minor and so irrelevant that they fail to remember it even needs to be said — just the claim to your husband's body, marriage and life.

When I finally moved to Alaska in January 2005, eight months after our wedding day, to finally be with my husband, I started to figure that out. Matt's body and Matt's life weren't mine — they were the Army's, and that meant they could do whatever they deemed fit with them as long as they could call him "Lieutenant Cuthrell."

With a war in progress, that's exactly what they told us they needed to do.

Just before my arrival in Fairbanks, the Department of the Army announced that the 172nd Stryker Brigade Combat Team out of Fort Wainwright would be rotating into Iraq for a one-year deployment beginning in August of that year.

After eight months away from my husband, I was given just nine short months to prepare to endure 12 long months alone.

I felt so cheated, and for so long, I was so angry. The logistics of my husband's job had already forced us to endure the first months of married life on two different coasts, and all I wanted, all I asked for, was some extended quality time with the man I absolutely could not live without. Every other married couple we knew enjoyed that privilege and took it for granted as one of the benefits of married life. It was so frustrating to know that the one thing every other couple saw as normal — living together on a consistent basis — wouldn't be a reality for us. At least not this year.

As the days got lighter and lighter in Alaska after the short five-hour winter days, I was forced to confront the fact that soon, my husband would indeed be deployed. As it got harder and harder to kiss him goodbye in the mornings or be away from him for even grocery shopping trips at night, I realized that if I was going to make it through this deployment, I was going to need some help from someone with far greater abilities than me.

I'd believed in a higher power all my life — I just couldn't fathom a mountain stream or a Maine sunset that *wasn't* created by someone greater than myself — but it wasn't until I was 13 that I decided I wanted to develop a relationship with this higher power. I asked Jesus to be my Savior in eighth grade, and spent the next 10 years praising and serving and questioning Him all at the same time. My crazy requests and ultimatums were nothing new to the Lord who had quickly become my best friend and confidant throughout my tumultuous teenage years, and I figured He'd just laugh at my attempt to play *Let's Make a Deal.* Maybe it would even charm Him into conceding.

"Yo, Jeez," I called out in my very best assertive-but-needy voice. "Listen, if you just give me the strength to get through this deployment, I promise to conjure up the strength to have a good attitude about it."

So there.

Although I'm sure the creator of the universe accepts ultimatums, especially from selfish 23-year-old newlyweds who think the universe revolves around them and their needs — not that I was one of them, of course — He did somehow humor me, in spite of myself. All of a sudden, I felt stronger, more sure that I could manage this deployment, and that I needed to manage it to support my husband. Out of nowhere and because of no other reason than I knocked and asked, God poured out incredible serenity and steadfastness, and I stood in the rain and absorbed like a sponge.

What a transformation it caused.

Instead of viewing the Army as this evil empire out to ruin my marriage and harass my hubby, I suddenly began to view it as an essential and invaluable organization to keep our country de-

INTRODUCTION

fended and our children safe. Instead of viewing my husband's job as this career choice that put me on the back burner, I began to see it as a noble commitment to freedom that, above all, he made to protect mine.

From that point on, everything began to change.

Rather than disassociating myself from the Army by telling people I was married to a military man, I would make a point of calling myself an Army wife — and a proud one at that.

Rather than evading conversations about the motives of the military in the United States, I began to engage in them, defending to the death my husband's strong convictions of service and country.

I stopped complaining about the long days and nights Matt spent away training in the field, and started thanking God that the Army was taking the time to properly prepare my husband before sending him off to war.

And the day my amazing husband said goodbye, I kissed him passionately and sent him off proudly, knowing I was sacrificing a year of time with my husband so that he could complete a job that would mean years of freedom for many, many others.

Of course, all this doesn't mean I love deployment, and it doesn't mean I agree with every decision the government makes and has made about the use of it. It doesn't mean I'm positive and upbeat all the time, doesn't mean that I sing songs and jog jigs about how much I love the Army.

And it definitely doesn't mean that I display a great attitude about deployment all the time; daily, deliberate attitude adjustments and perspective evaluations are just an everyday part of military wife life.

But it does mean that I stand tall and proud, knowing that the selflessness the Army demands from my husband — the same selflessness I resented so many months ago — also makes my husband the most self-sacrificing, altruistic and noble man I know. The very things that once angered me about the Army taking him away are the same things that make him the most amazing husband or friend a woman could ever ask for. I know above all that the reason my husband is gone for a year is not because he chose a job over me, but because he chose freedom, service and my personal protection over being physically with me 24 hours a day.

It's hard to complain about a man who prioritizes some of

BEHIND THE BLUE-STAR BANNER

life's most admirable qualities.

Today, I proudly associate myself with my deployed husband and hang a blue-star banner on the back door of our humble home. Though that flag no longer sits on the ledge of my Fairbanks front window, I display it proudly as I endure second and third deployments on the home front of our new duty station in Fort Lewis, Washington.

This symbolic flag means that inside sits an immediate family member of a deployed soldier — someone who is likely spending all her cash on flat rate boxes, all her time on late-night e-mails. It means that inside this home is someone exhausted from performing chores for two, acting as a parent for two and trying to maintain a normal life for two. But most of all, it means that inside this home, there is someone who is fighting her selfish human nature every single day so she can admirably honor a hero who deserves all the support in the world.

I hope these newspaper columns, journal entries, personal letters and emotional commentaries I've written as both a journalist and a struggling Army wife provide at least a small glimpse into the world of stress and satisfaction behind that sacred blue-star banner.

CHAPTER ONE
GOODBYES

You never think it's going to happen to you.

Deployment is supposed to be something someone else's wife deals with, something someone else's family endures. It's supposed to be that horrible, awful trial you watch in Hollywood movies — the kind famous producers use over and over again to draw in viewers and tug on heartstrings. It's something you read about in newspapers, something you hear about on TV. But it's not supposed to be something that happens to you or your family — especially not within the first year and a half of your marriage.

When you sign on to become a military wife, you have to face the fact that all those "it's not supposed to" moments can and do apply to you — no matter your age, marital status, location or preference.

I was 23 years old and 11 weeks pregnant with our first child when my husband deployed to Iraq.

As we drove silently onto the Fort Wainwright post that mid-August day, I couldn't help but think that it was all just a really bad dream. Everything around me, from the blinking Arctic Warriors sign to the uniformed soldiers packing up their rucks, seemed to be moving in slow motion, and the air seemed still, almost frozen in time. Nothing seemed real — not even my husband.

Several times on our short drive to post, the man I'd married just over a year ago leaned over and squeezed my hand, stared into my eyes and mouthed the words, "I love you." He seemed so serious, looked so staunch, and in this strange way, I felt like I was saying goodbye to this person I didn't even recognize, and this person I might never see again.

Matt was rarely a serious guy. He took his job seriously, and was certainly passionate about his family and his affairs, but when it came to us, he was always playful and fun. We were always that goofy couple — the kind who spent Saturday nights dancing in gas station parking lots, who got a kick out of playing Rummy on late afternoon picnics. We held dance parties in our home and played stupid rhyming games for fun. On date nights, we'd hold silly contests, at dinner, we'd make stupid faces.

BEHIND THE BLUE-STAR BANNER

So when he grabbed my hand and bit his lip, I knew this year away wasn't going to be like all the other long-distance dating games we'd played in the past. This was going to be serious. It was going to be for real. And not real like all the sappy war movies we'd rented on Saturday nights.

Not even the goodbye part.

You'd think if the Army was going to take away your husband for a year, that they'd at least give you the romantic, movie-star goodbye — the kind where wives dress in their Sunday best and take their men in uniform to the airfield or the airport, waving their silk scarves in the wind as their husbands march boldly onto the aircraft and wave lovingly from plane-side windows.

Practically and logistically, it just doesn't work that way.

I was wearing jeans and a cardigan when my husband pulled our little Corolla to a stop in front of the Headquarters Company of the 2-1 Infantry Battalion building. We had exactly 15 minutes to unload his ruck and pack, say our last words and kiss goodbye. There was no runway send-off, no getting-on-the-plane type of closure. In fact, the soldiers wouldn't even leave for hours after we'd dropped them off. But they couldn't very well keep emotional wives hanging around as they cleaned their weapons and packed their bags and bussed out to the nearest Air Force base, where they would deploy later that day.

So instead of at an airport, our farewell kiss took place in a car. Instead of the big running-hug goodbye, it was a lean-in, lean-out, start-the-car-and-go-before-you-can't-anymore type moment.

In our last moment together, I mustered up the courage to hand my beloved husband a sealed envelope with a letter I'd been trying to write for months, but just couldn't manage to put down on paper. Before he left me for a year, I just had to make sure in the deepest corners of his heart that he knew how much I loved him, and how every inch of my soul was so incredibly proud of him.

August 16, 2005

Dear Matt,

After all the long months we've been talking about the possibility of deployment, the reality of that situation is finally here.

GOODBYES

You're going to Iraq, and you won't be back for an entire year.

I think I've probably done a pretty good job expressing to you the hurt, frustration and disappointment I'm going through with this deployment, but I don't know if I've ever done a good enough job at expressing to you the pride and respect I have for the way you are viewing this mission.

Matt, I'm so very, very proud of you. You have volunteered for the hardest job in the United States; you have volunteered to be a soldier. And you haven't just volunteered half-heartedly — you have thrown your entire heart and soul into this job, at making your soldiers better soldiers, at making your men better men. You have brought this platoon of random boys to a place where they call each other teammates — a place where they have been able to bond and really care about the success of their unit. You helped do that, Matt. You have done wonders with these young men, and I see it every time I meet with them.

I also see the respect they have for you. I see the way they look at you when you're not looking, the way they shake your hand and honor you just with their gazes. You have earned their respect and their trust, and that's something that no OBC or ROTC course can teach, but something you, Matt, have instilled in them. And I couldn't be prouder.

I couldn't be prouder that, as a medical platoon leader, my husband is going to bring medical treatment not only to his soldiers, but also to hurt Iraqis. I couldn't be prouder that he is sacrificing the most important things in his life to put someone else's life before his. I couldn't be prouder that my husband is doing this all with honor, integrity and a fighting American heart. It's something I love so much about you that I never take the time to tell you about. I'm telling you now, Matt. I love your spirit. You make me proud to be an American.

I also couldn't be prouder of the attitude you are taking at completing this mission. While I've spent many long hours in tears, begging you not to go, you've spent many long hours in prayer, asking God to send you where He wants you. It takes a godly man to go where God takes him, and to trust in the Lord completely. I think you are that man, Matt. And I know He has a plan for you over there — I know He wouldn't take you unless He needed you specifically to complete that mission.

I think He's also sending you to learn more about being a fa-

ther. You are a father to the 31 men in your platoon — you shelter them, you protect them, you guide them, you love them. The things you are going to learn from this year in Iraq with your platoon will apply so much more to parenthood than you could have ever dreamed. Take the opportunity to be a father to these soldiers, as God will be being a father to your little one until you can come safely home. Remember always that this little child of ours needs a daddy — needs a strong daddy — and couldn't have even imagined a better father than the one who will be coming into its life come August.

Matt, you are going to be the most amazing father in the world. That's one of the things I'm looking forward to most — seeing you with our child, because I know that you will love this child, protect this child, cherish this child, nurture this child more than any other child has ever been loved or cared for before. You are going to be an incredible dad, and I couldn't have asked for a better man to parent my children.

For the baby, and for me, please come home safely. I know God's protective hands will be around you, and we'll be praying for you daily. Always. Know always that I love you with all my heart and that you always have and always will be my very best friend. I love you so much, Matt Cuthrell. Come home soon.

Love,
The Wife Who Adores You

As he clenched this letter in the palm of his left hand and I stared into those hazel-green eyes I'd fallen in love with for the past four years, I stopped to memorize every feature of my husband's face — the shape of his nose, the crook of his lips. I wanted to remember — I wanted to remember everything.

I never wanted to forget.

In seconds, I felt his warm breath on my cheek, and as he pressed his lips sweetly to mine for the last time, hot prickles crept up my throat.

"You are my world, Michelle."

A squeeze, another peck and then he was gone.

As I drove away, tears streaming down my face, I watched that precious man enter the side door of his building, knowing I wouldn't see that uniform nametape again until he returned one year

GOODBYES

later.

When I stumbled through our garage door 15 minutes later, I just couldn't stop weeping. I couldn't catch my breath, and I couldn't see through the pools collecting in the corners of my eyes. I felt as if I were hyperventilating, as if some other person were suctioning all the air from the room in one of those really bad dreams where you wake up choking and sweating and swearing you were near death. But when I opened my eyes, my life was still real. My husband was still gone. I was still alone.

My heart physically ached with a pain in my chest that felt like heartburn. I was pregnant, and I knew I had to calm down, both for myself and for the baby.

I made my way, hand-by-hand, through the hallway, steadying myself on the whitewashed walls of our post housing, as I headed for the family room. I knew if I could just cuddle up under my favorite fleece, I could distract myself with a TBS movie or a comedy of sorts. But when I flipped on the tube, my local news station greeted me with news that sobered my soul.

"More dead this morning in an explosion in Iraq. It is unknown whether any U.S. soldiers were injured or killed."

My stomach churned as a vomiting sensation crept up the back of my throat.

I was a journalist by trade. I'd earned my bachelor's degree in journalism nine months earlier, and I'd worked for local newspapers and interned at various magazines and television news stations throughout my college career. At the very heart of my professional life was a desire for truth motivated by deep curiosity.

In the midst of that tumultuous moment, my deep, inbred curiosity didn't know how to battle my raw human emotion. I wanted to know — I wanted to know everything about where my husband was going to be, who he was going to be working with and how that alliance was progressing. I wanted to know the groups who were his enemies and the tactics they used to devastate their foes. And yet, with the love of my life in danger there every day, I wanted to know nothing. Ignorance had to be bliss, at least for the next 12 months.

My mind spinning, I tried to steady myself on the arm of our black leather sofa as I stood to find yet another distraction. I tried turning to the fridge for some sort of comfort food, but all I found there were the remains of my husband's trademark jar of dill pickles and some leftovers from the last dinner we'd shared before deployment.

The reality baseball clocked me in the head yet again.

"Who's going to eat the pickles?" I wailed, falling to the floor like a 2-year-old girl who'd just been told she was banished from ice cream for the next 12 months. "I don't even like pickles!"

It was one of those moments you almost wished your mama could see, just so she could slap you upside the face, pull you to your feet and shake you silly until you snapped out of your theatrical tantrum.

But my mama lived thousands of miles away and calling her to pull me out of my pity ditch was not at the top of my to-do list the morning my husband deployed to a war zone. I liked my pity ditch, even if I knew I didn't want to stay there too long.

Our 9-month-old beagle puppy wasn't doing any better than me.

Poor Ranger sat by the front window all day long, waiting for Matt's black F-150 to pull in the driveway and for his favorite man in the world to come wrestle for a few minutes before dinner. Every time a black truck passed, the poor puppy barked and ran to the garage door, wagging his tail in anticipation.

"Ranger!" I yelled through snot and sobs. "Don't you get it? He's not coming home!"

But day after day, he followed the same routine, eagerly awaiting the arrival of his master. And day after day, it would break my heart to put him in his cage at night without that much-anticipated play date with Daddy. It took several weeks before he gave up the 6 p.m. routine and realized that Matt just wasn't coming home.

Through it all, I just cried and moped and prayed the day would hurry up and pass so I could be one day closer to reuniting with my love.

Before deployment, I'd always been a life embracer — the type to seize the day and make the most of it, the kind to count the moments and make them last. But for the first time in my life, I found myself just wasting those minutes and wishing for 9 p.m. so I could crawl into bed and sleep my heartache away.

For three days, I became a chronic time checker — glancing at the clock every five minutes to see how much time had passed so it could hurry up and be tomorrow. I found myself taking three, four or even five showers a day to pass the time and keep myself occu-

GOODBYES

pied. I couldn't read because every book somehow brought me back to Matt, and I couldn't watch the news because I couldn't handle the updates on Iraq. When I viewed movies, I found myself reaching my right arm across the rest on our couch trying to hold the missing hand of a husband gone to war. I was miserable, and I couldn't snap myself out of it.

I climbed into bed at the normal 9 p.m. the Thursday after Matt deployed, sad, lonely and wishing a year had already passed us by. As I snuggled under the comforter, staring at my ceiling and wading slowly into the pool of depression that was quickly becoming my life, my desk-side landline rang, shaking me from my stupor and startling me from my daze.

I glanced at the clock.

11 p.m.

My heart froze. Anyone calling my house at 11 p.m. when my husband was deployed could not be delivering good news.

Hesitantly I placed my hand on the receiver, took a deep breath and picked up the phone.

"Hello?" I asked, almost bracing myself for the worst.

Silence.

"Hello?" I repeated, louder and more irritated this time.

"Michelle?" it crackled in broken tones.

It was the sweetest voice I'd ever heard.

"Baby! Oh my gosh, are you okay? Are you hurt? Did you get shot?" My heart raced as the words tumbled out of my mouth.

"No, baby," he laughed. "I just made it to Kuwait."

Matt proceeded to explain the long few days of travel from Fairbanks to Kuwait and the ridiculously long lines to use the phone and Internet at their staging base in the area. It wasn't so much his words that touched me; it was the tone. That voice — I had missed it so much in the long three days I'd endured its absence.

"How are you, love?" he asked so gently, so calmly, so lovingly.

I pushed the hot prickles back down my throat and swallowed hard.

"I'm fine," I lied pathetically, trying to convince him with my very lame voice acting skills that I was just peachy.

"Are you really?"

He knew me too well.

The fire burned my throat as the first vocalizations of tears escaped from my lips.

"Matt, this is so hard — so much harder than I thought it would be. I don't know if I can do this. I don't know how I'm going to make it 12 months. I haven't even made it 12 days..." I brushed my pajama shirtsleeve against the side of my face, trying to wipe off the tears I felt dampening my cheeks.

"Michelle, you can do this. We can do this. And do you know why?"

Silence.

"Michelle, we can do this because we have asked God for the strength. He's not going to give us anything the three of us can't handle together. It's not going to be easy, and it's not going to be fun, but we have a choice to lean on God's strength, or to deny it and try to make it through this thing on our own."

I inhaled a deep breath, replayed his words in my mind and released the warm air again from my lips.

He was right.

"And do you know what's even cooler? I left a piece of myself there to be with you. To help you to remember to lean on God's strength."

The baby. Had I not been clutching a toilet that very morning from the sickness that first trimester of pregnancy brings, I almost could have forgotten about the fact that we were going to have a child. Together. We were going to have a child! The news was only a few weeks old and it still lit an unexplainable joy in my soul every time I thought about it. God had blessed us with a child. In the middle of this lonely time, God had blessed me with company — permanent company — and company who would be a piece of Matt for me every single day that I physically couldn't have him in my life.

Why was I not embracing that?

"You did," I replied, smiling for the first time in three days. "You left me the most beautiful piece of yourself with me."

I placed my free hand on my stomach and grinned.

"And you know what else?" I chimed in for the first time. "You'll even get to experience this little piece of you the day it gets to meet me!"

I could hear him smiling on the other end of the line.

"It's not for certain, Michelle," he reminded me carefully, "but the commanders said they'd do everything they could to schedule

GOODBYES

my two weeks of R and R around your due date."

All soldiers deploying to a combat zone for 12 months or more were allotted two weeks of rest and relaxation in the middle of the deployment to return home and spend time with their friends and family. While our other non-pregnant friends were meeting their husbands in exotic locations for their two weeks of leave, Matt and I were planning a glamorous stay at Bassett Army Hospital.

"We're not going to worry about it. God has a plan," he reminded. "And you know what? The good news is that today I'm one day closer to seeing my beautiful wife again."

Butterflies danced in my stomach. Even after nearly four years together, my husband still made me blush.

"One day closer to seeing my awesome husband again," I answered.

I couldn't wipe the smile from my lips. For a moment, I just basked in that glorious silence — that time that I knew my husband was safe, well and as in love with me as ever. I relished that second and let its warmth and glow chase away the shadows I'd been carrying around for days. I felt good.

"Well, baby, I'm so sorry to do this," he interrupted, "but I'm going to have to get off the phone now. There are a line of Joes 10 miles long to call their families, and I don't want to monopolize the phone time."

My heart sank. Matt could tell.

"But I love you with all my heart, and I promise to call you whenever I can. Please know that I love you, and give the baby a kiss for me."

The moment was over.

"I love you, too, baby."

"Sweet dreams."

"Sweet dreams."

I rubbed the bulge barely protruding from my stomach as I kissed the pad of my pointer finger and gently placed it on my belly button.

"This is from Daddy," I whispered, and I hung up the phone and turned out the light.

CHAPTER TWO
ADJUSTMENT

From my prior experiences with the long-distance relationship, I knew that the first few days (or weeks, in this case) were always the worst, and that once you made it through them, you could make it through anything.

So when September greeted me with its wonderful cool breezes and colorful crunching leaves, I knew the worst of the "goodbye" portion of deployment was indeed over. We'd said farewell in August, and once that month turned, there was this unwritten rule that you had to move on with your life. And so I did — with much more ease than I anticipated. At least at first.

After my encouraging and supportive conversation with Matt, I suddenly found myself surrounded by a flock of other incredibly supportive people. My coffee group members offered smiles and hugs, my hometown friends sent letters and love. My church set me up with an adopted family, my family set me up with care packages and roses. Even the town of Fairbanks donned yellow ribbons and American flags to help support the deployed soldiers and the spouses they left behind.

In addition to these wonderful new support systems and constant words of encouragement, out of nowhere, and after three months of unemployment and constant job-searching, I simultaneously scored two different jobs. My church offered me a volunteer coordinator position and my local NBC affiliate news station offered me a part-time cameraperson/reporter job.

Starting new jobs is always stressful and time consuming, but starting two at the same time my husband was deployed to a foreign country was almost overwhelming. I spent six hours a day, five days a week, at Friends Community Church, learning how to serve and coordinate the volunteers and ministry leaders in our church.

I'd leave Friends on Thursdays and Fridays to rush a few blocks over to KTVF, where I had just enough time to speak to the experienced cameraman and refresh myself on the camera shots before we shot the 6 p.m. newscast.

After we closed the Fairbanks Evening News, I'd rush home in time to let poor Ranger outside and complete all the chores my husband used to complete for me.

If that weren't enough, the book I had been volunteering to help produce for our church was released just 11 days into the month and marketed in Fairbanks bookstores.

With all these huge tasks on the table before me, I almost didn't have time to ponder deployment.

That didn't mean I didn't miss Matt.

Though I stayed busy all day long running between jobs, checking on *Free to Fall* status at the two Christian bookstores, taking over Matt's old chores and learning my new roles as volunteer coordinator and cameraperson/reporter, every inch of me felt heavy without Matt there to come home to at night. I hated not being able to share stories from my day or funny moments from my life. I hated not being able to come home to someone who would just wrap his arms around me and let me collapse in them after a tiring day on the floor. And I hated not being able to hug the one man who made my life worth sharing.

What I hated more than all of those, however, was not being able to communicate with the love of my life at all.

I hadn't heard from Matt since that first phone call when he arrived in Kuwait two weeks earlier, and though I'd sent five to 10 e-mails a day to his Army e-mail account, I'd heard nothing back. It was so difficult to hold a conversation with an imaginary image of a husband at war with no response.

Though I was surrounded by hundreds of people all day long and too busy to even clean my house or check my mail, I was somehow so completely lonely without the man who was my other whole (I learned long ago that, in marriage, it takes two "wholes" to make a "whole"). Though I deliberately worked crazily to forget about how much I missed him, somehow, filling that void with work made me miss him even more.

Two weeks into my hectic schedule, after a long day of writing, reading and chasing down volunteers to serve in the church, I stumbled in my garage door at nearly 9 p.m., flung my purse on the nearby futon and collapsed in my cheap computer chair.

I'd never received an e-mail from Matt, but I thought I might as well check before heading to bed.

There in my box for the very first time was the gift that would become my life and joy for the next 12 months of my life.

BEHIND THE BLUE-STAR BANNER

Hey, beautiful!
August 27, 2005

Hey, babydoll!!! Look who has joined the cyber age! Man, I miss you like crazy, and since the Internet is slow, I won't be able to read all your e-mails today. But I promise I will get to them, love. Did I mention how much I miss you? Man, I can't take it.

So how are you? How is the baby? The dog? Fill me in on the details. So you got two jobs?! God is amazing. I can't believe that. That is so cool. And it seems like you won't have any problems doing both with the baby and appointments.

Sounds as if you are keeping really busy, and that's good because it helps with the missing part. I know if I wasn't so busy, I would fall apart from how much I miss you and think about you. But that doesn't stop the time I sit in my cot trying to go to sleep just dreaming and thinking about you — and worrying, too.

I know you are such a strong woman. I know you can handle this with no problem. But I still worry a lot. I hope you are really doing well and taking care of yourself. I am so sorry that I can't be there for you and help with chores and sickness and the dog and baby stuff. I feel horrible that I am not there for you. But please know that I am there with you at all times. Because we are connected. I love you, Michelle, and please have an awesome day. And please pass on the following to all on our mass e-mail list:

Hey, everyone! Just dropping a line from Kuwait to let everyone know that I am safe and doing well. It is hot here — the thermometer only reads 120 degrees and the needle gets buried every day! The food is good, and we have kept really busy preparing, which helps me keep my mind off how much I miss Michelle. If you live in Alaska and have the chance, please give her a hug for me.

Aside from that, there's not much else going on. Thanks for the prayers and hope you all have an amazing day!

Love,
Matt

ADJUSTMENT

Though it was incredible to receive that first line of communication from my husband, it made the deployment so real, and it kicked in the missing-Matt reflex that I had tried to suppress with busyness for the first two weeks he was gone. My heart hurt, and I hated pain. So to combat it, I just made it a point to take Matt's advice and get busier and stay away from the places that reminded me most of that precious man. Namely, home.

For the first time in my life, I started making excuses to stay at work late and run around until dusk, which is actually quite late on the tail end of an Alaskan Midnight Sun summer.

As long as I wasn't sitting home alone, I didn't have to confront the fact that my husband wasn't there with me — that he was indeed deployed to a war zone, and a dangerous one, at that.

So all day long, I filled myself with even more busy work than I was assigned. At my church job, I volunteered to take work home. I spent one week of post-dinnertime activity creating and assembling welcome packets, the next, researching feature story ideas for Channel 11. I started making lists for myself of all the tasks that needed to be completed before Matt came home and convinced myself that they needed to be completed now, just one month into the deployment.

I cleaned out all the closets, reorganized the garage, detailed both vehicles and redecorated the house. Then I joined a pregnancy support group, a book club, Big Brothers Big Sisters, two Bible studies, a small group and even, for a short time, a scrapbooking club.

Mentally, I was doing great. But emotionally, I was struggling. Not because I was taking on too much — no, I'd always been one to multitask and dive into the involvement pool head first — but because I was being so heavily criticized by others for dealing with deployment by staying busy.

Some acquaintances told me I was in denial. Others told me I was being disrespectful to Matt. One woman even implied that I should honor my husband by taking the time every day to grieve for him — by staying home all day without any children to entertain or any jobs to perform and sulking because I missed my soldier.

I just didn't see that doing any service either to me or my husband.

If I was going to endure a year without the most important

man in my life, I was at least going to make it a productive one and use it to challenge myself, deepen my relationships and give back to others.

I knew in the back of my heart, too, that no matter how many people scolded me for doing too much or working too hard, staying busy and working three jobs was definitely one of the only things that was going to get me through this thing alive.

Well, that and a growing baby in my belly.

On August 30th, I attended my very first prenatal doctor's appointment — the big 12-week benchmark where I was told I could listen to the baby's heartbeat for the first time.

As I pulled up my candy-pink cotton sweater — Fairbanks cools down by September — to reveal the beginnings of a baby belly, Dr. O'Connor squeezed the remnants of a tube of clear gel onto my stomach.

My neighbor Heather had come with me to the appointment, and she smiled as Dr. O'Connor slowly shifted the stethoscope-type piece of the metal monitor across my belly. Heather had delivered a baby five months earlier and was eager to support me as I attended prenatal appointments alone and just beamed as I stared at the little device, listening intently for anything that even remotely sounded like a heartbeat.

Three minutes later, Dr. O still couldn't find the baby's beat. For a moment, I lost my breath. *What if I had a miscarriage?* I thought to myself. *What if there's no longer a baby? I don't know what I would do…*

Just as somber thoughts of dismal phone conversations with my husband crept into my head, I heard it — the faint but racing beat of a baby's heart. Dr. O'Connor pressed in harder, and the sound just echoed through the tiny white examination room. It sounded like a washing machine, or a dishwasher, and it just raced so fast!

Tears crept into my eyes as Dr. O'Connor timed the heartbeat and Heather grabbed my hand and squeezed it.

"That's your baby," she replied so sweetly.

My baby, I thought to myself. *We're really having a baby.*

But when I followed that hand up the arm to the beautiful feminine face peering back at me, my stomach turned. Those eyes didn't belong to the man who helped me create this beautiful, beating life. Those hands weren't the Army-groomed, calloused hands that framed my face during our first, fabulous kiss when I told my husband we were having a child.

I tried not to let the disappointment show in my eyes as Heather helped me up and handed me my car keys. She had been so amazing to attend this appointment with me, and I didn't want her to think that I wasn't appreciative. But what about Matt?

The father of your child is supposed to be the one holding your hand when you hear your baby's heartbeat for the first time. The father of your child is supposed to be the one whose eyes light up when he hears that first precious sound. The father of your child is supposed to be the one in there hugging you, loving on you and supporting you.

We weren't having a baby; *I* was having a baby. And though it would be *our* son, I was doing it alone.

Frustrated and disappointed, I literally scuffed my Sketchers and sulked all the way to the car.

"How could he not be here?" I kept asking out loud. "How could he miss something this big in both our lives? Why?"

While the most selfish part of me continued to mope as I shoved my keys into the ignition, the part of me that knew my husband would have given anything chimed in, and in remembering my vow to serve selflessly, God spoke up.

"Yes, Michelle, this is hard," He told me. "Yes, this is heartbreaking. Yes, this is not what you expected when two pink lines appeared on your pregnancy test back in July. But this is reality. This is the military. And if you're really going to serve and support your husband while he serves and supports this country, you need to realize that you're not the only one sacrificing. He hated missing this moment more than you hated the fact that he wasn't there. So if you want to support him, if you want to serve him, maybe you should put aside your own selfish pride and desires and check in to make sure he's okay after missing his child's heartbeat. That would at least be a start."

I hated humble pie, but I knew that He was right.

With my new, Matt-centered focus, I wanted to do something to include my husband, to let him know that, though he wasn't physically in Fairbanks, he was, indeed, a part of this pregnancy, and that I would commit myself to making sure he was included for all nine months.

On the way home from the hospital, I stopped at the drug

store to pick up some magazines and Daddy reading materials. I ripped out articles from parenting magazines about fatherhood and purchased a book about learning your child's love languages. I threw in an inspirational songs CD and a devotional, and, after carefully wrapping the digital recorder I had used to tape the baby's heartbeat in the examination room that day, shipped the box full of daddy-style goodies and baby heartbeats to my first baby in Iraq.

I was actually putt-putt golfing at the local Glo-Putt facility when he called me for only the second time since he had deployed to tell me he received the package. I had to hold my ears and run out on my friends at Hole 11 just to hear him speaking on the other end.

"Michelle!" He nearly hollered to overcome the machines and soldiers buzzing in the background. "I heard the heartbeat!"

He sounded like a little kid who had just sat on Santa's lap for the first time.

"I can't believe it's real! We're really having a baby!"

His smile echoed a million miles across the ocean and just penetrated my heart. I beamed as he told me how he'd replayed those 60 seconds of washing machine reverberation over and over again until he convinced himself that this was really his child.

My heart just melted, along with any remnants of resentment that he had missed the appointment in the first place. I always thought my husband was going to be a good father, but when he made sure to call me from Iraq to tell me how much a taped heart-beat and some parenting pamphlets meant to him, I knew he was going to be a phenomenal one.

CHAPTER THREE
STRUGGLE

The best military wives always make it look easy. They're the ones who are always composed, always encouraging and always positive about their deployment perspective. They're the ones who, in the middle of a spousal sob session about how difficult deployment is and how ridiculous the Army can be, remind the crowd with grace and love that at least their loved ones are still alive, and that the Army is providing the very freedom that allows them to complain about it. They're the ones who empathize with everyone but refuse to throw pity parties for anyone; the ones who always say the right thing when you just want them to give in and say the easy thing. They're the wives who should write the scripts for sappy wartime movies, because they've got all the right lines and all the right moves. They're always right on.

Three months into deployment, I wasn't one of them. I wasn't even one of the crying girls in the room with them. I was more like the girl who spent the sob session egging the Department of the Army's office building. With rotten eggs.

I wanted so badly to be that spouse — the one with the great, positive attitude who supported her husband 200 percent and then some. I wanted to be the one all the other wives looked to for strength and security. I wanted to be a rock. Sometimes, I even pretended to be. But it never lasted long. That's because, at my core, I was so consumed by raw emotion — sadness, bitterness, confusion, fear. With those emotions boiling inside, I just couldn't fill that perfect military wife role model position I wanted to fill so badly. There were moments when I saw glimpses of a strong Michelle who could encourage others instead of sulking by herself — in the same way she had encouraged her husband after the ultrasound that day — but most of those moments were overshadowed by tears and frustrations and decisions about how many dozen eggs would make the biggest mess.

I missed Matt terribly, and I wanted more than anything for him to feel loved, supported and at ease. He was the most fantastic husband, and I wanted him to feel that way. But every time we talked, I just couldn't help but think about my own woes and struggles — struggles I thought the Army had inflicted upon me that none of my civilian friends had to endure. The conversation often turned to what *I* needed and how *I* was doing, and before long, I felt needy and resentful and just wanted out of the whole deployment deal.

No needy and resentful person can truly lovingly support her husband. And she definitely can't support others. Not with rotten eggs to distribute.

That's the ironic dichotomy of military wife life — and the struggle. While you want to stand strong and proud, you really need to first be quiet and humble. It's only in a state of humility — a place where you can accept that it's not all about *you* — that you can truly rise to the occasion and proudly serve in a supportive way.

I spent the month of October struggling to find that balance. I thought I could stand proud and strong, and I could be proud and strong first. But I became self-proud and self-consumed and eventually convinced myself that the world revolved around me. That's because I hadn't first humbled myself. I was still too caught up in the me and the mine and the personal and the selfish. I needed to be humbled before I could truly be proud of my husband — not because I was supposed to be a proud soldier's wife, but because, after humbling myself to see all he did and sacrificed for, I couldn't help but let my heart burst with pride for the man he was. That kind of respect led to honor and patriotism for the causes he championed.

Humility sank in, and I soon realized that struggle was all about perspective.

As Christ had offered me so many times, I looked to the Bible to gain a different perspective — a more righteous perspective, and one that would allow me to remember the big picture. It was there that I rediscovered one of my favorite verses from my college days: "Consider it pure joy, my brothers, when you experience trials of many kinds, for the testing of your faith produces perseverance. Perseverance must finish its work in you so that you may be mature and complete, lacking nothing." (James 1:2-4)

I shut my Bible, and I put the eggs away. At least temporarily.

If I wanted to overcome my pain and my pride and my selfishness and my sorrows, I needed to consider my trials pure joy and my struggles opportunities to build character. I needed to humble myself to realize that no one owed me anything, but that one man was sacrificing everything, and in that trial, I could count that pure joy.

Joy, however, is hard, because joy is a choice. Happiness is easy; happiness is a response to a stimulus. Friends cause happiness. Husbands cause happiness. Families cause happiness. But deployment does not cause happiness. Happiness is not the normal response of a healthy, loving couple to spending 12 months apart on separate sides of the world while one rears children alone and the other faces terrorists and guns. But God was teaching me that joy, on the other hand, could be.

Joy is a choice. It's a decision. Whereas happiness is an emotional response, joy is a deliberate decision to look on the bright side and make the most of the situation. You might not be able to choose to be happy about deployment, but you *can* choose to view deployment *joyfully*.

It didn't happen overnight, and it wasn't a one-time decision — that kind of attitude change requires a deliberate daily dedication to seeking the higher road — but over time, humility and joy built a place in my heart and my perspective shifted yet again.

When I only got to talk to Matt on the phone every seven or eight days (for exactly 30 minutes, at which point the guy Matt called "Phone Nazi" held up a sign telling him his time was up and forced him off the phone and back to the barracks), I thanked God that I had been given the opportunity to talk to him at all. I looked at those seven lonely days between phone calls as opportunities to build my character and build myself up in new ways, independent of the husband I had grown so attached to. Of course I backslid, and of course I had my bad days. My friends may have even considered treating me for manic-depressive disorder. But leaning on Christ's strength and Christ's words, I was able to dedicate myself daily to "considering it pure joy."

I even started creating lists to remind myself of all the positive aspects of deployment, and to remember that this was a growing and learning experience, and that I wanted to really embrace it as such.

Before long, I found myself e-mailing my lists to friends and family, both to help explain what Matt and I had been doing in our free time, and also to help hold myself accountable for my new positive attitude. I couldn't exactly launch green eggs and ham from my super-powered slingshot when 300 of my closest friends were reading on a monthly basis about how positive I was being back at home. It would have killed my credibility, and that's something I took very seriously as a journalist!

The more I found myself *practicing* joy in my everyday life, the more joyful and enjoyable I actually became as a person and the more easygoing and lighthearted I became, too.

October 2005

Top 10 Things I Learned from
Dealing with Deployment in the Last Frontier

1. When your husband is in Iraq, you don't even need to put on the guilt trip to get what you want. He practically offers you all the things he told you you could never have before.

Since we got married more than a year ago, Matt and I have settled for this crappy $30 Wal-Mart bedspread in our bedroom. For a newlywed couple, we thought we were doing pretty well. I mean, we at least had a bedspread on our bed! But after about six months of Ranger beatings and sleepless nights, this poor little comforter was looking pretty sorry. I mean, really sorry. So I suggested we purchase a new bedding set. Of course, I may have suggested this after my adorable little husband was deployed and had no physical say in the matter.

So when I looked online for bedding (remember, no real mall in Fairbanks) and found the bedroom set of my dreams, I e-mailed the picture to Matt. He, of course, wrote back and commented on the, well, bright nature of the bedspread and suggested we get something that didn't look like a rainbow threw up on our mattress. I then pulled the "But I'm all alone in Alaska in the dead of winter and I need something bright to cheer me up when my husband is so far away and this bedspread would make me so happy" line, and one month later, I put that beautiful rainbow puke bedspread on my bed with all Matt's wonderful blessings.

2. Deployment brings out the neediness in everyone... including the family dog.

The day Matt left for Iraq, it was like this little switch turned on inside Ranger. He went from super independent dog who didn't want to be coddled or messed with and just wanted to play all

STRUGGLE

day and bite your fingers, to this dog who suddenly had to be sitting on your shoulders and head every time you sat down on the couch, and had to be touching you at all moments you were together. I started letting Ranger sleep in the bed with me. One, because I was lonely. Two, because I was scared. And three, because Matt wouldn't let him sleep with us when he was here and I felt super cool for making the bedtime Ranger rules for once.

At first, he was great. He'd sit by my feet and go right to sleep. But in the last month, he's gotten into this routine. As soon as I crawl under the covers, he pushes me onto my left side (why he prefers the left, I have no idea), nudges my arm around him and then spoons with me. Literally. He has to be spooning right up against my body all night long. And if I move or roll over or push him away in the middle of the night, he wakes me up, rolls me back over, puts my arm around his chest and makes me spoon, as if he wore the pants in the relationship and it was his bed to sleep in, not mine. Now I know how Matt has felt in the middle of the night all those days we've been married!

3. Mace is just not all that effective when you spray it into your own eye.

So I realize now that if you have a history of false key burglar alarms in the middle of the night (I once called a friend frantically at 1 a.m. because I heard a "burglar" in my house — a "burglar" that turned out to be a fallen set of keys in my kitchen), you probably shouldn't stay alone in your house in Alaska in the wintertime. Especially not when it's dark 21 hours of the day in the dead of winter.

So last weekend, I was cuddled all up in my nice bed (with my fabulous new bedspread!), fast asleep at 1 a.m., when all of a sudden Ranger bolted out of bed and started barking. Ranger never barks in the middle of the night, and it freaked me out, so of course, I started then hearing things, and I seriously thought I heard a door open and shut and whispers coming from the hallway.

I flipped out and called my next-door neighbor Heather, who ran out of her house in her bathrobe and checked all my doors from the outside and walked around the house and looked in all my windows. She called me back and said she didn't see anything.

But I, meanwhile, am positive someone is in my house. So I lunge toward my dresser drawer, where I store the can of Mace my neighbor bought me before he left for Iraq (he was worried that I refused Matt's offer to buy me a gun and keep it in the house and thought maybe Mace would help), and whipped the can out. Of course, I'm sure my attacker would have been just terrified if he could have seen through that door. A big pregnant lady with bed head, a telephone and a can of Mace with a sidekick dog who crawled back up on the bed and went right back to sleep — wow, I wouldn't touch that one.

But it was at that moment that I realized that I'd never actually sprayed Mace before. I didn't even know how the bottle worked. If this guy was going to break down my door and kill me, I should at least know how to make his eyes itch! So, thinking I was brilliant, I did a little test spray… right into my eyes. Of course, at that moment, I couldn't see anything, my nose got itchy and I started gagging from anxiety, as did poor little Ranger, who was attacked with Mace while trying to quietly go back to sleep on the bed.

Blind, itchy and coughing, I found my way to the bathroom attached to my bedroom, lifted Ranger up and we took a shower together — holding the stupid can of Mace defensively outside the shower curtain in case my attacker was the persistent type, puking together in the shower. It was beautiful. Lesson: Don't leave Michelle home alone in Alaska. She's more dangerous than the burglars she imagines in her head.

4. The Alaskan Army has its own priorities about providing for spouses of deployed soldiers.

For military wives anywhere else in the United States, deployment means lots of potlucks and girls nights out. It means sappy, teary-eyed get-togethers and fun-filled chick-flick movie nights while no man is around to complain about them. At least that was what I was hoping for. But I'm beginning to think that in Alaska, dealing with deployment might be executed just a little bit differently.

My first hint came two weeks after Matt deployed. I was cuddling up in my favorite chair with my cup of hot cocoa and my fuzzy red blanket to check my e-mail, and I opened a message from the activities director at our post inviting me to join the "Becoming an Outdoor Woman" class on post.

If that weren't enough to tip me off, the second e-mail I received offered free hunting equipment rental to spouses of deployed soldiers.

STRUGGLE

And that's not all.

Around town, spouses of deployed soldiers can get deals on everything from women's pistol-shooting classes to four-wheeling trips through the Alaskan wilderness.

Now don't get me wrong. It's not that I don't like the outdoors, or think that rumbling around the woods without a shower for three or four days at a time while I try to bait animals about five times my weight isn't attractive. It was definitely the number 10 thing on my Top 10 Things To Do list when my husband leaves the country for a year. It's just that I was kind of hoping for something a little more practical for me — like maybe free movie rentals, or giant buckets of Neapolitan ice cream, or a day at the spa.

After some inquiries, however, neither my hairdresser nor my local Blockbuster thought I deserved a discount for simply existing in Fairbanks without a husband around to keep me company.

But hey, maybe with all these awesome outdoorsy offers, when my husband returns from Iraq next August, I'll be a true Alaskan woman — a hunting, fishing, firing outdoor princess who keeps her tiara tucked just inside her camouflage. I'd just better have cute toenails underneath my Sorrels.

5. When your husband is deployed, the Christmas lights go up when you feel like it — even if that's in October.

When Matt and I were looking to buy a house in Fairbanks last year, we noticed a strange phenomenon.

At almost every real estate Web site we visited, we found pictures of beautiful, summertime Alaskan cabins for sale — with hideous, massive Christmas lights dangling from the front porch and the back fence. In the middle of August.

At the time, we were appalled.

Call me a Midwestern Christmas snob, but I always considered it pretty tacky to hang Christmas lights before Thanksgiving, or to leave them up all year long. Who really wants to be reminded about Christmas in the middle of football season? It's kind of just a mood killer. And it doesn't make Christmas very special, either, because when the fantastic holiday season does come around, you have nothing to celebrate with. Your Christmas lights have also become your Halloween lights, your birthday lights and your friend's second cousin's first date lights. Why even bother calling them "Christmas" lights at that point?

So when we moved into our first house just outside the city of

BEHIND THE BLUE-STAR BANNER

Fairbanks, we vowed that we would hang no light, light no tree, until after Thanksgiving had passed.

Of course, that was before Matt left his wife alone in Alaska with a staple gun and an extension cord in a city where snow covers the ground in September and neighbors scramble to dangle their Christmas lights before Columbus Day.

By mid-October, snow blankets the roof and temperatures drop below 0 degrees (some years, even to -30!), and it's just too cold and too slippery to bother with the winter wonderland effect. That's why all the hardcore Alaskans hang their lights in September, and the even harder core folks leave them up all year round. Because when the snow doesn't melt until May, it seems silly to take down the lights for three or four short summer months.

After all the work my neighbor and I spent dangling from the roof hanging them this weekend (yes, the first weekend in October), maybe we just won't.

If he's lucky, maybe Matt will even catch a glimpse of our beautiful October Christmas light display when he returns from Iraq next August.

After all, we're real Alaskans now. We have permission to be tacky.

6. If you want your husband to be able to reach you the one time a week he can call, you should probably not drop your cell phone in the toilet and fry it to a crisp.

Or if you do, you should make sure your cell phone plan is not one of those crappy prepaid plans with an Alaskan company you've never heard of before who won't give you a new phone just because you're stupid. Just a memo for all you future spouses of deployed soldiers.

7. Groceries and meals just lose their appeal when they're only intended for one — a pregnant one, at that.

First of all, cooking while pregnant is not the coolest task in the world. My cravings change from minute to minute, and the second I prepare that bacon-green pepper omelet I would have killed for just five minutes earlier, the smell of eggs makes me queasy, and I end up inviting my neighbors over for my breakfast while I chew on some celery in the far corner of the room where the horrendous odor of morning breakfast doesn't make me gag.

And if cooking breakfast isn't putrid enough, grocery shopping gets even better.

STRUGGLE

Do you know what my favorite part of deployment (and pregnancy) is? It's going to the grocery store alone when your cabinets are completely empty and you have nothing to eat but the mold off the heel of the bread that your husband used to eat but you refuse to consume but can't stand to waste, and you go to the grocery store and just push your cart down every aisle, bawling in your mukluks (because you went to the grocery store when it was 30 degrees and snowing and it was a big trip for you) because everything at the store makes you gag and the smell of the meat counter almost sends you into a deep upheaval and you leave the grocery store bawling with only a loaf of bread and six eggs and call your mom crying because you can't find anything to eat and she has to send you three loaves of cinnamon bread from Michigan via Priority Mail because that's the only thing that sounds bearable and they don't sell cinnamon bread in any store you've searched yet in Fairbanks. That's my favorite part. And after $13 in postage to mail me cinnamon bread, I think that's Mom's favorite part, too.

8. Naps are the answer to everything. Believe me. I take about four a day now, and I'm getting really good at them! You can't be depressed when you're sleeping, and you can even pull the "rest is good for you" card to get away with it. It's a win-win for every pregnant military spouse in deployment denial.

9. Learning the sex of your baby makes all the deployment woes disappear… unless, of course, they aren't sure if you have a three-legged girl or a not-so-shy boy.

Anything that has to do with your baby is just so exciting and serves as such an awesome distraction to the crappiness of deployment. Yes, we found out that Matt and I are having a little baby boy! Well, kind of.

So Matt and I were convinced for several reasons that we were having a little girl, so when I got the ultrasound done two weeks ago, I just made a statement to the ultrasound guy, like "So it's a girl, right?" and he just smiled, pointed to a little limb on the ultrasound screen and said, "Well, not unless your little girl has a third leg." But I just kept pressing him, "Are you sure it's not a girl? You're positive? Not a girl?"

After asking the poor guy like five times, I started crying, because it was just such an emotional thing to see my baby on a computer screen, and to know that my baby was going to be a real live little boy, but the poor guy I think thought I was crying because I wanted it to be a little girl, and he kept telling me it was going to be okay, little boys are awesome! He was a little boy once and he turned out okay.

Meanwhile, I'm shedding tears and super emotional because it made the pregnancy so real, and this poor man is trying to make me feel better about having a boy, so he starts trying to get me excited about a little boy by printing out oodles of pictures, inserting little arrows next to the pee pee (which he displayed very proudly in every picture) so I could get used to the idea of a penis when I got home or something. I don't really know.

So the poor guy leaves, I think, thinking I'm devastated about having a little boy. Meanwhile, I'm thrilled and go home and start registering for tons of boy clothes online and call my family and talk to Matt and am just thrilled with the idea of a baby boy... until I go to a doctor's appointment on Monday and my doctor tells me that, according to the ultrasound, I am actually three to four weeks behind where they thought I was in the pregnancy, my baby is now not due until April 4th, I am only 14 weeks (not 18 weeks) pregnant and that, at 14 weeks of age, little boys and little girls can look very much the same on an ultrasound. So we can't be 100 percent sure we are absolutely having a boy.

So, I get another ultrasound in November, at the correct 20-week period. Until that time, I guess we're just going to call our baby "It Cuthrell" or something.

If it does turn out to be a girl, Matt and I have a whole lot of questions for Mr. Ultrasound. We'll keep you posted. But we think it's a boy. Dear God, please make it a boy and not a girl with a third leg. Amen.

10. Having things to look forward to is a key coping mechanism.

On my calendar every month, I put an event on the top of the month that is my "looking forward to" moment for that month. That way, I have one positive thing to look forward to every month so that I don't just hurry up and wish that month was over. Although my October moment was ruined when Chili's restaurant decided to open its doors in November instead of October.

Hey, food is a big motivator for me! Especially now that it actually tastes good! And Chili's? Come on — I haven't had real chain restaurant food since I visited Dayton in the summertime. That's a total treat here in Fairbanks!

STRUGGLE

Shortly after I sent my Top 10 list to all my friends and family, the managing editor from the *Fairbanks Daily News-Miner* actually called. I had written him a letter a month before my husband deployed suggesting a new column for the local paper about dealing with deployment on the home front during the Stryker brigade's tour in Iraq. This, of course, was back when I actually felt strong and good about deployment — not after I'd suffered 5.2 million bawling breakdowns and half considered checking myself into a mental hospital somewhere far, far away from the Army.

But when Mr. Bostian called and asked me to meet with him about the idea, I couldn't exactly turn him down. I mean, I had written him the letter in the first place and it might be a bit unprofessional to tell a potential employer that you have since endured a psychotic breakdown and would no longer like to write for his paper, but please do keep you in mind for any future positions, thanks.

I met with Mr. Bostian on a Tuesday. The following Friday, the first of nearly 70 weekly columns appeared in the *Fairbanks Daily News-Miner.*

By that time, I'd already executed three major attitude adjustments and wondered how many more I would need to perform before making myself a public figure. I knew I wasn't the role model military wife I wanted to be, and it scared me to think that people who had perhaps never interacted with military families could form their opinions about military wives from the words I printed in a weekly column.

I knew that I wanted to be transparent about the struggles of being a military wife (especially my personal struggles), and I knew that I needed to be real about the responsibility of it all, too. In doing that, however, I needed to be a support, as well — not for a cause, not for a country, but for a husband who desperately needed to know that I was behind him, that I believed in him and that, with God, I could handle anything his incredibly important job might cause me to experience.

I wanted to consider it pure joy.

That perhaps was one of the most difficult balances I've ever tried to strike, and one that I'm confident I will still never be able to perfect.

As a journalist, I've always felt a responsibility to reveal truth — to dig for it, to find it and to print it, even when it finds people at their most vulnerable. Truth releases. Truth teaches. And truth offers compassion and understanding that facades and fake faces just don't. If I ever expected anyone to be a source in a journalism story for me ever again, if I ever expected anyone to trust me with his very precious, very personal story, if I ever expected him to allow me to take that story and to tell it in the context of history and use it to change minds and change lives, then I had to be willing to share mine, too — the good, the bad and the ugly. Putting up a façade of faux support wasn't going to help anyone to understand what it was like to be a spouse dealing with deployment on the home front, and it wasn't going to allow others to use my experiences and make more educated decisions about policies regarding military deployments and their effects on the family. I had to be real, I had to be honest and I had to be vulnerable.

At the same time, however, I knew I had to be a strong pillar of support for my husband. I had to be real in a way that would honor him, that would honor his work and that would bring others to support him and his comrades, even if they didn't support the war at large. I had to be vulnerable and, at the same time, bold and I had no idea how to be both. If I admitted that being a military wife was difficult and that there were days I begged my husband to resign his commission after his four years, how could I, at the same time, support him as a soldier? If I admitted that there were days during deployment that I emotionally did not think I would survive, how could I encourage him that he could take care of himself on the war front because I was safe and fine back home? And how could I one day claim that I would proudly serve as a military wife until I died and the next plot toilet-papering missions at the Department of the Army building?

For hours, I wrote and I prayed and I strived to strike that balance — that precious balance that would allow me to be real and relevant while still being positive and uplifting.

After several rewrites and many long Neapolitan ice cream breaks, I finally submitted my very first piece for my brand new "Until They Come Home" column and prayed for a good response.

STRUGGLE

Until They Come Home
October 21, 2005

After four years of long-distance dating and marriage, I was sure we'd be ready.

My husband and I had become the queen and king of goodbyes. We'd efficiently executed dramatic, sappy, teary-eyed farewells in airports from Alaska to Singapore, and we had almost mastered the cutting-off-and-moving-on part of long-distance relationships. After all, when you attend colleges in different states and one of you is in the military, departures just become part of the routine.

Thus when I drove my Army hubby to Fort Wainwright, Alaska, to deploy to Iraq for a year, I assumed I'd handle the venture just fine. There was no way I was going to be one of those out-of-control wives who cries, "I can't live without you!" as other soldiers pry her desperate hands off her husband and send her home sobbing in the family Corolla.

Not this woman.

So when we'd finished unloading my husband's ruck and pack and I was bawling hysterically and repeating over and over through snot and sobs, "I can't live without you," I knew this deployment was going to be a whole lot harder than I had first imagined.

Being a military wife isn't easy. No, I'm not on the battlefield, and no, I'm not the one facing the fire. Those are true heroes. But I do take some of the shots. I sacrifice, too.

While my husband faces the attacks of insurgents and the casualties of war, I face the attacks of depression and the casualties of worry and stress. It's not just a long-distance relationship I have to hold together anymore; it's my sanity.

And that task has never been harder.

For one thing, I'm pregnant. Between updating life insurance policies and completing burial worksheets, I schedule doctor's appointments and search out labor coaches who can assist me in the delivery of our very first child. I spend my free time mailing off ultrasound pictures to APO addresses and posting my most current schedule and emergency numbers around my house for possible injury informants to find when I leave for more than a few hours at a time.

BEHIND THE BLUE-STAR BANNER

It's a lot for one person to handle. And it's sometimes difficult to hold my tongue and be supportive when the only thing I want, the only thing I ask for, is to be a normal family — together in the same place for more than six months at one time. It doesn't seem like that should be asking too much. And yet, when it comes to serving our country, I'm starting to realize that sometimes it has to be.

Although I complain about holidays alone and long, lonely nights, I quickly forget that my husband endures those things, too — only he endures them in 100-degree heat with only a chow hall, an M4 and a platoon of all-male Army medics to keep him company. While I retreat tearfully back home for recovery weekends, he has no option for a vacation or even a night away. The craziest part about it all is that he actually considers this lifestyle an honor.

For a hero who sacrifices so much just to serve each day, the least I can do is serve him honorably in return — by staying strong, praying hard and realizing that sometimes my husband's call to serve is more important than my wish to be served.

After all, it's not just a career choice that causes those long, lonely nights and those dreadful deployment goodbyes — it's a passion and patriotism that keeps not just my husband, but this entire country alive. Through missed anniversaries and single motherhood, I choose to serve my husband, and my country, from the home front. I am a military wife.

You'd think once they appeared in print, I would actually be able to remember and live by the words I myself had put to paper. But it's a lot harder to stay strong and supportive than to vow to do it.

That's because selfishness and egotism are ingrained in the human race, and though this one reminder did adjust my attitude temporarily, I would need many more attitude adjustments throughout deployment to make it to the other end with even a "quasi-supportive military wife" title. Frequent attitude adjustments are just part of the job description.

I needed about a million in October alone.

October was a rough month because we had passed the goodbye part of deployment, wore out the exciting/romantic long distance part of deployment and were now entering the crappy, this-really-sucks part of deployment. Though I really tried to remember

STRUGGLE

every single day that it was indeed because of his passion and patriotism, not because of his job choice, that my husband was away from me during morning sickness and back pain, it was difficult to remain patient and not be upset when every other pregnant woman I knew had her hubby there to hold her hand during early-morning puking sessions. I almost began to resent those women, and I found myself even avoiding them, as well as other women who had their husbands physically with them to have and to hold.

It's easy to become bitter and cynical when you find yourself in the midst of a trying and tumultuous time. In the midst of your own pain, it almost becomes easier to look outward and criticize others for the ungratefulness in their own lives than to look inward and find something to be grateful about in your own.

Suddenly I found that I had no patience for women who told me that they never saw their husbands because they worked such long hours, or women who cried because they just didn't know what they were going to do with themselves while their husbands traveled away on business for a weekend at a time. I had no tolerance for women who moped and complained about not getting help from their husbands with their children, and I had no willpower to even listen to the women who turned their husbands down for sex.

I'd overcome my resentment at the Army and at my husband for joining it, but I replaced that resentment with a consuming anger against women who lived out each day things that I could only dream about and yet took them for granted or complained that they weren't enough. Soon I found myself berating them and rebuking them under my breath as I tromped through the grocery story mumbling, "I *wish* my husband would come home late. At least then he'd be home at all." Or "I *wish* my husband only left for a weekend. Maybe then I could see him the other 363 days out of the year."

I would have killed for those things — any or all of those things — and I lit up like a roman candle anytime I saw another woman taking those blessings for granted.

It was one day when I was speaking to a friend whose neighbor had lost her husband to a sniper bullet in Iraq that I realized I was doing the same thing.

I had become so addicted to analyzing the ungratefulness of others and using that as a coping mechanism that I had failed to look inward and reflect on my own attitude.

Maybe my husband wasn't here for the next 10 months, but he would be here. He would be here at that welcome home ceremony in August. He would be here for the birth of our child. And he would be here to help raise the child after his 12 wartime months were over. Those were blessings that I could thank my God for.

Until They Come Home
October 28, 2005

As the spouse of a deployed soldier, it's been easy for me to be complacent about the way I "support our troops" — to send my husband love letters and write a column about deployment and convince myself that I am really serving these soldiers in meaningful ways. I mean, really, I wear my yellow ribbon pin and carry on a long-distance marriage for months on end — isn't that enough of a sacrifice to say I support my troops?

This week, those somewhat shallow (and selfish) views of support were challenged.

First, by the wife of my husband's battalion commander — an incredible lady who balances several classes at UAF, a million community service activities and single motherhood while her husband commands the 2-1 infantry battalion in Iraq. She made an entire afternoon to visit one of the Stryker brigade soldiers wounded in combat who is now recovering at Bassett hospital, and follows up on his healing and progress regularly.

And then, by two complete strangers who called my home this week. One gave me information about free doula services, and the other invited me over for lunch to discuss how she could better support other pregnant women with deployed spouses in this city.

As I left that second woman's house Saturday afternoon and stepped into my car with the yellow ribbon plastered to the bumper, I couldn't help but wonder if I, like these ladies, made that yellow ribbon mean anything, or if I put it there so I could simply feel as if I were doing my part.

Here, complete strangers were reaching out, going completely out of their way, screaming "I care! Please let me help!" to soldiers wounded in battle and spouses left behind. And here I, the spouse of one of these soldiers, was settling for half-hearted help and for-show-only support.

STRUGGLE

It was disheartening, and it was disappointing.

On my short drive home, I tried to count all the things — any of the things — I had done to really act on my promise of support for the Stryker soldiers. Rather than developing a list of proud support moments, I was overwhelmed by the times I had disgracefully fallen short and told myself that someone else would get the job done.

Where was I when the brave soldier my friend visited was injured and wound up in the post hospital to recover before returning to war? Where was I last week when the first two soldiers from the 172nd died in Iraq? Had I even written their families? Had I prayed for their friends? What had I done? Where was I at?

Shamefully, I was in the comfort of my home, cooking my comfortable dinner, thanking my God that it wasn't my husband.

No, it wasn't my husband, but it was somebody's husband. It was somebody's brother, somebody's son, somebody's best friend, somebody's love. It was somebody that my yellow ribbon promised I would support. And somebody I had broken that promise for.

For me, the shallow yellow ribbon patriotism ends today.

This week, I'm going to break out some red, white and blue ribbons to tie to some packages I'm sending to the families of the two soldiers who were killed, and to some of the soldiers still very much fighting and alive. I'm going to write some letters, I'm going to make some calls, and I'm going to throw away my complacency to be served as a spouse of a deployed soldier and name that act "support." Although those small gestures don't make up for my lack of action thus far, maybe those colored ribbons will be a start to make the yellow ones plastered to my car and to my chest really mean something.

Ten minutes after I submitted that column to my editor, I felt so convicted that I headed to Wal-Mart, bought some American flag note cards and spent the night writing to the families of soldiers injured or killed in action. I found myself choked up and frustrated that I hadn't taken the time to write these hurting families before. How could I have been so consumed in my own deployment woes that I could forget about those who were experiencing losses much greater than my own?

I was almost embarrassed when I dropped those cards at the post office. How meaningless they were — how little they meant in the big scheme of things. But I didn't know what else to do for families hurting thousands of miles away. So I pretended like that was enough.

But when I walked back in my garage door, I knew it wasn't. Yes, I was honoring those soldiers who had died. But what about those soldiers who were still fighting so bravely? What about the men and women who had made a difference in my husband's life, and therefore mine?

I opened a second stack of note cards and began writing furiously to anyone who worked with my husband — his company commander, his chaplain, even his battalion commander, thanking them for the roles they played every day in keeping my soldier safe and effecting a mission that would change lives forever.

At 2 a.m., that still wasn't enough. I needed to do more.

So I started a roster of all the birthdays of the men in Matt's platoon and vowed that the least I could do for these hardworking soldiers was remember to honor them on their birthdays. I sent cards to the medics whose birthdays I had already missed, and started addressing new ones to the medics whose birthdays would come in the next month.

Finally, at 3 a.m., I headed to bed, still feeling inadequate and helpless, but at least knowing that I had taken a first step. I had done something — and that was a whole lot more than the nothing I had been doing the entire first three months of my husband's deployment.

CHAPTER FOUR
SOLITUDE

Until They Come Home
November 4, 2005

He's been staring at her pictures on the Internet and watching her from the other side of a Web camera for weeks. He's called her, sent her kisses and adored her from thousands of miles away. But this week, he will finally get to meet the little angel he's fallen in love with for the last two and a half months.

This week, SGT Adam Worthington will meet his baby girl for the very first time.

Adam's 4-pound 9-ounce daughter, Skyler, was born four weeks early in a hospital in West Virginia the day before he deployed to Iraq. Because he was scheduled to deploy from Fort Wainwright the next day, he was unable to leave Fairbanks to be with his wife, Angela, in the hospital or even meet his brand new bundle of joy during her first moments of life.

I saw the look on Adam's face the day he deployed, knowing the two most important women in his life were in a hospital 6,000 miles away. I saw the stoic expression on his face as he forced himself into the 2-1 Infantry Battalion headquarters and proceeded with his mission against everything I know must have been hiding deep inside.

I just wish I could see his face this week as he looks into Skyler's eyes for the very first time. And as many other soldier daddies do the same this year.

Although the Fort Wainwright public affairs office did not know the number of pregnant spouses of deployed soldiers, from my personal experience, I know there are plenty of them.

That means that for the next nine months, many others just like Adam will be present for baby deliveries only over cell phones and meet new babies for the first time only in airports. There will be born a whole generation of Skylers who will spend their first year without daddies and Angelas who will raise little children without Adams.

My husband and I are two of them.

BEHIND THE BLUE-STAR BANNER

Depending on the timing of our baby and the rest and relaxation two-week release date of my husband, Matt may or may not be present for the delivery of our child, and might not even meet the little one until he or she is nearly four months old.

Some people gasp at this concept — that military wives like Angela and like me can deal with the fact that their husbands might not be present in the delivery room to hold their wives' hands and cut the umbilical cords on their newborn babies.

But I've come to realize that it's not the movie-star perfect, happy ending Hollywood life that we live as military families. And the important job our husbands perform requires that we can't expect that. No, we're more of the movie box office flop — the kind that no one wants to watch because the husband never makes it to the delivery room and the airplane never arrives home on time, and babies are born without daddies present every single day.

It's unfortunate, but it's the reality of war. And it's the reality of military family life. Soldiers (and their families) sacrifice not just the comforts of home, but also the most important parts of home in order to serve. But sacrificing what's most important, not just what's convenient, is what makes their service so meaningful.

It's because I can tell our baby why Daddy wasn't there that I'm okay with the possibility of him not being there. It doesn't mean it's easy, and it doesn't mean it's fun — Angela and Adam can attest to that — but it means it's bearable. When you're serving your country, sometimes that has to be enough.

Well, it was — until, that is, I felt the baby's very first kick.

Before that time, I really was convinced that I would be okay enduring this pregnancy, and possibly this delivery, alone.

But when that baby kicked for the very first time as I was watching a TBS weekend movie and munching on pineapple at 11:30 p.m., I suffered yet another major pregnancy breakdown. Tears flowed freely as I experienced what it was like to be the mother of a living, kicking being for the first time in my life.

Ecstatic, flustered and completely overwhelmed with this new sensation, I turned almost instinctively to the black leather recliner chair where my husband always sat when we watched late-night movies — only to remember that he wasn't there to share this moment with me.

The tear rivers turned to floods.

SOLITUDE

Moaning and nearly hyperventilating, I reached for the phone lying on the other side of the couch and dialed my parents' number, not caring that it was nearly 3:30 a.m. their time, but simply needing to share my exciting news and be comforted about the fact that Matt wasn't there to share in it with me.

After two rings, my dad picked up the phone.

"Dad!" I screamed, without even giving him a chance to offer a "hello" or "good morning." "I felt the baby kick!"

I was nearly yelling into the receiver, alternating between a chorus of laughter and sobs at my big pregnancy news.

I don't even know if my poor dad realized at the time what psycho was calling him during a mental breakdown at 3 a.m. So, trying to be supportive but obviously completely exhausted, he replied, "Oh, that's nice, Michelle. Do you want to talk to your mother?"

He then handed the phone to my mom, and I repeated my yelling-crying-laughing announcement once again. But poor Mom, too, was completely out of it, and though she tried to sound excited, was just too tired to express the enthusiasm she might have displayed at, say, 9 a.m., or some other decent hour of the morning.

After saying our quick "I love yous," I hung up the phone and shed a few more tears.

Deployment stunk. I didn't want to go through it alone anymore. I was so sick and tired of playing Dr. Jeckel and Mr. Hyde. I hated that there were times I hated deployment, and I hated that I couldn't just maintain that strong, positive persona that my husband and my community so desperately needed. I was just so sick and tired of being so sick and tired of deployment, and I wanted the split personalities to end. No more attitude adjustments, no more bawling breakdowns. I just wanted to be normal, and I just wanted to be strong for my Matt without having to remind myself to do it every two days.

"God," I whispered, "please just give me strength."

Mail from Mosul
November 13, 2005

(Note: Matt sent me this e-mail completely unprovoked. I, in fact, had no idea that he was even slightly interested in writing

mass e-mails until this one appeared in my mailbox last night and asked if I would send it out in my next mass e-mail. But I decided that mass e-mails are very special and very personal things, and just like we have separate toothbrushes and pillows and towels, so I think we should have separate mass e-mails. Plus, he wrote a stinking book and if I added mine to his, no one would ever read our e-mails! Below is the letter I received from Matt last night and some pictures he sent from Mosul).

Hello everyone,

Just like she does with Christmas gifts and birthdays, my wife runs the show. So I had to give this e-mail to her so it would make it to everyone!

I am doing well here in Mosul. We have all gotten into our routines. Michelle asks me what I am going to do for Thanksgiving and Christmas here. The answer is always, "The same thing I did yesterday, which is the same thing I did today, which is the same thing I'll do tomorrow." I definitely feel like I am in a bad remake of the movie Groundhog's Day. *But I guess the routine is good, as long as we do not become complacent.*

It has cooled off here a lot lately. It stays in the 70s during the day and gets into the 40s at night. It's actually kind of nice. If the city only didn't smell like rotten cow and dirty feet I might think of building a summer home here. I really can't complain, though. We have it pretty nice. The chow is good — steak and shrimp every Sunday — and I have someone to do my laundry for me. We have received a lot of care packages — all the fattening threats you could ask for. So thanks to all that have sent stuff and cards. The guys here really appreciate it. It is definitely a morale booster... Thanks for the prayers and support.

Matt

P.S. So sorry I turned into my wife. I can't believe I just wrote a mass e-mail. If you are smart, you'll do like I do and delete it without reading it first. I mean, um, sorry, Michelle, just kidding. You know I love you, and I read all your e-mails!

Upon receiving that e-mail from my husband, the jocular Dr.

SOLITUDE

Jekyll returned and Mr. Hyde hid in the barn for a few days. Matt was always the more quiet one — the complete opposite of me, actually. While I thrived in large groups and lived for interaction with people, he preferred to spend his free time alone or with one or two close friends. While I sent mass e-mails to a list of 200 people every month revealing my deepest darkest feelings and trials, he hardly wrote letters to any of the handful of guys he called his best friends. So the fact that he sent me an e-mail to distribute to the group was an unexpected and unanticipated event — and one that made me smile inside. After a year of marriage, his wife had finally worn off on him, at least a little bit.

He'd worn off on me, too, in ways I would have never imagined before marrying a military man.

While November had always been the month of Thanksgiving and corn pudding for me, for Matt, the autumn month had always been a time to honor soldiers and veterans.

Before I met Matt, I ashamedly never paid much attention to Veteran's Day, or any military holiday for that matter. I knew it fell on the 11th of the month, and that in elementary school, we had a bugler play taps at 11:11 a.m. to honor the soldiers who had died performing service to our country. But it was never a holiday I had marked on my calendar, never a day I considered especially important.

Maybe that was because all my life, I had never really understood veterans. My papa had served in the Army when he and my grandma were first married back in the 1950s, and I can remember from the time I was little how upset he would get when people talked through the raising of the colors, or forgot to remove their hats when singing the National Anthem. And he hated it when people thought Veteran's Day was just another day off from school and away from work.

To me, these were just traditions — nothing to take so seriously. And I just didn't understand why veterans like my papa held them in such esteem and became so irate when others refused to.

That all changed when I started dating an Army boy.

Every year, in his own quiet way, Matt honored veterans on the 11th day of that sacred month. He became more serious, was deliberately more reflective, and took that special day as a time he could ponder the sacrifices of those of the past. He removed his hat, was silent at the raising of the flag and would appear almost on the verge of tears when someone sang "God Bless the U.S.A." It was always something I admired about him, but never quite understood — until this year.

Until They Come Home
November 18, 2005

I can still remember the awkwardness I felt a year ago last week when I stumbled into a Veterans of Foreign Wars post in Ithaca, New York.

I've never felt comfortable around large groups of men, especially large groups of military men, and standing in my high heels and power suit with a pen tucked behind my ear in the middle of a canteen filled with large Vietnam vets in Harley T-shirts didn't exactly allow me to blend in and feel at home.

At the time, I was just a rookie reporter, working part-time for my local newspaper as I completed my final semester of my journalism degree at Ithaca College, attempting to speak to some very experienced former military personnel about what Veteran's Day meant to them.

As these vets humored me with stories about war and recovery and country and service, I sat shyly at the canteen bar, waving away clouds of smoke, trying to even slightly comprehend where these former soldiers were coming from. Even though I was married to an Army guy at the time, I still didn't understand these military men, their culture or their stories. It was all so foreign, and I felt so foreign in that place.

It's amazing what one year, a blue-star banner and a deployment can change.

Last Thursday, I once again entered a VFW post to report on the importance of Veteran's Day — this time, at the Golden Heart Post in the city of Fairbanks.

When I trudged through the door with my Newscenter 11 camera and tripod and two men offered to carry my equipment and the post commander practically gave me a hug, I knew that something must have changed.

All around me, veterans of various ages and wars sat at the bar and collected around tables, laughing and talking and hugging and smiling. Over the lull of the classic country tunes, I could hear bits of "remember when" conversations and many "I'm so glad you're here now" exchanges. Even the same smoke that had bothered me at the canteen bar just a year ago set a kind of aura that made the place feel oddly approachable, homey.

As I focused my camera and took shots of the room, a few of the vets approached me with smiles, asking me questions about who I was and what I did. And when they found out that my husband was soon going to be one of them, they embraced me with even wider open arms. One even thanked me for my service.

For 30 minutes before and nearly an hour after the Stryker brigade adoption ceremony I had come to tape for my package, I felt included as I chatted with veterans about the importance of country, the meaning of Veteran's Day and the pride of service.

And in the middle of their presentation, when Post Commander George Ison stopped the ceremony and presented me with a blue-star pin and banner to hang in my window until my husband returned from Iraq, I felt accepted, even loved.

With the experience of a deployment under my belt, I somehow now understand these veterans and their culture. In so many ways, we are so alike. We've both dealt with the hardship of being away from family, both dealt with the realities of war. Though they did it from the battle ground and I do it from home, they somehow understand me, and we've made an odd connection that I would have never imagined just one year ago.

Though deployment has taken my cherished family far away, it has, in return, offered me family much closer to home than I would have ever expected.

A new family was one of the amazing and unexpected blessings of military life, especially military life in Alaska — especially during deployment. I'd never been so closely associated with a group of people, simply because of a family member's career choice. I never hung out with Matt's coworkers at his old Dayton gym, and I certainly didn't hug and haw over his old roofing buddies summer after summer. I don't even think I ever met them. And it was such a strange sensation to build such a tight bond around a career, especially one I wasn't actively involved in.

In Fairbanks, though, all you had to say was "military" or "spouse" and you were in — part of the club, a part of the team, in it for the gold, high-fives all around.

Of course, that could have partly been on account of the Alas-

BEHIND THE BLUE-STAR BANNER

kan culture, as well.

Although my military friends and vets embraced me with open arms, my new Alaskan friends took me under their wings and completely adopted me. Most people I knew in Alaska lived there because they didn't want to be anywhere near their families; they went there to get away, to be away, to embrace an outdoor life.

In the meantime, they embraced me and made me part of their Alaskan family lives.

Until They Come Home
November 25, 2005

"In sickness and in health" used to be my very favorite part of my husband and my wedding vows.

Maybe it was because I'd never been really sick, or maybe because I could count on one hand the number of times I'd seen a doctor for anything but a regular checkup. I've generally been a pretty healthy girl — I've never even so much as broken a bone or chipped a tooth. So the idea of this magical guy promising to hold a cold washcloth to my forehead and massage my feet as I lay home in bed sick seemed like this lovely, romantic idea to me. After all, every princess needs a prince to take care of her.

Of course, somebody should have told me when I married into the military that just under the finely printed words "in sickness and in health" in our wedding vows was an asterisked disclaimer in 10-point font that read, "only when the princess is in a terminal or unstable condition and the American Red Cross considers her condition bad enough to contact her prince in Iraq."

Monday afternoon, for the first time in the nearly five years Matt and I have been together, I was sick. Really sick. And my prince wasn't there to take care of me.

Looking back, I really think it was my husband who missed out on the whole ordeal. I mean, I was feeling pretty sexy as I sprawled out on my bathroom floor in mismatched pajamas and a ski cap to keep me warm, smelling like dirty feet and regurgitated orange juice as tears streamed down my face and I cried, "I want my Matt," between puking episodes for six hours straight.

I'm sure had he been there, he would have rated it one of our top 10 romantic moments together. Hands down.

Though he might not have missed much, it was so hard for me to lie there and not feel cheated that the man who promised to be there in sickness and in health couldn't be. I needed him there — and it was so hard to overcome my selfishness and try to remember that, at that moment, other people needed him more.

Fortunately, God put two very special substitute spouses in my life.

Within minutes of calling a couple very dear to my husband and me, Todd Thompson had picked me up and taken me to the post hospital while his wife, Teresa, ran to grab me comfort food and ginger ale. Todd let me claw his arm while I received my very first IV — five different times before my dehydrated veins would cooperate — and Teresa prayed over me and tucked me into bed. That day, they were more than just my good friends — they were my "in sickness and in health" extended family.

But they still weren't Matt. No matter how incredible they were, they still weren't my husband.

No matter how many times I tell myself I can't expect that dream, and I have been so blessed by other people who fulfill it, I still want it. Knowing that it's not realistic doesn't keep me from hurting when I can't have it — from being sad when another couple has to take me to the hospital, or frustrated when I have to wait 24 hours before my husband reads my e-mail and even realizes that the baby and I had an overnight visit.

The only thing that keeps me going is the hope that someday, in a land far, far away from Iraq, my prince and I will get to live out the real marriage dream that every other couple takes for granted every day, and hold each other in hospital beds until death do us part.

When I submitted that column to my editor, I really did think that I was being real with myself, and with my readers. The night I wrote it, I was missing my husband like crazy and I was battling that constant egocentric voice that told me I deserved my husband there. Mr. Hyde was shoving Dr. Jeckel's fingers out of the way and inserting typos right and left. But when I read the column on Friday after it appeared in print, I was hit immediately, once again, by my own selfishness.

Teresa and Todd spent a night in a hospital holding the hands of a dehydrated, puking pregnant woman and all I could say was, "Gee, I wish you were my husband." How ungrateful I was for the love and assistance of others!

Unfortunately, that's one of the many traps of dealing with deployment, or any trying issue, on the home front. You become so consumed with your own life and the fight each day just to emotionally survive that you fail to see the way others sacrifice moments of their own lives to make yours better. If you're not careful, you can quickly start viewing your life through the lens of what you don't have instead of what you do, and that dangerous perspective leads not only to unhappiness, but to egocentricity, self-pity and sloth. Egocentric, self-pitying sloths have a pretty tough time supporting their husbands, encouraging their families or making any kind of positive difference in the world.

I decided at that moment that I no longer wanted to be one. So once again, I adjusted my attitude — a daily practice during deployment — and tried once again to embrace the blessings of my life as just that. Blessings.

"Dude, Jesus!" I literally yelled one night. "You need to hurry up and teach me how to consider it pure joy! Like, stat! I'm failing miserably here!"

Later that week, Teresa and Todd took me under their wings once again and invited me to Thanksgiving dinner at their place. With Todd's whole family and Teresa's amazing gourmet cooking, the event was wonderful.

Though I tried to count it all joy (especially Teresa's sweet potato casserole), it was still difficult to not miss my Matt.

Though we'd missed nearly every other holiday in our four years of long-distance relationships together, we'd never once missed a Thanksgiving since the day we started dating. And as I dug into the potatoes and passed around the rhubarb pie, a part of me felt empty without my awesome husband there to share in what would have been our very second Thanksgiving as a married couple.

That empty feeling only got worse when I returned home and read my e-mail the next day.

My husband's rear detachment commander had sent out a notice to the spouses of the soldiers in the 2-1 Infantry Battalion, my husband's unit, to let them know that the first soldier from 2-1 had died that Wednesday, the day before Thanksgiving.

PFC Christopher Alcozer had been guarding another wounded soldier when he himself was shot and killed by enemy fire. He was 21 years old, and he had just given his life for his country.

Alcozer's death really hit me hard. The unit had been deployed for three months without any fatalities, and this brave young man's sacrifice reminded me that our soldiers were not invincible, that they were not immortal. This was a young man who had served in the same unit with my husband, who had been in the same platoon with our neighbor, and who was now dead.

I read the e-mail and read the e-mail and read the e-mail, and every time, I just found myself in tears. With nowhere to go and no place else to find comfort, I pulled out my stack of sympathy cards, wrote one to the Alcozer family and then spent the rest of the night writing letters to my husband telling him how much he meant to me.

CHAPTER FIVE
SACRIFICE

Until I married Matt, I'd never really been asked to make meaningful sacrifices in my life.

I'd grown up in an upper middle class home and both my parents were educated people with great jobs, great attitudes and a real heart for providing for their children. They paid for my clothes, my car and what my scholarship didn't cover of my college board and travels. Time and time again, they sacrificed for the happiness of my siblings and me. When my dad received a promotion that required him to move from Dayton, Ohio, to Washington, D.C., my parents even allowed me to remain in Dayton to finish my senior year of high school.

They made sacrifices that I never even realized and never really ever appreciated. But they rarely asked me to sacrifice for them — at least not in ways that involved investing any emotional energy.

When I married Matt, sacrifice seemed effortless. I was so absolutely crazy in love with this amazing military man that picking up my life every two to three years and moving across the country sounded like an exciting adventure, not a sacrifice. So what if I had to change jobs every 48 months? I had a short attention span, anyway, and change thrilled me.

It wasn't until that military job required Matt to miss our first anniversary (he spent that month training for Iraq in Louisiana) that I first started to grasp the depth of the sacrifice he might be asking me to make. When he deployed three months later, it really hit me.

Matt never asked me to sacrifice. I pledged my love and loyalty willingly and unconditionally without any contracts or concerns. Sacrificing for him was a joy and an honor.

But as soon as he left for Iraq, sacrifice suddenly became very challenging — a chore and a task that consumed all my physical and emotional energy. This was my husband's career choice, not mine, and one he had signed up for long before he met me. Why should I have to sacrifice for a decision my husband made when he was 18 years old? And now, why should our *child* have to sacrifice?

SACRIFICE

Sacrifice is hard. But if it weren't difficult, it wouldn't be meaningful, either. And it wouldn't have the ability to refine us.

I battled my selfish human nature tooth and nail every single day of deployment so that I could supportively and honorably sacrifice — not in a way that made my husband feel guilty or horrible or regretful (although I know there were times my selfish actions made him feel that way), but in a way that allowed him to focus on what he was doing — making sacrifices for his family, his friends and his country.

How could I ever complain about sacrificing for someone who was sacrificing in bigger and more meaningful ways than me?

I couldn't.

So I learned to live with the sacrifices, and even embraced them as a part of my decision to choose joy in the face of trials. Sometimes the sacrifices were easy — a dinner by myself, a Friday night alone — but sometimes, they were difficult — my feelings of security, my assurance of safety and, worst of all, my need for sanity.

Until They Come Home
December 2, 2005

The ring of my front doorbell used to be this exciting, welcoming sound. I'm a pretty big people person, and unexpected visitors have always been such a thrill.

It's amazing how that same tune changes so drastically once your husband is in harm's way.

Last week, at 2:30 a.m., my doorbell rang.

I immediately bolted up in bed, not knowing what to do. And for a moment after that terrible ring, I just sat there, clinging to my quilt. Maybe if I didn't answer the door, no one could give me any bad news. I was terrified, and my hands started shaking as I grabbed my sweatshirt and stumbled down the stairs to the front entryway, my barking beagle right behind me.

When I opened the door, there stood my worst nightmare: a police officer.

I shook my head back and forth and bit my lip, fighting back the tears, but becoming hysterical inside.

"Are you the wife of Matthew Cuthrell?" she asked me very officially.

BEHIND THE BLUE-STAR BANNER

I just shook my head violently and murmured, "No! No!" as she let herself in the front door. I didn't want for this moment to come, and I could feel my heart breaking. I was gasping for air, and my eyes began building up the tears. Police officers don't stop by in the middle of the night unless someone very close to you is hurt, or dead. My knees started quivering, and I suddenly felt nauseous. Until she spoke her next words.

"Well, may I please speak with him?"

I paused, my mind not catching up with what my ears had just heard.

When I told her that he was in Iraq, she seemed puzzled. After a few more inquiries, we together discovered her fatal flaw: She had come to the wrong address, and had therefore asked for the wrong name.

And my heart beat a million miles per minute.

Had I been thinking properly, I should have been relieved when I opened my door to find a city police officer instead of a uniformed soldier standing on my stoop. But ever since Matt deployed, I suppose I've been a little more paranoid, a little more jumpy — and not just with police officers at 2:30 a.m.

Yesterday, a couple of really sweet neighbor kids stopped by my house around dinnertime to see if they could help me shovel my driveway. But when my bell rang and I wasn't expecting visitors, my heart just sank, and that horrible, unmentionable thought just settled into the back of my mind as I forced myself to go answer the front door.

It's so hard when you're constantly worried about someone you love to not be paranoid, to not think the worst. You do all these things all day long to keep optimistic, to stay busy. You post lists of all the positive aspects of deployment on your refrigerator, recite a million reasons a day why your husband is safe and there's no need to worry.

But when you're home alone at night in a house that seems empty and with a family that's split apart, part of you just can't be the same. You don't sleep as well at night; you don't feel as secure during the day. Part of you always feels like you need to be on edge when people come knocking on your door, or worried when the phone rings a little later than maybe it should.

Maybe in eight more months my doorbell will once again be a happy thing, late night phone calls great surprises. But until my husband is safely home, I'm afraid paranoia is going to be an unavoidable part of my door-answering routine.

And I wasn't the only one.

After my column appeared in the paper that Friday, I received phone calls, e-mails and in-person comments from other spouses who told me tales very similar to mine.

One woman lived on post and had a military police officer show up at her front door at 2 a.m. He waited just long enough for her to panic before he told her there had been a bomb threat at the facility across the street, and he needed to evacuate her from her home temporarily until they checked it out.

Another woman told me stories of how her children's friends rang the doorbell late at night or early in the morning, scaring her into believing that maybe, just maybe, it was a uniformed soldier standing at her front door at such odd hours.

It's hard to combat that kind of paranoia, especially when you care about someone so much. It's every military spouse's worst fear to see that uniformed soldier pull up, to hear that battalion commander on the other end of the line. And though you try not to think about those things, it's hard not to remember that they are real when women like your next-door neighbor and friends down the street have experienced them firsthand.

Back in Iraq, I knew Matt's unit was completing some very intense missions. His battalion, the 2-1 Infantry Battalion of the 172nd Stryker brigade, was responsible for safety and security in the city of Mosul. They spent most of their time patrolling neighborhoods and detaining terrorists. And there had been losses. The brigade lost four soldiers from August to December, one of a non-combat related injury. It had been hard on the guys, and it had been hard on the families back home. And it hit much closer to home than I ever imagined.

Our neighbor had been seriously injured by a grenade and was transported to Walter Reed Medical Center for treatment. His near-fatal wounds occurred the day after Matt sat down with him at breakfast. It was scary how many faces I knew, how many friends' friends or neighbors or commissary cashiers or PX workers or acquaintances I'd interacted with who had faced the injuries or deaths of loved ones with the brigade. It was a much smaller community than I anticipated, and every injury, every fatality, affected all of us much more than I would have ever dreamed. It was hard, and it was real.

I sent cards and notes to all the parents and spouses of soldiers who had been killed, but the rear detachment commanders weren't allowed to release the names or contact info for soldiers who had been wounded, so it was hard to reach out to them and let them know we cared. No matter how much or how little I did, I couldn't help but think that it wasn't enough. And it probably wasn't. Nothing I could do could be sufficient for those who had lost loved ones to the realities of war. Not for guys who were putting their lives on the line every single day because they believed in the kind of sacrifice required to serve their country.

It was sometimes really overwhelming to think about, really overwhelming to bear. So I dealt with it all by staying busy and trying not to let it consume my thoughts, my life.

But every spouse has her bad days — the days she doesn't want to get out of bed and she's just so worried sick about her husband (no matter how safe she thinks his job is) that she can't hardly focus on anything else — and her good days — the days that go by so quickly that she can't believe it's already December and she only has eight more months of deployment to endure. I'd found myself in both positions. What I found really hard to deal with was the way people reacted to the way I personally reacted to deployment.

Many of my friends and family from home had called, only to have me answer the phone in a great mood with everything going really well. My far-away friends told me, "You don't have to be okay — this is so hard. Let it all out. You seem like you're taking this too well. Why aren't you crying right now?" As if I were putting up a front, or trying to put on a happy face when I was really stinking at life.

I would face those complaints only to turn around and be real about deployment struggles in the town newspaper and then receive an e-mail from a military wife who told me that I need to be stronger and support our soldiers by staying strong at home — basically, telling me to suck it up and not let everyone know that deployment stinks sometimes. One person implied that I was being unpatriotic by expressing some of the difficult aspects of deployment in a public forum. I just felt like I couldn't win. And I didn't feel that fronting — pretending that I was happy-happy, joy-joy to be pregnant in Alaska without my husband during the holi-

SACRIFICE

days — did anyone in our community a service. That's not what my column was for. And it sure as heck wasn't a service to myself, or to my husband, to be that fake.

No matter who I spoke to, I tried to be real. I was honest when I had bad days, and I wasn't afraid to express how hard it was to deal with deployment. But I also was not afraid to look on the positive side and express my joy when I'd had some really great weeks, either. And as long as I was writing a column or talking to friends or relating to my husband, I was going to be real — whether that was really happy or really down, I promised, I'd be real. Dealing with other people's reactions to my own reaction to deployment was probably one of the most complicated and difficult things I dealt with, outside the deployment itself.

The pregnancy, however, was going great. We found out officially that we were having a little baby boy, and since my husband wasn't around to share my joyous, funny pregnancy moments, I created a list to send to my friends.

December 2005

Michelle's Top 5 Favorite Pregnancy Moments

1. Matt's response when we found out, for sure, that we are having a boy. He called my work about 20 minutes after my ultrasound appointment, and when I told him it was a boy, he asked how I knew. I then proceeded to tell him that the doc had printed me out a close-up of the baby's penis. To that, my wonderful Army husband, of course, asked, "Really? Is it big?!" Remind me how I am going to live in a house with two men and a male dog again?

2. Midnight pineapple cravings. My food aversions have finally passed, and I have now started experiencing some pretty normal cravings: chocolate, Neapolitan ice cream and pineapple. But not just canned pineapple — fresh pineapple. Okay, I'm not sure whose funny trick it was to make Michelle crave pineapple. In the wintertime. In Fairbanks, Alaska. In the middle of the night. Can we discuss how few good pineapples there are in Fairbanks, Alaska? I mean, had I craved reindeer or moose roast or Eskimo pies, maybe I would have been set. But pineapple? So, yeah, once I finally found some decent pineapples, I took them home, cut them up and ate two of them in one night. Two whole pineapples. It's

BEHIND THE BLUE-STAR BANNER

almost 11 p.m. now and I'm thinking I might just have to make another Safeway run. That's why, along with my Mace, my military ID and my keys, I now carry a pineapple cutter in my purse at all times. You think I'm joking.

3. Receiving stuffed giraffes in the mail from my friend who swore she sent me a moose. Matt and I decided to decorate the baby's room in moose and other Alaskan décor, and my awesome friend Miss Jenny Marsella decided that she was going to be super sweet and send me a stuffed moose to put in the baby's room. Too bad she sent me a giraffe instead. When I called her to thank her for the baby's gift, she said to me, "Um, yeah, I think I don't know what a moose looks like, because my roommates just told me I sent you a giraffe." The best part: She was convinced the baby was going to be a girl, so not only is there a giraffe in the baby boy's moose room, but there's a giraffe with pink tags on its neck telling him what a beautiful princess of God he is. This is going to be a keeper.

4. Filling out a cow costume for Halloween. Even though I still had to stuff a pillow in there to make it look real, all the kiddies at the church carnival I volunteered at that night were convinced I had grown a baby in my stomach overnight. I'm sure our baby boy will love looking back at pictures in the womb and really appreciate the fact that I included him in Halloween even before he was born. He was, after all, my set of utters.

5. Picking out baby names. Matt vetoed my favorites — Atticus and Amadeus. I vetoed his pick — Sun Tsu. For two weeks, we thought we'd reached a compromise and actually found a boy baby name we loved, but even that's now down the drain. We're taking recommendations!

Of course, like any pregnant woman, I experienced my share of ups and downs, which, I'm sure, were only enhanced by the emotional ups and downs of deployment. Even after my most joyous pregnancy moments, I still suffered from bouts of depression and resentment that I had to physically push out of my mind in order to remain emotionally healthy for my husband and myself.

68

SACRIFICE

Until They Come Home
December 16, 2005

Less than a week after my husband deployed to Iraq, I was already spending every spare second browsing discount airfare Web sites, searching for the cheapest fare I could find to be back in the Lower 48 for Christmas.

I realize Mary and Joseph probably didn't have a lot of company or daylight as Mary was popping out a baby in the hay by a manger, but I wasn't a big fan of spending my Savior's birthday pregnant and alone in the dark in Alaska. So I bought tickets to my well-lit, people-filled and restaurant-ready hometown of Dayton, Ohio, for the holiday season instead.

Dayton would be my answer, I told myself, the cure-all to all my holiday missing-Matt woes.

But as I loaded up my suitcases and packed up my puppy to head home last Wednesday night, I found that the trip back home that I had been billing for months as my missing-Matt medicine suddenly seemed a little less healing, and a little more heartbreaking.

As I unplugged my Christmas tree and "I'll Be Home for Christmas" droned in the background, I choked back building tears and wondered if "home" would really be the same without the man who has always made our hometown feel like one.

Though Fairbanks was our first home as a married couple, everything we are today sprouted from the seeds planted in Dayton. It's where we met, where we dated and where we wed, and every corner of the city has some kind of special memory associated with my husband that I never realized until I visited it without him.

I walked the Dayton Mall for the first time in months — and nearly cried when I saw the Santa Claus portraits my husband refused to take and buy every year.

I ate at the Olive Garden restaurant I'd been craving for weeks — and started sniffling when I saw his favorite Tour of Italy meal on the menu.

I spent the night at our sister's house — and almost broke down when I slept in the same tiny twin bed that we'd both squeezed into on our last Dayton visit because we couldn't bear to spend a second apart, even for one night.

BEHIND THE BLUE-STAR BANNER

Maybe I'm just overly emotional and super hormonal. Hey, I'm pregnant with a deployed spouse — I don't feel too bad about it. But there were bigger, more legitimate Matt reminders, too.

Like when I attended the wedding last Friday of a couple I set up several years ago — in the church where Matt and I got married.

And when our niece told the story of her school field trip on Wednesday — to the dinner theater where Matt proposed.

And, of course, perhaps the most awkward moment, when Mom and Dad rented us a hotel room for the night when we attended a late-night wedding and the clerk oh-so-kindly upgraded us — to the exact same room where Matt and I had spent our wedding night.

Really, there's nothing like sleeping in the honeymoon suite of the Holiday Inn with your parents who know exactly what you did in that suite for the first time with your husband just a year and a half ago.

Though I never planned on sharing a heart-shaped hot tub with my parents, planning my trip in Fairbanks, I thought that all these things would make me happy for the holidays — would bring out the Christmas spirit and kill the depression of spending it all without a husband. But without Matt, I've realized that these things are just empty facilities, and this town that I've always adored is still just a town. It takes my Matt at Christmastime to ever consider it a home.

Besides the fact that the airline cancelled one of my flights, rerouted me to a new airport, delayed my last flight and lost my luggage, coming home wasn't everything I had been anticipating.

The people, of course, were amazing. And being with family during the Christmas season was so wonderful. But being there without Matt was really hard.

I spent my first week home in Dayton, Ohio, with his family. They laughed with me, they loved on me — they were more than I could have ever asked for. But still, it was very difficult to be around these people I loved so much without the person they loved more than anything in the world. Everywhere we went, it seemed like there was this empty car seat or this unexplainable void that only Matt could fill. Our conversations weren't as light, our days weren't as full. Matt just added something very special, and his family and I both knew that it wasn't the same without him there.

It wasn't the same attending events with my friends, either, even though many of them didn't even know Matt. But wow, did they ever try.

To keep my mind off missing Matt for the holidays, my friends took me to weddings and malls, Lonestar Steakhouses and Arby's restaurants. They reintroduced me to everything I had been missing for the last year living in the Last Frontier, and even told jokes and performed skits to make me laugh. Three friends even humored me by driving me "30 minutes to my aunt's house" — and even laughed when the adventure, like Gilligan's, turned into a three-hour tour.

To help celebrate my new mommyhood and make me forget about my geographical bachelorette lifestyle, two beautiful friends from high school even threw me a baby shower.

With hand-stained wooden alphabet cubes and mini beanbag moose on every table, Mandie and Melissa spent hours preparing for the baby shower of a lifetime. There were moose lights, moose stuffed animals and even a moose cake topper on my favorite white cream cake. (They apparently figured out that we were decorating the baby's room in moose.)

For two hours, Mandie and Melissa, along with the 20 friends and family who attended the beautiful affair, made me laugh, made me cry and made me remember that pregnancy was a joyful occasion. We giggled as we tasted jars of baby food, threw our Bingo sheets as the girl across the way won when I opened a new pacifier. For two hours, I was transported from "pregnancy is so difficult alone" world to "pregnancy is a joyous occasion" world. It was a service that meant more to me than all the money or pregnancy pep talks in the world.

Unfortunately, you can only hide from your life so long before you have to face it again.

As I was helping my daddy and my papa pack up all my beautiful gifts after the shower, I just couldn't help but think of Matt. Everything made me think of Matt. I wanted him to see the beautiful party my friends had planned. I wanted him to meet all my friends who had never gotten the privilege of getting to know my husband before we got married. I wanted my husband to see all the wonderful onesies and sweet little slings and gosh-darn-awesome gadgets and toddling toys we'd received for our unborn child. He was missing so much. I just wanted him to be a part of the wonderfulness that was my friends and family, and the amazing gift that was our unborn child.

But Matt was in Iraq, and I just had to get over myself and what I wanted out of my life.

One week later, I said goodbye to my hometown and hello to road trip one. Though part of me was really sad to leave, part of me was very ready to go. Dayton was just not a happy place without the man I'd married there in that town.

I gave my new family all big hugs, hopped into the truck my aunt let me borrow, shed a tear or two at the thought of saying goodbye to the people who meant so much to me, and then, with almost a sigh of relief, hit the road and weathered a snowstorm to head up to New York to visit with some old college friends. Matt and I had no memories in New York, and I hoped this would be a welcome emotional break.

As I stood in the snow and knocked on the door of my college roommate's new place, I just breathed in the chilly Ithaca air and expelled it from my lungs once again. It felt refreshing to be somewhere away from Matt memory land.

And when my amazing friend Lindsey answered the door with her long chocolate hair and her memorable smile, I just felt lighter, easier. Something about being around best friends brings out the best in you, no matter what kind of crappy life situation you're in at the moment.

Linds and I spent the night chatting about our life, our dreams and how I felt about deployment, and the next afternoon, we piled into a car with our other former college roommates and hit the road for the Adirondacks as snow began to blanket the highway before us.

There's nothing like New York snowfall in December. It was just somehow happier than the snowfall back in Fairbanks. Maybe because it snowed less. Maybe because it happened less frequently. Maybe because when it snows in New York, you feel classy — like the girl on all those romantic comedies that take place in New York City and feature couples holding hands on the ice at Rockefeller Plaza as snow sprinkles their perfectly matching hats and gloves and they stare into each other's eyes and kiss under the moon-kissed shadows of the New York City skyline. Even when

SACRIFICE

you're not going to New York City, you still feel classy. (Although after my adventures in the Adirondacks, I was fortunate enough to actually visit my wonderful friend Morgan in the Big Apple. And at six months pregnant, she and I walked the town like we owned it, shopping at the three-story Babies R Us and the cutest maternity clothing stores I'd ever seen, which, after shopping at the maternity section in the Fairbanks Wal-Mart, was not saying too much.)

It snowed the entire three-hour drive to our picture-perfect cabin, and when we arrived and our friends Jon and Nikki greeted us with hot chocolate and a tour of the most beautiful mountain cabin I have ever seen, I just felt at home. I never liked living in New York. And yet there, in that small cabin surrounded by friends I'd missed for a year of my life, I felt comforted and safe. And happy, though I couldn't help but wish Matt was there to cuddle by the crackling fire with some of the most caring friends I'd ever made.

Until They Come Home
December 23, 2005

I was nestled under a handmade fleece blanket in a cabin in the Adirondack Mountains last weekend when some college friends and I got into a conversation about Christmas.

"Is it hard to spend Christmas without your husband?" my former roommate asked me as we sipped on smoothies and munched on mint cookies on the couch in our friend's remote cabin.

"Very hard," I told her, tucking my toes into the blanket that reminded me so much of the ones I always cuddled under with Matt. The red-orange fire crackled, and I glanced away from my friend, fighting back tears. "It's all about family this time of year, and it doesn't feel like Christmas without Matt here."

But is it really?

Society tells me Christmas is all about friends and family, caring and sharing. You're supposed to sing Christmas songs around pianos and kiss under the mistletoe. Everything is about what you do and who you're with.

With this concept of Christmas implanted in my brain, it's been so difficult for me to say that I can actually celebrate mine joyfully without the most important family member and friend there to share in it with me.

But the thing is, Christmas is not about the days we spend decorating the tree or the nights we spend attending holiday parties. It's not about the cookies Matt and I used to eat by the handful, not about the prime rib dinners and festivities we look forward to on that day. It's not even really about the awesome people we might spend it with. Christmas is all about the birth of Jesus Christ, and that's something that you don't need family or holly or Christmas trees or even your husband to celebrate.

Some 2,000 years ago, in a manger in Bethlehem, the son of God was born. And 2,000 years later, most of us are so preoccupied dressing up and making family plans that we forget the reason we get together in the first place.

Jesus was born only so that he could make the ultimate sacrifice — his birth alone was a gift to us, and his death, an unreturnable sacrifice that none of us could ever match.

If Christmas is really about the birth of this messiah and the importance of the sacrifice he would make 30-some years later, why was I not taking joy in the small sacrifice I myself could make? Jesus gave his life so that I could live. On the anniversary of his birth, isn't it appropriate that I give up something meaningful in my life so that the true meaning of his birth can live on, too?

The funny thing about sacrifice is that you can make one meaninglessly. You can sacrifice something so important for years, and never truly grow from it because of the way you choose to view it.

For the past four and a half months, I've been so busy considering this yearlong deployment a trial to endure that I have failed to see it as an opportunity to grow. Rather than seeking out ways I can use it to better myself, my marriage and my faith, I've gotten caught up in the "woe is me" moments and the "it's just too hard" mindsets that are so easy to fall into when something hurts your heart so much.

That ends today.

This year, on Christmas, instead of reveling in the family moments and the mistletoe kisses, I am going to revel in the fact that I can somehow share in Christ's sacrifice, and grow closer to his character because of it.

SACRIFICE

Though it might not be the most traditional Christmas, I know that this Christmas will probably be the most meaningful and significant I've celebrated in years.

And it really was meaningful.

On Christmas Eve, my mom and dad and sister and brother and aunt and uncle and papa and new grandma-in-law and aunt-in-law all gathered at my parents' Michigan home for two days with family and a whole lot of home-cooked food.

Though I did have memories of Matt in this place, Christmas was so full of joy and so warm and welcoming that I was able to step back and really appreciate the kind of sacrifice I was being called to make. Though I missed him tons, especially when I opened gifts intended for the new baby, I took joy in knowing that this sacrifice would not only bring me closer to my husband later, but also closer to the character of Christ. It was marvelous, it was memorable and it was meaningful, for both my family and me.

Until They Come Home
December 30, 2005

Since my husband and I were married more than a year and a half ago, I've always kind of carried the label "Matt's crazy wife." So when I told friends that, though he was deployed, I was planning to share a New Year's Eve kiss with my love, they didn't ask questions about the logistics of tongue-tying from thousands of miles away. They know I'm just ridiculous enough to make that kiss happen.

And I plan on it.

It's just that this year, it's going to have to be made out of chocolate — a dozen Hershey's Kisses, a picture of me in my New Year's formal and a CD kissed with too-bright red lipstick that plays the traditional New Year's Eve song, all of which should arrive in Iraq sometime this week.

Not too shabby for a long-distance New Year's Eve date.

After three years of long-distance dating and another year of long-distance marriage under our belts — not to mention the seven and a half additional months we've yet to endure — Matt and I have become pretty good at maintaining romance over the miles. We've learned that not every anniversary comes with an in-

person date, not every New Year's Eve comes with a goodnight kiss. But that doesn't mean that we can't turn the obstacle of a long-distance relationship into an opportunity for some very creative romance.

And believe me, we definitely have.

I once ordered pizza to be delivered to Matt's dorm on a day I knew he was too busy to eat — and just may have tipped the driver extra for scribbling a cute message on the inside of the box and humming him a tune at the door.

Matt has called me on more than one occasion to tell me jokes and sing "sweet dreams" in the middle of the night.

I have sent him a series of goofy pictures of myself acting out the lyrics to his favorite "I Love You Period" song to keep him laughing when we can't be together.

He has driven 550 miles overnight just to surprise me with a rose, a kiss and a dinner.

Together, we've held long-distance pizza and movie nights (where we both order pizza and rent movies and then talk on the phone as we enjoy both from afar), regular instant messenger dates and played half a million creative "I Love You More" games in between.

Admittedly, it's a little more difficult to maintain that same romance when you only get to speak to your husband for 30 minutes once a week and you can hear the conversation of Johnny soldier at the next payphone. But as Matt and I are constantly learning, there are several small ways Army couples can keep the flame lit from Fairbanks to Mosul. A few of them include:

- Sending pictures. But not just of the everyday things. Send posed pictures of winks, smiles, seductive grins and all those funny expressions you know the other person misses about you most.
- Handwriting long, snail-mail letters on a weekly basis.
- Mailing dates in a box. If he likes Friday ice cream and movie nights, send Astronaut ice cream and his favorite DVDs. If her fondest memory includes dinner and dancing, order a dress online and have it delivered with a CD of all the songs that make you think of her. Create a dinner and dancing out coupon dated for when you return.
- Sending a kiss — chocolate if need be — for every day you

SACRIFICE

have to spend apart. Staple cute messages to each kiss so that your spouse has something to look forward to each day.

Finding new and more creative ways to show my husband I love him from afar is my New Year's resolution this year.

Because my column space was limited to 620 words, I wasn't able to list all the creative ideas Matt and I had conjured up in the newspaper. But there were many more — ideas we'd tried, ideas we'd always wanted to try, ideas that might just be too weird to try.

Even with fabulous, romantic and creative New Year's ideas sent to your hubby afar, when the clock strikes midnight, it's still pretty lonely to be standing all by yourself in your black formal.

I was attending the wedding and reception of a good friend in Philadelphia on New Year's Eve. All around me were beautiful flowers, close friends and lively music to keep me happy. Gold and cream decorations glistened on my round table and accents of cranberry and pine filled the room with a festive spirit. But at midnight, when all the other couples were kissing and ushering in the New Year, I had to make a bathroom run to go dry my tears.

For some reason, New Year's hit me like a brick. Maybe it was because it was such a beautiful event. Maybe it was because it was a wedding and love was all around. I'm not sure. All I know is that I just wanted more than anything for Matt to be there sharing that precious moment with me.

As I took a deep breath and opened that bathroom stall door with "Auld Lang Syne" droning in the background, I sent a little love note via mental telegram to my husband.

"I hope you know how much I love you," I whispered.

And I grabbed my black velvet purse and marched back out on that dance floor knowing that it was at least now 2006 — the year of my husband's return.

CHAPTER SIX
BUSYNESS

Christmas in Mosul
January 2, 2006

Greetings from Iraq!

I haven't sent anything out in a while, so I figured I'd write and wish everyone a Merry Christmas and a Happy New Year! (Basically my wife told me I had to send out a mass e-mail because I haven't done so in a while. Yes, dear.)

So, anyway, things are going well. We had a good Christmas complete with an official tree lighting ceremony and all the non-alcoholic beer we could stand, commonly referred to here as NA.

We have been pretty busy over the past couple of months. We recently assisted the Iraq agencies in completing the national elections — a huge success for the new government. It all ran relatively smoothly. I guess the biggest news was that one of my medics, SPC Crowe, saved the life of a 2-year-old boy who had drowned in the basement of his family residence. The kid was not breathing and was blue when Crowe brought him back to life. The story made CNN and he received the Bronze Star from Secretary of Defense Donald Rumsfeld. That was pretty cool, except for the fact that I personally had to brief the Secretary on what had happened.

First off, I didn't know how to address him, so I reverted to the always-safe "sir." I guess I should watch more The West Wing. *Secondly, I was so nervous I almost threw up on his shoes. But all went well and Crowe was recognized as the hero that he is.*

Aside from that, things are the same as they always are. Today is just like yesterday, which will be just like tomorrow. Some days I am lucky and get to attend four meetings instead of just two. That's the Army way — have a meeting to coordinate what you are going to discuss at the next meeting.

I would like to thank everyone for all the gifts, packages and letters. Your support really means a lot to all of us over here away from family during the holidays. And thank you to all who sent letters with Michelle's care package. They all meant a lot!

In the absence of friends and family, we do a lot of weird

BUSYNESS

things to keep motivated around here.

My sister sent a 27-pound bag of cookies in a care package. Now that's a lot of cookies! Some of my guys bet another guy that he couldn't eat the whole bag in 24 hours. Let's just say there was a lot of money in it for him if he won. Well, he tried, and failed miserably, and his excuse? I didn't have any milk. So we all got to enjoy the cookies for the next week. Krysti, I can't wait for the next batch!

I got frocked to 1 LT last week. (Yes, frocked is a military term, not a nice way to say the expletive.) So we held the ceremony in front of the battalion and all is good. I am no longer the only 2 LT in Task Force 2-1.

So really we live pretty boring lives. This is already way too long, and I haven't learned much since the last e-mail, but I'll try anyway. Here are the most important things I've learned in the last two months:

1. Intelligence reports are awesome. We always get reports to beware of this activity or watch out for that person. But sometimes you really get the detailed report that will save the day, such as: "Beware of a red Opel Vectra with unknown license plate number driven by an unknown number of military-aged males. They are suspected of doing such and such activity." What the heck? Now I had never heard of an Opel car before I got to Iraq, but it is the car of choice for insurgents — and everyone else in Mosul. This report narrows the search down to about 500,000 people. Awesome.

2. IEDs and mortar rounds still blow.

3. I still get yelled at just as much as a 1 LT as I did as a 2 LT.

4. E-mail and digital paperwork saves time — but it lasts forever! Watch out what you send. I had a memorandum I wrote months ago resurface out of context and really bite me in the butt. I love technology!

5. Iraq will never be known for its plumbing feats. The pipes to the toilets here are very small. So small, in fact, that you can't flush toilet paper or it will get clogged. So you have to throw the paper in the trashcan. Now it was hard at first to undo 27 years of conditioning and throw the stuff in the trash as compared to the toilet. But now it's a habit. I can already hear Michelle yelling at me for that one when I come home: "Why is that stuff in the trash? The dog will get in it!" It takes the not-putting-the-toilet-seat-down argument to a new level.

BEHIND THE BLUE-STAR BANNER

Well, that's all I have. Thanks again for all the support and prayers. It means a lot. Stay safe and see you all soon.

Matt

Until They Come Home
January 6, 2006

I had just enjoyed the first sips of my morning Ice Rage and blown a kiss to the picture of my husband that sits next to my computer on my office desk when I came across an e-mail from Matt's rear detachment commander.

CPT Tim Sawyer regularly sends informational e-mails about Fort Wainwright services to the spouses of deployed soldiers in our battalion. But the subject of this e-mail was "Alcozer family," and I knew right away that this wasn't positive news.

PVT Christopher Alcozer was the name of the soldier who fought so bravely in Iraq in November and was shot as he protected a fellow wounded soldier. He was the first soldier killed from my husband's battalion — only 21 years old and engaged. Often throughout the holidays, I prayed big prayers for his fiancée and family, and hoped they were dealing okay without their loved one this time of year.

But when I opened CPT Sawyer's e-mail, I realized that they needed more than just big prayers in the face of even more tragedy.

This week, as the family watched movies upstairs in their Illinois home, a candle left burning on a shrine to their son caught his picture on fire and sent the house into flames. They all made it out safely, but everything they owned was gone — including most of the memories that remained of their son.

This tragedy, of course, piled atop the other challenges the family faced this year.

First, Christopher's father lost his job. Then, his veteran's benefits were cut. On November 19, the family lost their 21-year-old son. Days later at his funeral, they faced half a dozen protesters who stood across the street with signs that read, "Thank God for dead soldiers."

And now, according to the Chicago Tribune, a fire had taken away everything they had to remind them of their beloved child *except for the flag that draped his coffin and a collection of his medals, which one firefighter was able to retrieve after Christopher's father mentioned that he had nothing left of his son.*

As I read this e-mail and the newspaper articles attached to it, I looked around me and realized I had everything in my tiny office space that this family had lost in a matter of one year — a job, three pictures of my soldier and letters from a family member still alive in Iraq — all things that this family no longer could call their own.

As I fought back tears, I opened the next attachment to this horrible e-mail.

But it was in that second attachment that my heart saw some hope and I remembered why, though it was sometimes very difficult, I was always proud to be a member of the military community.

It was a flier created by a member of Matt's battalion that explained the Alcozer family's situation. The bottom line read, "Donations will be collected by Company 1 Sergeants and turned into the 2-1 S1 by the 10th of January 2006. Get the word out! Let's help the family of one of our own."

One of our own.

If I've learned anything in my year and a half as a military wife, I've learned that no matter how hard the circumstances, no matter how difficult the job, military families take care of their own like no one else I've ever seen. Soldiers and families of soldiers are families of the military — and family is always looked after.

Whether you are part of Christopher Alcozer's military family or not, you are, in fact, part of the Fairbanks family where he once lived. I encourage anyone who still has a living son, a standing home, an active job or a tangible family photo album to donate to this grief-stricken and needy family.

Matt heard about the situation around the same time as I did, and we knew that we had to help out this family. I couldn't even imagine going through what this family had endured in just the last 12 months. As if losing a son wasn't unbearable enough.

So Matt and I scrounged up all the extra money we had for the month and sent a check to the Jesse Alcozer Family Fund, hoping that our small donation might be able to make some sort of difference for this tragedy-stricken family.

BEHIND THE BLUE-STAR BANNER

But gathering this money also made me realize something else: We had done a pretty poor job of financial planning if we had to scrounge and pick money together to help out a family in need, especially when the Army was paying us more during deployment. We should have been able to give freely and generously, not just out of the change we had left at the end of the month. I wondered what we were spending so much money on when we should have been saving so much more. That's when it hit me: Deployment costs money, too.

Until They Come Home
January 13, 2006

Theoretically, deployment should mean big money.

When we found out that Matt would receive hostile fire and imminent danger pay, hardship duty pay and a family separation allowance each month of his deployment to Iraq, plus earn his entire income federal tax-free, we thought we'd be rolling in the dough.

We were going to pay off the credit card, buy a treadmill and take a trip to Hawaii. Oh, and, with my new income, we were going to put away $10,000 in a savings account, besides — you know, all the super realistic things that young couples say before they realize that they're really just stupid, naïve kids who think big dreams and bad budgeting gets them debt-free and on vacation.

But when I nearly bounced a check last month trying to pay a routine bill, I realized that, although you do indeed get paid more during deployment, you also spend a lot more during deployment, too.

Especially now that the U.S. Postal Service raised its prices.

When I tried to mail my regular flat-rate cheer-up package to my husband on Monday, I was informed that the cost of flat-rate boxes had now increased from $7.70 to $8.10, along with everything else at the post office.

With the number of flat-rate packages I mail my husband (about one every other week for 52 weeks at $8.10 a package), and the number of letters and cards I try to send in the mail (at least one each week for 52 weeks at now 39 cents a card), I figure I'll be spending close to $231 this year on shipping costs alone. And that doesn't even include the contents of those packages and envelopes.

BUSYNESS

Cards, at least the cute ones, run close to $3.50 a pop. Multiply that by 52 and you're spending $182 in cards in a year. Granted, sometimes I send handwritten letters on Xerox or notebook paper, but you still have to pay to write on something.

The packages are worse. I try to fill them with fun things to distract Matt from the routine and sometimes hardship of deployment. But everything from books to games to DVDs to candy — all my favorite mailing items — cost money. I generally spend about $30 per flat-rate box. Multiply that by the 26 or so boxes I'll probably send this year and that's $780 in deployment goodies.

Then, of course, you have to include phone cards, which cost us about $25 per month ($300 for the 12 months of deployment), the Web camera that many of my fellow spouses have purchased (anywhere between $20 and $200, depending on the type and quality) and the phone and Internet bills you have to pay to use those phone cards and Web cams.

And don't forget the unexpected extra costs on the home front, either.

Whereas Matt would normally shovel the driveway without a problem, since I'm pregnant, I now pay the neighbors to do it for me.

And even though you'd think I'd be saving money on food with half the number of people in my house, I'm finding that I'm spending even more because, rather than cook for one and eat alone, I tend to go out three or four times as much to be around people and get a decent meal.

Other costs: The cost of plane tickets to go home when you can't stand to be alone in Alaska anymore, the cost of travel once you get there and the monthly "don't get depressed — go do something fun" fund that my husband so graciously allows me to help make it through this deployment.

So much for the treadmill and the savings account. But at least we'll be out of credit card debt when we charge our trip to Hawaii next year.

After I submitted that column, I sat down with our bills and a Bic and reworked all our finances. I wanted to use the resources God had given us in a responsible way, and I knew that we weren't quite doing that at the moment.

I reworked some numbers, made an actual on-paper budget

and actually developed a plan to pay off our credit card and pay for some of our upcoming needs (like baby supplies) without going back into debt.

As I removed my calico glasses and took one last look at the spreadsheet I had created on paper and now typed into the computer, I nodded in approval. For a girl who hadn't taken math since her junior year of high school, I was pretty proud. And I think Matt was pretty proud, too.

So for a few days, we sailed on this "we finally have our finances under control" high. Things were good, we were good. Though our budget caused us to restrict our spending, in one sense, I just felt so free. I didn't have to feel guilty about spending money on groceries, or blowing money on retail therapy. Now I had a budget, and now I had limits, and that made me feel so comfortable, and somehow, so safe.

But just when things seemed to be going great for us as a married couple during a deployment, that's when the emotions kicked in, and I wondered why we had to do all this financial planning in the first place. Why did I have to take over this role when it was normally one my husband would gladly assume? Why did I have to manage not only the finances, but the home, the baby preparations, five jobs and all the meals?

In fact, why did I have to do any of these things alone at all?

Resentment built in not just the area of finances, but also the area of relationships and quality time. All these little incidents I had shoved off in far-away places for months started creeping back into the picture.

And when I came home from work the next day after a very long day and found only a couple e-mails instead of the normal five or six, something inside me just snapped. I realized I had to sit down and talk to my husband about this building resentment before I started lashing out instead. So I sent him an e-mail.

Until They Come Home
January 20, 2006

It had been a long day.
A really long day.
I had no food in the house, my lower back killed, my baby brother and I were fighting and I was craving pineapple I didn't

BUSYNESS

have. The -30 degree Fairbanks weather didn't help my pregnancy woes any, either. All I wanted at the end of my day was to come home and just nuzzle under a blanket with my husband who would let me know that everything would be alright.

But when I got home and checked my e-mail, not only did I not have a husband to snuggle up with, but I only had two e-mail messages from a husband who normally sends me five or six.

Being pregnant and emotional and unable to deal with deployment alone any longer, I wrote back something really grounded and down-to-earth, like, "I can't believe you only sent me two e-mails today. I don't feel like a priority in your life anymore. I hate the Army."

You know, something totally reasonable like that.

A long, sweet letter and a single red rose delivered to my door the next day reminded me that maybe, just maybe, I was being the unreasonable one.

Resenting your husband's job can become a real issue during deployment. Sure, the Army is great when it provides free post housing, free healthcare, great benefits and solid job security. And the community is a lot of fun when you get to attend balls, join spouses' clubs and run from social event to social event on post. But as soon as your hubby deploys, all of a sudden, that job you thought did so many great things for your family suddenly becomes your enemy, and you find yourself, at times, bitter and hardened that it is indeed a job that takes him away from his family for a year at a time.

It's a real feeling, and it's a real issue. When your husband can only contact you once or twice a week via telephone and the rest of the week via the Internet, it's hard to feel like you really are a priority in his life. You know how many hours a day he gets to spend with the guys in his platoon and the soldiers in his shop, and you feel cheated that that time isn't spent with you.

I don't know a single military wife who, if she's being real, at one point or another, if even for one moment, has not resented or been frustrated with the military lifestyle, or the job of her soldier.

It's a hard life, and deployment is a hard issue. And the truth is, we are in general selfish people. Everyone deep inside at some point wants what is best for herself and her family, with disregard to what that means for others. Even if those others are the people her husband protects.

BEHIND THE BLUE-STAR BANNER

In order to battle that resentment, I have to make a deliberate decision to sit down every day and remind myself of the real reason my husband is gone for a year. It's not because of a job, not because he's trying to be Superman and add a combat patch to his arm for good measure. And it's not because he loves the Army more than he loves me. In fact, it's just the opposite.

It's because 10 years ago, my husband made a decision that someone had to put his life on the line and sign up to protect and defend our country, and when his children and spouse did come along, he wanted that protector and defender to be him.

When you remember what it means for your husband to be a soldier, it's hard to resent a job that demands so much selflessness from one person.

I seriously have the best husband in the entire world.

I can't say enough about the importance of patient and supportive spouses during deployment. And I'm talking on the warfront side. Here I was lashing out at my husband, resenting a job that he had felt called to perform for years of his life — an important and vital job to the success of our country — and I could only think about myself. And here he was, sending me roses, apologizing for not making me feel like a priority, when it was, indeed, my own decision to let those feelings creep into my life.

Matt had never shown me such unconditional patience, love and support than he did that week my emotional, hormone-driven little heart snapped. And our marriage grew 10 times stronger because of that patience and love.

After mending our fences and recommitting to a loving and passionate marriage, the next day, we tackled — via the Internet, of course — the next biggest issue in our marriage: the name of our child. We were sure now that we were having a boy, but the only names we agreed on were for a girl. She was going to be either Denali Joelle (for the mountain our cabin sat under when we conceived the child) or McKinley Ashlyn (the more common name for Mt. McKinley) and we would call her Kinley.

But Matt wasn't a big fan of McKinley for a boy.

"He sounds like he should play tennis and tie a sweater around his shoulders as he uses words I'll never understand at the golf club we'll never be rich enough to be members of," he wrote me in one of his e-mails.

BUSYNESS

I kind of had to agree. Although I loved the name McKinley, it did sound a little hoity-toity for our casual family. So we brainstormed new names.

Matt had already turned down two of my favorites — Atticus and Amadeus, named after the great literary character Atticus Finch and the famous composer Wolfgang Amadeus Mozart — and wasn't a big fan of my other favorites, including Quinton (for the alliteration in Quinton Cuthrell), Austin-Blake (a combination of both our mother's maiden names) and Noah-Joel (for the Biblical references).

After what seemed like a hundred e-mail exchanges, Matt finally suggested Connor and Colin, and I suggested Joel. We agreed that, even though the other person's names weren't our favorites, we really did like any of those names and could definitely live with any of them as the name of our child.

Because we lived in Alaska, we felt that our family and friends missed so much of our lives, and now, so much of our child's life. They wouldn't be able to see the baby for months after he was born, and they wouldn't be able to play a physically active role in his life until we moved closer than the often 20-hour plane flight from Dayton or Detroit. We wanted them to be a part of our joy and play a part in our child's life. And so we decided to let them vote.

We sent out a mass e-mail and gave voting cards to all our family without e-mail addresses and asked them to vote on the names Conner Clarke, Colin Clarke and Joel James, and gave them an end-of-the-month deadline to complete their responses. It was wacky, it was crazy, it was unconventional. But it was a lot of fun, too. As votes came rolling in, Matt and I couldn't help but read the e-mails from two separate sides of the world and grin. Our friends were deciding our child's fate. What a way to go.

Dear Friends and Family…
January 2006

I'm sitting here cuddled underneath my new yellow ribbon fleece knot blanket, curled up into a ball with my unpolished fingers wrapped around a mug of steamy hot chocolate to stay warm, just staring out the window at the snow and ice in my backyard and wandering how long this Fairbanks winter is going to last.

BEHIND THE BLUE-STAR BANNER

The temperature has been a consistent and frigid -50 degrees all week, hitting -55 at its low. The newspaper even reported yesterday that, if temperatures stay like this for the next three days, this could be the coldest January on record since 1971. Great, glad I could be here for that one, thanks. I'm sure there's nothing more exciting than watching a pregnant woman waddle-run to her car to go start it every three hours in the middle of the day because her place of employment (the church) forgot to put outlets on the outside of the building when it was being constructed, and if you don't start your car or keep it plugged in in this weather, it dies. I bet Jack Frost gets a kick out of that scene every day.

If you remember my rants from last winter, you'll remember that Fairbanksans plug in their cars everywhere they go from October through March, and sometimes longer so that the engine doesn't freeze up. Every place from the Whirl Pool store to the Wal-Mart has little outlet boxes in the parking lot for customers and employees to keep their cars warm and running. I have the plug, I have the battery blanket for the car, I just have nowhere to plug the dang thing in. That means that every Monday through Thursday, I have to make a cute little trip to my car every three hours to start my vehicle so that it doesn't freeze up by the time I leave around 3 or 4pm. Loads of fun, let me tell you. But sometimes I cheat and play the pregnancy card and my pastor runs out and starts my car for me. But I try to reserve that card for the really bad days.

Lately, I've noticed visitors to the church parking lot "tucking in" their cars — wrapping their hoods and engines in thick wool blankets to keep the engine at a normal, non-freezing temperature. But I just can't bring myself to stand outside at -50 degrees long enough to tuck my car in. Please, in just nine weeks, I'll be tucking in a little baby boy every time I want to go anywhere in the Fairbanks frost, I don't need to add my car to the list of items that have to be swaddled this winter. But thanks, anyway.

Although I can't complain much today. The freeze finally broke, and we actually saw a high of -25 degrees for the first time in more than a week! Let me tell you, here, that's a heat wave. People were coming to church without gloves and hats, tromping in again with high heels and open jackets. You'd have thought we'd welcomed in spring already. I even got an e-mail after church from a couple from my small group talking about the "great weather" and reminding all of us to take advantage of it while we can. Yup, mental note: Take advantage of my nice warm house (where the Army pays for my heat — score!). Already on my list, thanks.

It's funny — though I complain quite a bit about the frigid Fairbanks temps, I'm actually really happy to be back here in this chilly town. Although my three weeks at home were relaxing and a lot of fun, I somehow missed this place and these people.

For the first time in my life, I feel like I can call a place other than Dayton "home." It's a really comforting feeling, and not one I would have anticipated feeling about this crazy little Alaska town. But when I stepped off that plane on January 1 and took a nice big breath of cold mountain air, I just felt safe, comfortable, right somehow. For the first time, my post house — off-white hospital walls and all — felt like home, and my post facilities, like my hometown stores. And the people felt like real neighbors and good friends rather than these crazy people who somehow chose to live in Alaska on their own, or just happen to hang out with me because we live in the same town.

Of course, this homey feeling could be because we now have not only a Chili's, but also an Old Navy and a Famous Footwear in town, so Fairbanks feels much closer to a real civilized society than it did when we moved here just a year ago. Either way, it's been an awesome experience for me right now, especially during the fifth (and hardest) month of Matt's deployment. During that roadblock month where the white surrender deployment flag just kind of goes up and you feel like you can't do it anymore, having a real home in Fairbanks has been settling.

Deployment, like at any other time in the last five months, has had its highs and lows. And since I made a New Year's resolution to be more real and more transparent, I'm not afraid to admit that anymore.

There have been days this month where I've just come home and cried because I've felt like I just can't do it anymore. I'm not gonna lie — it's lonely to come home to an empty house when you're pregnant and alone in the dark at -55 in Alaska and just want more than anything to have your husband there to share dinner with, tell jokes to and just laugh with and cuddle on. I realize more and more that it's those small things that I miss the most — like the way he checks the alarm clock exactly 12 times before going to bed, or the way he takes off his boots when he gets home *from work and chases me around the house trying to make me smell them, or the way he'll walk in the door and come give me a hug and a kiss and just hold me for five minutes before he does anything else. I miss the way he makes fun of my "foofy" decorating and the way he literally jumps up and down like a little boy when we decide to do something fun like go out to dinner or hit up a movie. I miss our movie marathon sleepovers on the pullout couch in the family room and our dinner and dancing dates under the stars. I just miss him like crazy, and it's really hard to be without the man you love more than anything else here on earth. Though you have your really good days, too, you never stop missing your husband, not for one second, and you always feel a void that you just can't explain. And of course, it goes beyond just the part where you miss your husband like crazy.*

The other half, the un-talked-about and untold half, is the part where you worry about your husband. And that's the part that's different from doing the long-distance relationship Matt and I have perfected in our four years apart.

Believe me, I know that God has a plan, and I know that Matt is a great and a safe soldier. And those two things alone should keep me from even pondering the subject. But no matter how many reasons people give you not to worry, no matter how many you give yourself, you can't help but care about the safety of the man you love.

Every time my doorbell chimes or my phone rings, part of me hesitates for just one millisecond before answering, because though your head tells you you're being paranoid, somewhere in your subconscious, your heart tells you that bad news on the other end is a real possibility. Your husband is at war, and this war is not one fought on battle lines and with infantrymen alone. That means that everyone is a possible target. If you leave the base, you could hit IEDs. If you stay on the base, you could be attacked by mortars. There's no safety in numbers, safety in job MOS, safety in anything else that you might convince yourself protects your husband more than anyone else's.

Even if his armor does protect his physical body most of the time, it doesn't protect his head, his emotions or his heart. Though I know Matt is a solid guy, and I know by our conversations and letters that he is the same old Matt, I still wonder how he will be emotionally affected by this whole war experience.

BUSYNESS

Matt has seen men wounded and killed, seen and heard things that most of us will never see and hear. He's had guys hit by bullets, men in the middle of grenade fire. I wonder if these images and experiences will haunt him in future years — how this all will affect him when he gets home. I worry that he might not be the same person, or that he will feel differently about life, love, or even me after he returns from an experience like this, no matter how many times he reassures me that he won't.

Being a soldier is such an emotionally dangerous job, and being a soldier's wife is a hard one. Turning over my worries, concerns, paranoid visions and deepest fears to God is a daily activity in my home these days — along with a few other coping mechanisms I've picked up along the way.

Like it has been most of my life, my second biggest coping mechanism to deal with all these worries is staying busy. That has been both a blessing and a curse. In one light, I've accomplished a lot of personal goals, participated in a lot of extra activities I wouldn't have otherwise taken part in, and put in a lot of extra work hours I would have never considered before. And I've definitely grown quite a bit as a person.

The down side to all the busyness, of course, is that I'm burnt out and nearly running on zero. Today is the first day I haven't had to work one of my many jobs in 27 days, and the first time I've had more than 15 minutes to sit on my couch before 8 p.m. Yes, I can hear all the motherly types in the group screaming, "Michelle, what are you doing!? You are pregnant! You need to stop this right now." Believe me, I get enough mothering from my own mother (who has been awesome) and all the other ladies at church and work who lecture me on a nearly daily basis.

The truth is that, although staying this busy burns me out physically, sitting around my house burns me out emotionally. I'm never more down, depressed or lonely than when I'm home alone in my house for extended periods of time. If I can still get eight hours of sleep, maintain a normal bedtime, eat three meals a day and not physically overextend my body for the baby, all of which I have been doing and following very closely, I know myself well enough to know that I deal much better with physical burnout than emotional burnout. I know, I know — there should be a balance somewhere in between. There is. I just haven't found it yet. But I'm working on it.

BEHIND THE BLUE-STAR BANNER

Ever since Christmas, I've been really trying to focus and view this time away from Matt as an opportunity to grow rather than a trial to endure. And with the New Year, I decided that I needed some hard and fast goals and some new rules for myself so that I would stop overextending and start really living a normal and healthy life. I needed goals to find that balance. So I made a list (four pages typed and single-spaced — I know, you would have never guessed it, right?) of my goals (I have 12), and listed several actions points underneath each of them. Some of my favorite 2006 goals: to spend more time pursuing my relationship with Christ (6 a.m. daily quiet times are actually really nice), to spend more time learning how to better love Matt (with his help, of course!), to learn how to be a good mom (I'm in the middle of two books and Parents *magazine as we speak, as well as spending a lot more time observing mothers I respect), to run a marathon in 2006 (before I got pregnant, Cara and I were up to three miles a day, but now Matt is going to train with me when he gets home), to get in better shape (I started daily pregnancy Pilates workouts and weekly yoga classes at my church), to eat healthier (I've taken the time to develop an eating plan rather than stopping by Subway every day on my way home from work), to better learn sign language (I am getting back into this at my church) and to read 12 for-fun books this year (*Buffalo Soldier *and* Captivating *are down, and I have a wish list with 20-something books on it to tackle next). I realize some of these might be a little ambitious, or possibly a little unrealistic, but hey, dream big or don't bother dreaming at all.*

I am officially now 31 weeks pregnant — only nine more weeks to go! And I absolutely cannot wait to meet our child! I would tell you how long that is in months, but I never know how to translate the months. One of my pregnancy books says I'm now at eight months, while the other one says I'm at seven, so I guess it just depends whether or not you consider the ninth month an actual month, or whether you count 40 weeks as hitting the first day of the ninth month. So I just go by the week numbers to keep myself straight.

Last week it kind of hit me that this is about more than just the pregnancy, and that in just nine weeks, I'm actually going to be a mother, responsible for the life of another little person. Talk about a wakeup call. You know, you'd think that fact would hit me when I gained 20 pounds (I'm at 22 pounds now! Yeehaw!) or maybe

BUSYNESS

when my friends threw me a baby shower.

Nope, not Michelle. I'm on the slower side.

It hit me when I was reading my weekly pregnancy book chapter and realized that the book was almost over and I would have to start the next book: What to Expect the First Year*! Yeah, so since that time, I've finished my little pregnancy books and have been voraciously reading two different parenting books recommended by my doctor and my friends (not my friends with ill-behaved kids, but the ones who have kids that I actually respect and think have turned out pretty good — just don't tell them that). And I am learning so much! So, to celebrate, I've developed a list of all the things I've learned from my new baby books and my preparing-for-baby life experiences.*

Top 5 Lessons Michelle Has Learned About Preparing for Babies

1. It takes seven men to assemble a baby crib.

My fabulous crib set arrived the first week in January, and because I'm super mechanically inclined and couldn't figure out how to open the box, not to mention the crib, I asked for some help. My amazing church small group jumped in right away and offered to do everything for me. So a couple Sundays ago, all the women came over and helped me make lunch while all the guys crammed into the tiny baby-to-be's room and assembled this ridiculous crib.

When I walked in to check on their progress, I found seven burly guys with their big manly toolboxes all crowded around a crib directing the one guy who actually had a tool in his hand. It was classic "how many men does it take to screw in a light bulb" joke material. But hey, after three assembly attempts, I now have a crib and dresser set for baby! I just hope it holds the kiddo safely.

Although I wasn't too confident when one of the guys came downstairs to ask me if I had any towels that they could get super-glue on... when superglue didn't even come in the crib assembly package. Mental note: Ask Matt to test crib before placing child in construction built by men using superglue, check.

2. Seventy pounds of moose make for great baby room decorating.

When I went home for Christmas, my amazing friends and family threw me a few baby showers — one in Dayton, one in the Adirondacks and one in Philly. I got the most beautiful items ever for the baby!

But when I went to pack my suitcase to return to Alaska, I realized that it wouldn't even come close to fitting in my two suitcases. So I (or rather my lovely daddy) shipped it — all 70 pounds.

It all arrived in Fairbanks last week, and I have to admit, the baby's room does look pretty Alaskan fabulous with 70 pounds of moose sitting on shelves on the wall. The stuffed moose head really makes for a great finishing touch.

Oh, and of course all the moose that make sounds. Elvis Moose was on what could have been a very long rendition of "Love Me Tender" when he arrived at my front door, and the Moose on the Loose animal was pretty content shouting his little line from above the crib. This is going to be one melodious nursery!

3. Baby equals back pain.

Okay, so I've never really had to deal with back pain in my entire life. But the last month or so I have just been dying. I now hobble around like an old man with my hand on my back in that typical pregnancy pose that I swore I would never strike. It hurts!

My doctor suggested massages and sex to relieve the pain. So, yeah, great timing on that one, Matt! You'd think he planned to be gone for the entire pregnancy. I just hope he arrives before baby comes (he's due back here the week before my due date), because I have hours of foot and back massages to guilt out of him before we bring another life into this world.

And no, I'm not going to feel guilty about playing the "but I've been alone and pregnant in Alaska" card to get them, either.

4. Exercising to keep baby healthy is a little different when you live in Alaska. Especially if you try the recommended-by-doctors swimming route.

I thought I was brilliant when I scheduled a date with my Big Brothers Big Sisters little sis, Breannah, at the Fort Wainwright post pool. It's free, it's open when I'm off work, I had the whole thing planned out. What I didn't plan on was the fact that my one-piece bathing suit would no longer fit. Yeah, I kind of missed that one.

Because I'm a planner, and Bre was already anticipating our pool date, I was determined to make something work. So I pulled out my two-piece suit. A word of advice to all those lovely women out there who haven't had kids yet: Please make note that it's not just your stomach that grows during pregnancy — it's also your

BUSYNESS

boobs, your thighs and your butt, and that cute little modest tankini you got so much coverage in last year looks like a skank outfit on a pregnant body.

But again, I didn't care.

I was going to swim, and I was going to get some exercise for my baby. Besides, who is really going to be checking out the blubbering pregnant lady? So I squeezed myself into my little tankini, cut off all my circulation and went to the pool and swam around like the scantily-clad Hawaiian freak I was. Thankfully, my fabulous little sister was one of the most gracious people I knew and didn't capitalize on the opportunity to point out my blubber bottom.

Hey, I realize that they do indeed make maternity bathing suits, but you know what? I'm not about to spend money to ship a bathing suit to Fairbanks, Alaska, when the daily high is near -35 degrees this week. Thanks, I'll pass.

5. If you're going to let people vote on your baby's name, you'd better be prepared for the responses.

Most of the votes — though not all — are in (thank you to all 100 people who participated in the vote so far! We are very impressed!). Among other things, we've had e-mail suggestions to name our kid Kal-El (to follow the whole Smallville theme — justified by two different people who suggested it and by the fact that Nicholas Cage named his newborn Kal-El this year, which I guess makes it the cool-cat thing to do) and Jesus.

Jesus came from the fact that I mentioned we were looking for a good role model to name our child after, and I said that it wasn't like we could name him Jesus.

Our friend LT Roger Garcia responded to this e-mail with, "You can so name your kid Jesus! I'm Hispanic, and my parents named me Roger. So you can be Caucasian and name your kid Jesus."

Valid point, Rog, but I think we're going to pass on that one, but thanks for the input!

Of the people who actually voted for the names that were options (thanks for following directions), we noticed an interesting trend.

The Connor Clarke voters (yes, we've changed the spelling to Connor instead of Conner because several of you pointed out that the name sounded like "one who cons" when spelled with an –er) *were steady and consistent, but have been submitting their votes as late as yesterday. They've seemed very nonchalant about their name voting privileges, but have been very firm and very certain.*

The Joel James voters, on the other hand, have been a little more passionate, writing back with three and four exclamation points after their name votes with a list of reasons why Joel James is a better name than Connor Clarke. We had one lovely lady write back and suggest that we name the baby Joel Clarke, a combination of the two names, because then his initials would be JC, and "there's no better role model than the big JC, Jesus Christ!" she wrote. Interesting, but I don't know how well that would go over in kindergarten class.

Then, we had 11 people who wrote back and voted for Connor James — again, not an option on the ballot, but one we liked upon counting up votes. Right now, the voting is extremely close. So this is your last chance — if you haven't voted yet, vote now by sending me an e-mail with your name vote in the subject line. All votes will be tallied on Friday, so don't miss your chance! We'll then announce the baby's name when he is born.

In other interesting news, my puppy almost got eaten by a moose, my husband sent me super-sweet and totally unnecessary apology roses when his very hormonal wife had a breakdown and told him that she was devastated because he only e-mailed her two times instead of the normal five or six that day (um, guess I'll chalk that one up to pregnancy — oops!) and I only have 55 more days until Matt will be home for his two weeks R and R leave and we get to have a baby!

And that's about it from Fairbanks. We love you so very much, and thanks so much for all your cards, prayers, phone calls and packages, and for reading my 11-page e-mail, if you made it that far. Keep us updated on your lives!

Love,
Matt and Michelle

CHAPTER SEVEN
LONELINESS

The month of love, especially in the dark winters of Fairbanks, Alaska, can be quite depressing without the one you love. All around you are sappy couples sending roses and signing cards, and there's you — the single pregnant lady, for all practical purposes, waddling around the Valentine's aisle at Wal-Mart searching for the perfect card to send to the hubby in Iraq. Instead of dinners out, you send coupons for future dinner dates. Instead of roses, you send pictures of roses and pretend it's the same thing.

It's all kind of depressing.

Fortunately, February was a positive month for Stryker spouses, because it marked the exact halfway point in the deployment. That was definitely something to celebrate and something to keep us all going.

It was also something to reflect on.

The soldiers had now been gone for six months — six months of missed marriages, missed births, missed bonding time and missed memories. That was also six months of combat fire, manic missions, grenade attacks and platoon fatalities.

Six months is a long time for any person to endure those kinds of assaults. And the soldiers still had six more months to go.

Part of me worried about my husband's emotional health, having been deployed for so long without marital and with very little female interaction for months. I worried about six months of seeing guys injured and killed, six months of living in the middle of a war zone. What would six months of that do to a person? And what would six more affect?

As I reflected on this half a year and all the things my husband must have endured during this time, I was reminded about a neighbor of mine who had endured a whole lot more in his short few months overseas.

SFC Pete Lara had been injured the same day that PFC Alcozer died, and neighbors told me he had finally returned to Fairbanks for recovery. Up until that time, I hadn't taken the time to go visit. There was something so real about seeing a man who worked with my husband who was now seriously injured. I didn't know what to

BEHIND THE BLUE-STAR BANNER

make of that emotionally. But when another soldier came to my door looking for his brave sergeant, I knew that it was something I needed to do.

Until They Come Home
February 3, 2006

It was around 8:30 p.m. and nearly 50 degrees below zero when one of those scary, late-night knocks resounded at my front door.

"May I help you?" I asked the man with the high-and-tight haircut standing staunchly on my front stoop, not really wanting to hear the answer.

"Yes, ma'am. Is SGT Lara available?" he asked.

With a sigh of relief that this man obviously wasn't a military injury informant, I unclenched my fists, smiled and replied, "No, I'm sorry. You have the wrong address."

SFC Pete Lara was my neighbor — a man I'd seen plenty of times skidding around on his four-wheeler on long summer nights, playing with his children in the front yard after work on short fall days.

I had heard that he'd been seriously injured in Iraq, and was recovering at Walter Reed Medical Facility in Washington, D.C., and was expected home any time.

After meeting a man willing to make the visit at 50 below, I was inspired to do the same. But what I was sure would be a simple cheer-up chitchat and some wartime story telling turned into an amazing and touching lesson in loyalty and love.

As I entered Lara's homey post house, the proud soldier approached me immediately with a firm handshake and a grin. Though he had indeed received a bullet both to the jaw and the arm, the sergeant simply smiled as if he'd endured something as painless as a tooth cleaning or a flu shot.

While he shared with me the story of the November day he and 12 other soldiers found themselves shot, injured or killed in the midst of grenade and small arms fire, I couldn't help but ponder the details he chose to include. Though he told me where and when and why and how, I was surprised by the amount of time he spent on the "who" part of his story — his men.

It's rare that I've seen a man express so much emotion when

98

speaking about the people he works with. As a platoon sergeant in the Charlie Company of the 2-1 Infantry Battalion, I expected him to speak about these men as employees or peers. But instead, he spoke about them like friends, even soul mates — able to share every detail of their lives with me from the songs they played when they were down to the way each missed his family back home.

All around me was evidence of this relationship that I hadn't noticed on first glance — pictures of his platoon in Iraq, CDs of the songs they listened to together, even the bronze star one soldier was awarded for saving Lara's life.

As he touched each memento, his eyes lit up and you could feel the deep hunger he possessed to be back with these men he called brothers. It didn't matter that he'd already endured two major surgeries and was heading for several more in the next few years. It didn't matter that he couldn't move his right arm to the side, or that he had permanent nerve damage in his mouth. It didn't even matter that he had a piece of shrapnel forever implanted in his head.

What mattered to him was that these men, these soldiers, were his brothers, and more than recovery or revenge or anything else in the world, he wanted to be with them again, and to know that they were safe.

And I don't need to talk to his platoon members to know how they feel about him. I can tell by the constant e-mails they send and visits they make at 50 degrees below zero that this brotherhood extends many miles beyond Fairbanks, and it's not something that either a deployment or a couple bullets could ever alter.

I was so touched by SFC Lara's story that I took it to my news director at the station and asked him if we could run a two-part series on this brave soldier. He gave me the go-ahead, and I spent the next week interviewing, recording, editing and packaging Lara's story. I wanted it to be perfect — to tell the tale of camaraderie, loyalty, brotherhood and bonding that Lara had experienced. I wanted it to tell the story of bravery, the story of trials, and I wanted the package to tell it perfectly.

The two-part series aired during sweeps week.

BEHIND THE BLUE-STAR BANNER

Until They Come Home
February 10, 2006

It finally hit me.

After living in some kind of euphoric "Oh, yeah, I get to be pregnant and wear cute maternity clothes" land for quite a few weeks, I finally realized that gee, this whole pregnancy thing probably wouldn't last more than, say, nine months, and that soon, I was going to be a mother. But even with this new revelation, I somehow missed the whole part where the baby had to actually exit the womb for that all to happen.

It only took 22 pounds, 12,000 pineapples and a very informative birth preparation class at Bassett Army Hospital Tuesday night for that itty-bitty reality to kick in.

Ouch.

I have to admit, I had always pictured my first birth preparation class and the labor itself as this wonderful, romantic bonding experience between myself and my husband. I imagined us walking in together hand in hand, carrying beautiful blankets knit by our great-grandmothers as we entered into the world of baby preparation. We would sit together on our delicate blankets, propped on our perfectly-fluffed down pillows and he would hold me from behind as harp music resounded and I stared magically into his eyes as we hee-hee-hee-hoo-ed until the sun came up.

Needless to say, I was wrong — on all counts.

Instead of husbands sitting supportively at our sides, most of us had girlfriends, moms or other female relatives cheering us up and cheering us on. Of all the attendants that filled the side of the dining hall facility where we met, I counted only four or five men. Of course, with the entire Stryker brigade deployed, that wasn't exactly a surprise.

Dr. Suzanne Temple, chief of obstetrics at Bassett Army Hospital, told me that there was an increase in the number of pregnancies on post right before the Stryker brigade deployed. That means as we approach months six, seven, eight and nine of deployment, there's going to be an increase in the number of deliveries — and the number of women who, like me, have to find alternative birthing coaches to enter the delivery room.

In all my childhood fantasies about babies and deliveries, I had never imagined that my husband, not a good friend, would be my birthing backup plan.

Of course, after Tuesday's class, I realized that labor and deliv-ery were probably not going to be the romantic bonding experi-ence I had always anticipated, anyway. All of this was made quite clear to me as we watched a video about different comfort and coping mechanisms during the various stages of labor.

Though there might be big birthing balls and beautiful bath-tubs at Bassett, there sure as heck wasn't going to be any harp mu-sic — unless it was the music of me harping on the nurses to hurry up and get the baby out of my body in less than the average 14 hours.

As I learned more and more about the actual labor process, part of me was glad it was my good female friend with me and not my husband at the class. Whereas Teresa asked questions and took notes, I'm pretty sure Matt would have just stared around the room uneasily, looking for anything from a clock to a candy bar to get him out of the awkwardness that results for a man when a room full of women gather to talk about pushing a 7.5-pound baby out a 10-centimeter-big hole. And really, I just don't think Matt would have taken the whole "imagine your cervix opening like a rosebud" visualization as well as Teresa did.

Chalk up another big "I owe you one" to great female friends during deployment.

Besides the childbirth preparation class, I also chose to take another class at the post hospital — a class on breastfeeding. And once again, part of me was so glad my poor shy husband wasn't there to endure it. I just don't know how well he would have done as we discussed flat, inverted and pokey nipples by pushing in the gumdrops on our breast-shaped cupcakes before consuming them.

Though I was sad that he had missed these things, I had to laugh that at least I could experience them with other women who knew what they were doing. With him missing events like child-birth preparation classes that meant so much to me, I told myself, I was at least assured one fantastic Valentine's Day present to make up for it all!

In our five years together, Valentine's Day had never really been the glamorous holiday Hallmark always made it out to be. The first three years, we were attending college in separate states and spent our Valentine's nights enjoying pizza and phone dates

BEHIND THE BLUE-STAR BANNER

from the comforts of our cinderblock dorm rooms.

By our fourth Valentine's Day, we were finally married and in the same state together, but it was -30 degrees in Fairbanks and both of us got off work late. Matt forgot to plan anything special, and when I handed him a card and stood, batting my baby blues waiting for him to hand me one back, he just looked at me with a blank stare on his face.

"You said we weren't doing anything for Valentine's Day," he responded, almost defensively. "You said no presents!"

"This isn't a present," I began, slowly. "This is a card." He paused, smiled and tore open the card I'd spent 45 minutes perfectly picking out. As he read the left side and then the right side and then the back and then the extra note I'd slid in the middle because I couldn't fit all the wonderful things I wanted to tell him on three sides of a card, his cheeks began blushing and I could tell he was focusing on something else.

Again, I looked up at him, hugged him and smiled. He half-hugged back, looked at the floor and then broke into an "I'm-in-so-much-trouble-but-if-I-laugh-maybe-I'll-break-the-ice-and-your-evil-stare" giggle. When I just stared back, he took a deep breath.

"When you said no presents, I took that as no presents. As in, no spending money. So I didn't get you a card."

I felt heat rising up the back of my neck, but I paused, took a deep breath and practiced the technique Matt and I had learned in premarital counseling before our big day.

"So let me see if I understand you correctly. You didn't get me a card because you thought that cards cost money and money constitutes a present and we weren't giving each other presents, is that correct?" I asked through the beginnings of clenched teeth.

"Yes…" he replied, smiling meekly and lifting his eyebrows the same way our beagle puppy did every time he got into the trashcan and we caught him and he pulled the "I'm-too-cute-to-be-mad-at-trick" so we wouldn't put him in the time out kennel for 10 minutes.

"But I love you!" he squeaked in his cutest "please-don't-hurt-me" voice.

"So what you're telling me is that I spent 45 minutes picking out a card for you four weeks ago because we've never spent a Valentine's Day together in our relational lives and I wanted this one to be really special because you're going to be deployed next year at this time and we don't know when we're going to have one together again and I spent an hour pouring my heart out about how amazing you are and you can't even take the time to print a card on the computer?"

Okay, so it wasn't exactly the technique Pastor Cahoon had taught us, and I may have broken, well, all the rules about not placing blame and trying to understand the other person's position before spreading accusations. But I was ticked.

"But you said no gifts! It would cost money for ink and paper to print a card…" he started.

"Then write on a napkin! Write on the mirror! Stamp a message in the snow! I don't care! Just tell me you love me in writing on stinking Valentine's Day!" I bellowed back, and then stomped downstairs, being extra sure to dig my three-inch high heels into the carpet to emphasize my frustration. What can I say? I always have been a very mature woman.

Ten minutes later, Matt found me hiding very maturely in my corner, picked me up, held me, told me I was beautiful and apologized. Then he even got dressed up in my favorite shirt and tie and took me out to dinner to make up for it.

One week later, he surprised me by cleaning the entire house, baking a cake and buying me a set of for-no-good-reason-except-to-say-I-love-you bubble baths and fun fashion sets. Then I apologized for being a needy drama queen and let him off the hook. But I filed the incident away in the bank of IOUs and set an alarm to promptly remember the event the following year.

And after the last four years of botched Valentine's Days, that alarm buzzed precisely on February 14 of this year.

It was a Tuesday, and as I entered the church office to begin my regular daily routine, there were flowers everywhere. A large bouquet of massive yellow roses sat on the corner of our facilities coordinator's desk, and all around me were women giggling about the adorable things their husbands had done to make them feel special. It was 10 a.m. and although Matt had called me that morning to wish me a happy Valentine's Day, I hadn't received a card in the mail, or even an e-card that I could print out and hold when I felt lonely that night. There was a 12-hour time difference between Fairbanks and Mosul, and I knew he would be heading to bed in minutes.

Matt's an awesome husband, I kept telling myself, *and a fast*

BEHIND THE BLUE-STAR BANNER

learner. He won't goof up two years in a row! Besides, I told my-self, *I didn't tell him no presents this year! He'll definitely send a card.*

I mean, come on, it wasn't like I was asking for a Lexus. All I wanted was a card. A card with a long letter about how wonderful I was and how I changed his life and how he couldn't live without me and how he was just so in love with my non-neediness and subtlety and maturity. That's all.

As the day wore on and more and more ladies walked in and out of the coffee shop in the church foyer with roses and daisies and chocolates and stories, I began to think that he'd forgotten.

When I turned to switch my nightstand light off at 10 p.m., I sent him an "I-love-you-but-I'm-really-kind-of-disappointed" e-mail. Though I'd sent a Valentine's Day date in a box to Iraq, complete with a chocolate kiss for every day of the month with an in-spirational message attached to each kiss and a letter I'd written and rewritten 10 different times, he'd forgotten a card. Again. And I was depressed.

It wasn't that I needed a card to feel loved. And it wasn't that I needed Matt to buy me things to make me feel special. He made me feel special in millions of ways, every single day. But my love language was words of affirmation. I needed those precious words from him in written form, especially around Valentine's Day when I was pregnant, alone and spending my holiday in the -30 degree temperatures of Fairbanks, Alaska, in order to support his passion and support his call to serve. I didn't need a card. I just needed my husband to remember something that meant a lot to me. Because he loved me, not because he loved the idea of writing out a card 12 days before the big day.

The next morning, I woke to an apology e-mail in my box from the man I loved so much. He told me about how he'd pur-chased a Valentine's Day card weeks in advance this time, spent 20 minutes writing it — a feat for my English-challenged husband — and simply forgotten to send it until the holiday actually arrived. And with a 10- or 12-day snail mail lag time, I probably wouldn't receive it until nearly March. But he still loved me! And at least he tried.

With a chuckle, I told him I'd forgive him for a pregnancy massage and total slavery once he came home in 30 days for his R and R. He agreed, I laughed and we mended fences. And I decided that in the big scheme of things, something as stupid as a Valentine's Day card on a Hallmark-fabricated holiday was not worth wasting one second of precious marriage happiness on. Especially not when my husband was in a war zone.

Of course, it didn't hurt that I received a spa and massage kit in the mail the following week from my hubby, either. I was singing songs of forgiveness every night as I soaked my big fat pregnant feet in that nice warm water.

Until They Come Home
February 17, 2006

This week marks the halfway point in the Stryker brigade's deployment to Iraq. The strong soldiers we never thought we could let go in the first place have now been gone for six months.

Though it's a relatively short period of time in the grand scheme of things, six months can feel like a really long time when you're missing your spouse and managing everything for two (or in my case, two and one in the oven) in the freezing cold winters of Fairbanks, Alaska.

When I think back on all the times in my life where six months was a marker for me, all of them were very slow, very drawn-out ordeals — or at least they felt like slow-moving months at the time.

Six months is the same amount of time it took to complete my last semester as an overly-eager high school student with major college fever.

It's the same amount of time it took me to finally establish a regular exercise routine, the same amount of time it took me to land my first writing gig upon college graduation.

And six months is the same amount of time it took me to meet my husband, fall in love and trick him into believing I was the girl of his dreams. Talk about a long, exhausting six months. It only took two and a half years after that to con him into saying, "I do."

I think about all the things that have changed just in the last six months since that same man deployed to Iraq. Before he left, I was unemployed, barely pregnant and had established no real roots in the community. Now, I work three jobs, carry around a child the size of a basketball and volunteer or involve myself in more than five clubs, studies or activities per week.

BEHIND THE BLUE-STAR BANNER

Sometimes I'll sit curled up on my couch at night and fantasize about life with Matt just half a year ago. That was back in the day before television dinners and Bamboo Panda became my best dinnertime friends, when I actually cooked a full, three-course meal every night and sat down at the dinner table with my husband to eat it. That was before my nighttime routine consisted of running from one event to the next, and the only thing I needed to worry about come 6 p.m. was which show or game Matt and I were going to enjoy after he cleaned the dishes that night. Oh, and how nice it was to have him clean those dishes.

After six months, unless you make it a point to remember, you start forgetting the little things you and your husband used to make routine, and you simultaneously and inadvertently discard all the quirky things he used to do that drove you nuts. In your mind, he quickly becomes the husband who can do no wrong — except, of course, on those emotional prego days when you wake up irritated by the world, hate the Army and blame him for all your problems.

But through it all, there is one thing I always make a point to remember and make sure to take advantage of while my dear deployed soldier is gone. That's how much that wonderful man hates cheesy theme parties and "foofy" things anywhere near our house.

It's only proper, then, that to celebrate the halfway point of his deployment, I am inviting all my military wife friends to a very foofy Happy Hooray Halfway Candle and Spa Party at my place where, for two hours, we are going to remember that there are upsides to having six more months of girliness and non-complaining men left to go.

In that one and only respect, maybe it's good that six months can feel so long.

CHAPTER EIGHT
PREPARATIONS

In the military world, preparations are a sign of victory.

When spouses start preparing their hair, preparing their homes and refining their habits, you know a husband isn't too far behind.

March was my month of preparation — my 31-day window to prepare for a husband who'd been gone for eight long months to enjoy two relaxing weeks at home. I'd composed a list a mile long of tasks I wanted to complete to make my house and myself look perfect before the big Fairbanks R and R vacation, and I was ferociously tackling my list like a linebacker on a running back.

It's just that car preparations weren't priorities on my to-do list before the big day.

Until They Come Home
March 3, 2006

I couldn't believe it.

I stared down at my gas gauge and the little lit-up gas tank sign that indicated that yes, my tank was indeed empty.

I started jumping up and down in a rocking, forward motion, screaming, "No! No! No!" at the top of my lungs, hoping that maybe the combination of the sound and the weight might be able to scoot my car the rest of the way home. But the poor little vehicle had come to a complete stop, and the best I could do was let the fumes glide it to a resting point in a parking lot off Airport Road.

Had my husband been there, I think he would have shot me.

I realize that maybe it's not the greatest idea to let your gas tank run low in the wintertime in Alaska, especially when you don't own a cell phone or have a husband around to come rescue you. But I'd been running late to work that morning and was sure I could squeeze just a few more miles in before my Corolla went kaput. After all, I'd never run out of gas before.

I was wrong.

As I stumbled out of my car, I looked around and realized that there was no one to come rescue me from my car troubles this

BEHIND THE BLUE-STAR BANNER

time. Matt wasn't going to take off work and come pick me up, wasn't going to fix my car and tell me, "It's okay, honey, I've got it all taken care of."

This time, I was on my own.

So, at 16 degrees and more than eight months pregnant, I zipped up my jacket and started trucking down Airport Road. I made it all the way to Fred Meyer, bought myself a gasoline can, walked to the gas station, filled it up and then waved at all the curious onlookers who shot me the "What idiot lets her car run out of gas in the wintertime?!" look as I trudged back down Airport with two gallons of gas, a squirming baby in my belly and some freezer-burnt fingers.

And when I arrived back at my car and filled up my tank, though I was tired, cold and felt pretty much like a blubbering idiot, I was proud.

Just one year ago, I would have never even attempted to remedy a situation like this on my own. I would have called my husband to bail me out, and he would have come running and fixed it all for me.

It's amazing what you find you can do when you don't have that backup option.

I'm realizing more and more that, though I make a lot of stupid mistakes and I hate taking care of these situations on my own, deployment has been so good for teaching me how to be independent and to think on my feet. It's forced me to learn all the skills I was too lazy to perfect before, forced me to do some of those things I always labeled as "Matt's responsibilities."

Since he's been gone, I've learned to mow the grass, schedule house maintenance, assemble small appliances and change my own tires. I've made the budget, paid the bills, taken care of the cars and now, even learned how to get myself out of a breakdown situation.

Though I'll gladly return these duties to my husband the moment he returns, it feels good to know that I can be strong and take care of what needs to be done on the home front so he can serve worry-free overseas. And I think it makes him feel good to know that slowly, and admittedly mostly through my mistakes, I'm learning how to care for myself — and how to appreciate everything he does more and more every day.

PREPARATIONS

After the gas incident, I was more ready than ever for Matt to come home. I didn't want to deal with the cars, didn't want to deal with the gas, didn't want to deal with any more life without him, really. My physical capabilities tank was on empty. How much more did I have to endure before I'd get to see his face again?

God used that opportunity, in the midst of my self-pity, to remind me of my blessings and once again, adjust my attitude.

Until They Come Home
March 10, 2006

It seems nearly every time I turn on the network news or check out the newest national news Web site, I hear about another U.S. soldier who has died in Iraq, and what that soldier's death now brings the U.S. death toll to. But, unless he's a high-ranking officer or a Pat Tillman-type figure, rarely do I hear on these national reports anything specific about the recently-killed soldier, his passions, or even so much as his name.

As a reporter myself, it's always disgusted me how easily some of my fellow journalists can turn the sacrifices of soldiers into simple statistics. But this week, after complaining about this phenomenon to my colleagues for months, I found myself guilty, in my own way, of the very same thing.

Wednesday afternoon, I had the great privilege of attending the memorial service of Stryker soldier SPC Joshua Pearce who was killed when an improvised explosive device detonated near his Stryker vehicle on February 26.

I initially attended the service to honor one of those many fallen U.S. soldiers.

As I entered the Northern Lights Chapel at exactly 2 p.m., though, I was immediately hit by the revelation that this wasn't just some nameless soldier. The place was packed, and though I was on time, I had to grab a seat in the overflow area set up in the chapel lobby.

From my place in the back, I listened as friends, commanders and chaplains spoke about this man I had just minutes earlier counted as "another fallen Stryker soldier." I learned how SPC Pearce had been voted "best looking" in his high school, and how he was largely considered the life of the party. I heard the story of the day he painted a local water tower, and the time he dressed up

BEHIND THE BLUE-STAR BANNER

as a Spice Girl and performed a song with his friends. I was told where he hid the dirty dishes his mother had assigned him to clean, and what color wig he donned the previous Halloween.

And I learned that on September 11, 2005, this young man who I knew nothing about just five minutes earlier had published a letter to the editor in his hometown Oklahoma newspaper stating, "I do not want to die, but if that's what I was put on this earth to do, then everyone should know that I went for a cause that in my heart was worth dying for."

And he did. At 21 years of age — the age most of us revel in our first legal glass of wine and our first bar-side ID check — this young man laid down his life to serve a country and a cause that he sincerely believed in, for people who would probably never even remember his name.

I heard gasps and whimpers and the sound of rustling tissues as I felt tears swell in my own eyes. This young man was not just another fatality in an overseas war. He wasn't just another number to chalk up on our Fairbanks losses list. No. He was a real person, a real soldier with a real story. And he was a real hero.

I left that place with tears in my eyes and a conviction in my heart that I would never again allow myself to consider a lost life a simple statistic — and would refuse to be okay with others, especially national media outlets and politicians, doing the same.

My duty — our duty — is to remember Joshua and the thousands of soldiers like him who have a story to tell, and to honor them every day by telling those stories and remembering those names. Maybe then we can actually revere the sacrifices of our fallen soldiers the way we claim we do here in this land of the free and home of the brave.

When a soldier dies, especially one in your husband's unit, your first reaction always shames you, because it's always, "Thank God it wasn't my husband." It takes a minute to breathe that sigh of relief before you start really coming to grips with the fact that this man was indeed *someone's* loved one, even if he wasn't yours.

Pearce's memorial service really shook me. I couldn't stop crying, even hours after I returned home. Men were dying — men that Matt knew, men that Matt worked with. I wondered how this soldier's family would deal with his loss — how they would be able to wake up every day and know that their son wasn't coming

110

PREPARATIONS

home. That their countdown was over.

I worried about Matt — worried how these deaths would affect him and his soldiers once they exited the war zone and had to face the fact that Joshua Pearce wouldn't be on the softball team next spring, or at the bars next fall.

Pearce's death made me more ready than ever for Matt to come home. I just wanted to hold him, to look at him, to tell him that I loved him. I hated that someone in his unit had died, and I hated that this death reminded me that my husband wasn't invincible, either. I needed Matt, and I needed him now.

Until They Come Home
March 17, 2006

In less than one week, the day I have been anticipating for months now will finally arrive — my husband will be returning home from Iraq for his two weeks of rest and relaxation.

To me, that means two things. One, I am going crazy counting down the minutes until I get to reunite with the man of my dreams (he's only been away from me for 216 days now, not that I'm counting). And two, I have exactly four to five days to readjust my lifestyle and pretend like I have not been living like a bachelor for the last seven months of my life.

Oops.

Okay, so I admit that maybe a few things changed the day my husband deployed. Besides the fact that I started allowing my puppy to sleep in the bed with me — he's a great cuddler, and little white beagle hairs all over the sheets are a small price to pay for some much-needed nighttime loving! — I also started picking up the habits of the hundreds of bachelors I chastised throughout my college career. Including my husband.

Before we were married, I used to make the nine-hour drive from my college to Matt's for weekend visits, only to find the apartment he shared with three other ROTC guys in shambles and his refrigerator a mess. Without fail, there would be dishes hardened with last month's Hamburger Helper and pizza boxes peppering the living room. There would be bed sheets that hadn't been washed for years and laundry that had been lying around for months. And don't even ask about the collections of junk and gunk that reeked from all four corners of the room.

BEHIND THE BLUE-STAR BANNER

*As I tried to help tidy up the place, I'd always make very posi-
tive and encouraging remarks to my husband, like, "This is the
grossest thing I've ever seen in my life. There is no way we are living like this once we're married."*

*Well, Matt didn't anyway. And then he deployed to Iraq, and
suddenly, it was me who picked up all the bachelor habits I had
protested all those years.*

*It started out with the small things, like letting the dishes sit
for a few extra days, and pushing that vacuuming job off for another week.*

*But then it only took a month before I stopped making the
bed, and one more before I stopped putting the toilet seat down. A
month after that I stopped washing my sheets, and a month after
that, I started drinking milk from the carton. Seven months into
deployment, I now never wash dishes, hardly ever clean the house,
drink all my liquids from containers and consider it a good day if I
transport the trash from the kitchen to the garage. It's a really good
day if it makes it all the way to the curb.*

*And because there's no one else here to remind me that it's
rude, all those bodily functions I've been holding in for all those
years now resonate throughout the entire house, and are met only
by my own proud comments of, "Wow, that was a good one!"*

*So maybe I'm not exactly the prim and proper princess my
husband left behind. But I'm working on getting back that way.*

*Sunday I washed all the dishes, and Monday I used a glass
when I poured my morning juice. Tuesday I vacuumed the living
room and Wednesday I even considered making my bed — before
I decided that a long nap sounded like a much better idea.*

*So the process of unbachelorization is a little tougher than I
thought. But I have a plan. I figure if I can just hold in my bodily
functions for the next two weeks, the husband won't even notice
that I backwash in our Barq's and encourage mold growth in our
shower. It's at least worth a try.*

Note to self: Though it may be tough, unbachelorization is
especially important around large groups of women — even if
they, themselves, have been living like bachelorettes for the last
eight months, too.

In the two weeks before my husband planned to return home
for R and R, two beautiful friends threw me two more beautiful

PREPARATIONS

baby showers; Kathie, our kids' church coordinator, threw me a surprise bash for all our church friends at her house, and Laurie, my best friend from the Army spouse coffee group, threw me a party for all the other military spouses we knew.

At both lovely events, I had to stop myself from drinking out of two-liter bottles, slurping from Coke cans and eating my casseroles with my fingers with my mouth hanging open.

My grandmother would have rolled over in her grave.

I'm just so glad I had great friends who blamed my cave woman tendencies on pregnancy and hormones.

When I returned home from those showers and washed all the new blankies and baby clothes in Dreft and unpackaged and sanitized all the toys, I realized just how much cleaning really needed to be done before my husband came home and before we brought a baby into the world. Nesting kicked in, and I caught the urge to clean with a bang. Only I was too pregnant to bend over, and I wasn't technically supposed to be around most cleaning chemicals while carrying a child. So I hired a professional.

As we embarked on the Cuthrell house deep cleaning adventure — or rather, the friend from church I paid to clean my house embarked on the adventure while I sipped lemonade on the sidelines — I began to concentrate on the last weeks of pregnancy. My hospital bags were packed, the baby's room was set, and I only had a few more doctor's appointments to go. I was ready. Matt was coming home, we were going to make love and *boom*! Five hours later, I was going to deliver a healthy, beautiful baby. It was all going to be a dream come true. Or so I thought.

Until They Come Home
March 24, 2006

For months now, I have been anticipating not just the return of my husband, but also the arrival of our first child.

I knew our timing had to be just right for baby and husband to coincide, but I also realized that I didn't have a real choice in the matter. Matt would come home for his two weeks of rest and relaxation when the Army said so, and baby would enter the world when he thought it was time.

But that doesn't mean that I haven't been studying up on ways to make the two events coincide. We only have two weeks (from week 38 to week 40 of the pregnancy) to get this baby out into the world in time to meet Daddy and bond before he returns to Iraq. And if there's anything I can do to make that safely happen, I'm willing to try it.

So, while my husband has been reading up on being a father and returning to family life after wartime situations, I've been reading up on inducing labor. And getting lots of advice from my family and friends.

Of course, the first tip people always offer is to take a nice, long walk. But at this point in the game, walking is just not as enjoyable as it used to be. In fact, it really just stinks.

I stopped by the post gym the other day to hit up the treadmill for 20 minutes. I didn't want to have the baby, I just wanted to get some exercise and see if this whole walking thing was as overrated as it seemed to be. But by the time I had completed .2 miles at 2 mph, I had to pee so bad that I almost didn't make it to the bathroom. And when I got back on the stupid machine, I found that about every .2 miles, I had to repeat the mad dash to the bathroom routine, and I probably exerted more energy running back and forth to go pee than I ever did on the treadmill. So I gave up and went home.

The other little gem people not-so-subtly suggest is to try sex. One acquaintance told me, "You know, you should really have sex, but just beware that it's not going to be very fun or comfortable for either of you." I could be wrong, but after more than seven months of abstinence, I'm pretty sure my husband is not going to be worried about the quality of our performance, or if this one rates in our Top 10 category. And if that wonderful bonding experience can also start the process of getting this baby out of my body, neither am I, no matter how uncomfortable it may be.

Our church accountant told me that hand mashing potatoes did the trick for her, and another lady swore it was all about the hardcore cleaning. I've had friends offer to lend me everything from their children's trampolines to their mother's spiciest Mexican dinner recipes to get the process started. And of course, I've heard over and over again the tales about the wonders of castor oil — although I'm not such a big fan of pooping out my insides the same day I push a child through a 10-centimeter-big hole. But anything is worth a try.

Ideally, by the time you read this column, Matt and I will have

PREPARATIONS

reunited at the Fairbanks International Airport and will be in the process of delivering our little bundle of joy at Bassett Army Hospital. But if you don't find us there, don't fret — we're probably just out in a car somewhere driving on a bumpy road while having sex, mashing potatoes, chomping on chili peppers and downing castor oil. Whatever works.

On Friday, March 17, I attended my 38-week appointment. I had been experiencing cramps for the last few days, and when Dr. O'Connor checked me, she said I was dilated to 2 centimeters and partially effaced.

"You're experiencing cramps?" she asked, almost worried.

"Yes, why?" I asked, starting to grit my teeth.

"Those are the beginnings of contractions," she said. "That usually indicates oncoming labor. But you never know — you might still have three or four days left in you if you're lucky."

Small problem: My husband wasn't coming home for five days. Beautiful.

If I delivered this baby 24 hours before my husband arrived in the country, I was really going to strangle someone. We'd made it this far, and I knew I needed him there. I didn't want to embarrass myself in front of my backup labor coaches screaming, "I'm dying, I'm dying!" Matt already knew I was a sissy — but all my friends didn't need to find that out in the labor room.

I had a slight stress attack and didn't know what to do. So I slipped on my hated elastic-waisted maternity pants and headed to church, where I was finishing up my last day of work before I took maternity leave, and suffered a small breakdown.

After talking to the other women in the office, all of whom were mothers or expectant mothers themselves, I vowed not to do anything strenuous, not to lift anything heavy, until Matt arrived. Maybe if I squeezed really hard, the baby wouldn't come out. I mean, if I didn't push, he couldn't exit, right?

I went home that night and looked up every Web site I could find on delaying labor. That weekend, I reread my *What to Expect When You're Expecting* chapters on labor and started calling experienced family members to get tips and advice. That's when my husband called from his forward operating base in Mosul.

The sound of his voice was such a comfort on the other end of the line. Just hearing it gave me permission to breathe and to know that everything would be okay. It was Sunday morning, and I knew by now he was probably in Kuwait, or maybe even Texas, where his plane would enter the United States.

"Where are you at?!" I asked excitedly, thinking maybe there was even a remote possibility that he was calling from a nearby airport.

"Michelle, I have bad news," he replied.

At that point, I was stressed to the max. My legs hurt, my back hurt, my skin hurt and now my eyes hurt from reading so many articles on my computer. I peed when I coughed, I hurt when baby kicked, and I was pretty much just done with pregnancy. It was not the ideal time to tell me that something had gone wrong.

"You are coming home, Matt," I said slowly, annunciating every syllable like a school teacher. "I don't care, you are coming home. I am having this baby, and you are coming home."

It was a command, not a question.

I don't think Matt really knew what to say, because I heard him gulp before he opened his mouth and told me the bad news that the plane he had boarded to leave Iraq for Kuwait had broken down, and it could be a few days before they could fix it.

I started bawling.

When you've counted down for seven months to see your dear husband and your doctor tells you that you're going to have a baby any day, one day makes a difference, not to mention a few days.

"I can't have this baby without you!" I hollered at him, tears streaming down my face. "What am I supposed to do?"

I could hear his frustration on the other end of the line, and at once, I felt horrible.

Here I was angry and upset that he wasn't coming home to me — to the home I had enjoyed with warm water, hot meals, a comfortable bed and all the movies and free time I wanted for the last seven months. And I was angry at him that he was going to be delayed in coming home from a war zone to all the things he hadn't seen in more than half a year, as if this delay were his choice.

"I'm so sorry, baby," I whispered. "It's just that I don't want to wait anymore."

Being the amazing husband he is, Matt calmed me down, told me he loved me and promised that he'd find a way home in time for the baby.

The next day, God did.

PREPARATIONS

While the other soldiers sat around the FOB waiting for their plane to be fixed, Matt was "randomly" chosen to fill one of the three remaining seats on another plane and began his journey home. That Wednesday night, he called me from the airport in Anchorage as he hopped on a plane to complete his last leg into Fairbanks.

I arrived at Fairbanks International like a good little impatient girl an hour before my husband's anticipated flight. I'd decided on a classic black turtleneck and an elastic-waisted, knee-length jean skirt for the occasion, one, because those were some of the only maternity clothes that still fit, and two, because the cotton-ribbed turtleneck clung to my belly and showed off the new baby that Matt had never seen before.

For a good hour, I sat in a pair of cold metal chairs by the luggage claim where Alaska Airlines attendants told me my husband could come directly. I played Solitaire, I played with my calendar, I made lists of things the two of us could do together that week, all the while checking to make sure my candy-pink lipstick and coal-black eye liner were in perfect order. Anticipating the emotional floods of pregnancy and reuniting with my husband, I even dabbed on an extra layer of waterproof mascara for the occasion. I was ready to see my baby.

The Fairbanks airport is a small one. With only one terminal, a handful of gates and two luggage conveyer belts, it's really hard to miss someone you love walking by. But even so, I kept glancing up from my intense game of Solitaire, just to make sure I wasn't missing him.

And then I heard a microphone crackle, and an airport attendant turned up the loudspeaker.

"Alaska Airlines would like to welcome the arrival of Flight 141 from Anchorage," the lady bellowed, "at Gate 4, by the luggage claim. Again, that's the arrival of Flight 141 from Anchorage at Gate 4 by the luggage claim."

My heart stopped. My fingers raced to cram all the playing cards back into their box and stuff them back into the matching black purse I had brought for the occasion. I grabbed my mirror, checked my hair and makeup one more time and then jumped to my feet — quite the feat when you have 35 extra pounds hanging off your belly — and tapped my right toe nervously as I waited for my hero to disembark.

BEHIND THE BLUE-STAR BANNER

Businessmen carrying briefcases and mommies holding children disembarked and smiled politely as they walked past me, wondering what special person I was waiting for with my "welcome home" balloons and my big fat smile. And then there was a gap in the crowd, and I spotted sand-brown desert boots. I looked up, and there was my baby — camo-clad and smiling with a green ruck the size of King Kong on his back. I waddle-raced 20 feet across the room and jumped him before he even spotted me. Throwing his camelback to the ground, he freed up both arms, threw his arms around me and held me tight for three or four minutes. And then, when he looked into my eyes, he kissed me softly.

And as I clung to that man for dear life, I breathed a sigh of relief that we were indeed going to have this baby together.

Until They Come Home
March 31, 2006

I hadn't seen my husband for nearly seven and a half months when he stepped off his plane and into the terminal at the Fairbanks International Airport Wednesday night.

I'd run the reunion scenario in my head about a million and a half times before he arrived — what I would wear, what we would say, how long we would kiss, what it would feel like to touch him again. But in all my little fantasy meeting scenes, I never imagined his first words to me: "Oh my gosh, baby, you're pregnant!"

Good job, honey. It's only been nine months now.

I guess the fact that I'd been confronting morning sickness, attending doctor appointments, assembling cribs, enjoying baby showers, reading parenting books and gaining weight during Matt's entire deployment didn't really tip him off to the fact that yes, we were indeed going to have a child. Because when he saw me 30 pounds heavier with a belly that made our first hug a little awkward, his deer-in-the-headlights gaze told his story of shock. And excitement. The kind, I suppose, that is only made truly real when you actually get to hug your pregnant wife and feel the little kicks of your child on the surface of her tummy.

So for the past week, I've had the thrill of watching my husband be completely mesmerized by all the little things about pregnancy that have almost become a nuisance by month nine.

When it takes me twice as long to put on my clothes in the morning, he just grins and bends down to tie my tennis shoes for me.

When I crave pineapple in the middle of his favorite television show, he jumps at the opportunity to go cut me a fresh batch.

And when I have to walk through Wal-Mart at the pace of a turtle, he stays right there with me, holding my hand and complimenting me on my newly-acquired trademark waddle.

But it's not just helping with the challenges of pregnancy that has impressed me so much. It's also the extra pampering and care he has shown that has really touched my heart.

Here has been a man, fresh off a five-day plane trip from Iraq, straight out of a war zone, who is completely physically and emotionally exhausted and who deserves to be spoiled in every way possible, and who, rather than asking for anything, has spent his first days at home asking me how he can make me feel more comfortable and loved.

I don't know any other man who, in one week, could make his wife feel as if she had been completely and utterly spoiled for all nine months of pregnancy.

His first morning home, he woke up at 5:30 a.m. to make me my favorite bacon-and-egg, full-out breakfast and refused to let me do so much as pour the juice or wash one dish.

His second night home, he made me sit on the couch while he gave me an hour-long shoulder, neck and foot massage to make up for all those massages he said I missed along the way.

And his third day home, he dressed in a shirt and tie and took me out to my very favorite restaurant for a three-course, fancy meal together — and must have mentioned 500 times how beautiful my big belly looked in my black formal.

Yes, at nearly 40 weeks of pregnancy, I am definitely more than ready to deliver this child and tie my own shoes again. But with a husband at home as incredible as mine, I can handle dealing with some of those annoyances of pregnancy. For a few more days, anyway.

In a great twist of irony, the baby didn't arrive before the day my husband came home. In fact, he didn't arrive the week after my husband came home. In fact, he didn't arrive at all. And in just a matter of days, we went from doing everything we could to keep the baby in to doing everything we could to push the baby out. We

BEHIND THE BLUE-STAR BANNER

tried the castor oil, we tried the walking, we tried the sex. And nothing, I mean nothing, worked.

The last day of March, Matt and I attended a checkup appointment together. And after examining me, Dr. O'Connor agreed that Monday morning at 7 a.m., she would be willing to induce. Matt squeezed my hand, pecked me on the cheek and we collectively let out a sigh of relief, shared a huge hug and smiled, knowing that yes, we really were going to have this baby together.

CHAPTER NINE
ADVENT

It was 4 p.m. on Monday, April 3, and between the pain of contractions, I was starting to wonder what on earth ever possessed me to induce labor. My doctor had just broken my water, and the contractions were stronger now and much harder. And though the breathing techniques I learned at my child preparation class were offering me some control, they sure as heck weren't taking away the sharp pains I was feeling in my uterus.

You idiot, I thought to myself, wincing and bracing myself against the back of my hospital bed. *Who asks to be put in pain earlier than necessary?*

Matt and I had arrived at the hospital at 7 that morning, and after settling into our labor room and taking some quick measurements, the nurses discovered that I was already contracting — I was already in early labor. So instead of hooking me up to the Pitocin IV drip, as originally planned to induce labor, they simply placed a quarter of a cervix-softening pill on my cervix. Within hours, I was in active labor.

I'd never been in labor before, and I didn't exactly know what I was supposed to do. Was I supposed to read? To sleep? To play games? To talk about the baby?

Matt and I guessed — correctly, I might add — that at the very least, it wasn't going to be a short process and planned accordingly. So we brought games — cards, Yahtzee, Monopoly, all the games we could think of to keep us entertained for hours at a time.

As my contractions grew stronger, Monopoly became less and less fun. Rather than the usual "You stink!" emerging from my mouth every time I landed on my husband's properties with houses and hotels, new words were surfacing — words like, "Oh my gosh, you are a tyrant and I hate you, you little house-owning, hotel-building meanie head! I'm never playing Monopoly with you again. You stink, you poopy face!" as I'd slam the money on the board and cross my arms.

Of course, the arms only stayed crossed between contractions, because as soon as one hit — and they were hitting frequently by that point — I grabbed for Matt's hand to help brace myself. Poor guy — not only did he get money and dice thrown at him through-out the day, but he also got nail marks etched into the palms of his hands.

Labor only got worse from there. I went into that hospital room with the idea that I was Superwoman — that I was going to have this baby naturally with no drugs, no matter what. I'd told Matt not to let me get an epidural, to remind me that women have been doing this for years, and that I could manage. I mean, how bad could it really be?

Eighteen hours into labor and at 8 centimeters for the third hour in a row (though the midwife later told me that I was likely only at 5 at that point), I decided: bad. I had a breakdown, started bawling and begged Matt for forgiveness as I asked for that omi-nous epidural. As the nurse called in the anesthesiologist, I cried and cried, telling Matt I was so sorry that I was letting him down.

"Michelle, baby," he said as he grabbed me and held me, "I would have backed into the room asking for an epidural in the first place. I'm not disappointed — I'm so proud of you."

It was then I knew that I just couldn't have done labor and delivery without him. He was exactly what I needed.

Four hours and one epidural later, I was in labor transition and ready to deliver. Matt held my hand and whispered encourag-ing words in my ear as I pushed for more than an hour.

"You can do this, Michelle," he'd whisper in a calming tone. "You are amazing — you're doing a great job."

He coached me and petted my right hand and brushed my cheeks and wiped my forehead as I pushed and pushed and nearly gave up when I felt I wasn't making any progress.

"I think she's going to need an episiotomy," Dr. O'Connor told the nurses assisting with the delivery matter-of-factly from below my bed. Two minutes and one cut later, Connor James broke free into the world and gasped his first huge breath of air at 8:38 a.m.

As the nurse set him gently on my chest and wrapped the sheets around him to keep him warm, I just lay in shock. There was a real person inside my belly this whole time, and I wasn't just some lady who had been handed a child — I was now a mommy.

My mouth just gaped open as I stared at the beautiful baby boy my husband and I had created together. As Matt videotaped our first introduction as mother and son, I just kept repeating the

ADVENT

words, "Oh my gosh, oh my gosh."

And as I leaned up and kissed the forehead of our brand new baby boy, I knew for certain that our world was changed forever.

Until They Come Home
April 14, 2006

I knew the pain of labor was bad when I almost hanged my husband over a Handi-snack.

I had been in the hospital in labor for 10 hours on a diet of only lemon Jello, ice chips and beef broth, and after nine months of mega-sized meals and steady snacks, 10 hours without solid food seemed nearly unbearable.

The contractions were coming faster and stronger, and besides thinking to myself that I never wanted to have sex ever again, I just couldn't concentrate on anything else but the pains in both my stomach and my uterus. Since I couldn't do much about the uterine contractions, I zeroed in on the hunger pangs.

"Matt," I whispered in my super-secret spy voice once my nurse had taken my blood pressure and exited the room, "I brought cheese and crackers in my overnight bag. Could you please go grab me a Handi-snack?"

My husband had eagerly waited on me hand and foot his entire week and a half home for R and R thus far, and I was sure he wouldn't mind sneaking me a cracker or two.

So when he refused my request on the ground of ethics — I had been put on a clear liquid diet for a reason — I hit a wall.

I don't remember the exchange exactly — I was in a lot of pain by that point — but I'm pretty sure the words "Handi-snack Nazi" left my mouth, along with a few others I probably don't want to remember.

Until I experienced it myself, I never really realized how strenuous and ridiculous labor and delivery could be. Or how ridiculous I could be. Sure, I'd seen all the movies where the wives cursed at their husbands and screamed, "You did this to me, you little [insert choice word here]." But I always kind of dismissed those women as either psychos or wimps. I didn't think labor could really be that bad.

When I lost my cool over a Handi-snack, I knew it really was that bad.

BEHIND THE BLUE-STAR BANNER

While I labored for 23 hours in that hospital bed, I had a lot of time to dwell on the pain I was experiencing. For such a joyous occasion — a birthday that would be celebrated with cake and gifts and crayons and clowns for years to come — it sure did involve a lot of torture.

As I hee-hee-hooed through contraction after contraction, I began to develop a new perspective about childbirth and birthdays. I never realized that it was really the parents who endured all the pain — who encouraged each other until their voices gave out and tackled those not-so-nice Handi-snack moments at 2 in the morning. They were the ones who deserved the birthday gifts, not the kids who simply slid down a birth canal and received all the credit for that day year after year!

No more presents for kids, I told myself as I went into labor transition, all my birthday presents from now on are going to the parents as consolation! This stinks!

That was my last thought, anyway, as I took one more deep breath and finally pushed our little boy out into the world at 8:38 a.m. Tuesday. But once little Connor James looked me in the eye and curled up on my chest, I absolutely melted, reconsidered and decided, despite all the pain and insanity he'd caused, that maybe he could have a birthday present, too.

So next April 4, on his first birthday, we're going to compromise. Little Connor will definitely receive a gift — his grand entrance into the world is too important to ignore — but I'm also purchasing a little something for my husband as a "thank you for enduring 24 hours of labor with a psycho" gift. I may even splurge for Handi-snacks.

Because of an infection and some concerns about Connor's health, our hospital stay was extended for several days, and Matt's commanders extended his R and R leave for an additional week. It wasn't something we asked for, and it wasn't something we expected. In fact, we felt guilty taking an extra week when everyone else we knew only received two. But we were so thankful to have another week together with our little boy.

Bringing Connor home was one of the most exciting and crazy things my husband and I had ever experienced in all our five years together. Driving home from the hospital, I couldn't believe that they had let us go. I mean, all they did was check our car seat for safety features and that was supposed to somehow indicate that we were qualified to be parents. They didn't give us a pamphlet, didn't give us a quiz, just checked our car seat and sent us off with a child, as if we knew exactly what we were doing.

Although we were excited to be leaving the hospital, we were, at the same time, terrified.

Having Matt there with me, though, made the experience calming and absolutely incredible.

Every time Connor cried, Matt was the one to reach for him. He changed every diaper that week he was home, got up every single night. The only thing he couldn't do was feed little CJ, and even when I had finished, he would be the one to burp and hold him.

I just watched him every day as he took care of Connor in all the little things, and as I fell in love with our new little boy, I also fell in love with my husband all over again. He was incredible, and I knew he was going to be an amazing father.

Maybe that's why it was so hard to say goodbye.

Taking Matt to the airport to return to Iraq was one of the hardest things I've ever done — in some ways, harder than dropping him off the first time.

As Matt held Connor in his arms for the last time, I saw his eyes glaze over, and what could have been a tear forming in the corners. One camo-clad arm cradled Connor's back while the fingers of the other one caressed his cheeks. He gave Connor one last hug, kissed his forehead, told him he loved him and placed him back in his car seat. He was trembling as he stood up and immediately brought himself to an attention position, as if to shake off the emotion of the moment to make it less difficult.

Watching a father say goodbye to his son for four months was one of the most heart-wrenching things I'd ever seen. And when we kissed goodbye and I forced myself to leave that gate, hysterical and completely torn apart, I could feel Matt's gaze following the two of us all the way down the corridor.

It was horrible and I hated it. But like I'd done so many other times in my life, I came up with a schedule to keep me busy. When I was busy, my brain was occupied and the missing-Matt reflex didn't kick in so hard.

My first order of business: preparing for Matt's birthday.

Birthdays were always huge deals in my home, but ever since he turned 25, Matt had tried to pretend like they didn't exist in ours. He dreaded turning 28 and didn't want anyone to know he was really that old.

So I helped him out and sent a box full of SpongeBob SquarePants hats, blowers and streamers, along with some other party materials and some cookies, to his platoon sergeant with a big sign that read, "Happy Birthday, Matt."

SGT Walker sent me pictures of the surprise party they threw for my adorable husband on his birthday, and I almost peed my pants when I saw the "you-are-in-so-much-trouble-Michelle-Cuthrell" look on my husband's face as he donned a SpongeBob party hat and blew out the candles on a cake that read, "Happy Birthday, Ranger Matt" as members of the medical platoon clapped on the sidelines.

Good thing I had several more months for Matt to forget about the whole event before he came home.

Until They Come Home
April 21, 2006

Before I delivered little Connor James, I had a plan.

I was going to wake up every morning at 6:30 a.m., work out for exactly 47 minutes before changing the baby and completing my morning devotional, and then, while he breastfed, I was going to write in my journal and read exactly 2.5 chapters in my new parenting books. We would eat a freshly cooked healthy breakfast every morning, I would do my hair every day, and by noon, I would have finished all the laundry, cleaning, chores and errands for the entire week. Oh, and we would also spend six hours Monday through Thursday at work where CJ would be a perfect angel and let Mommy complete all the church chores before returning home for a relaxing night of playtime and cuddling, followed by at least eight hours of uninterrupted sleep.

Okay, so maybe I'm an optimist. Or just a super-Type A psycho. But I really didn't think having a baby would change my life all that much. I've always been surrounded by these incredible women who manage to do it all after having children, and I assumed, with my list-making and organization skills, I would be able to do it all, too.

I lost that bet.

The first week of CJ's life, my husband and I slept exactly 12

ADVENT

hours — for the entire week. We didn't do the laundry, we didn't make a meal. Instead, we struggled to wake up and soothe a crying baby, change about 5.2 million diapers and figure out why the heck someone would trust us enough to take an innocent child home from the hospital. It's pretty scary when the only test you have to pass to be a parent is to own a safe infant car seat. It's even scarier when two of you together can't figure out how it works.

I took my husband to the airport at the end of his R and R with bloodshot eyes and sent him off on a plane back to Iraq to get some R and R from his R and R. And I stayed back, determined to make my little schedule of events work.

Once again, I failed miserably.

The second week of CJ's life, I spent three hours trying to leave the house the day my schedule slated 30 minutes. I'd wake up, feed the baby, change the baby, clothe the baby. And just after I showered and dressed myself, he would poop his diaper, wet his onesie and cry for another meal. Of course, after I would feed him a second time, you could bet he'd spit up on my shirt or poop his atomic feces onto my pants, and I'd have to change my own clothes. If I was lucky, this routine only cycled once or twice before I set him in his car seat and held my breath that he wouldn't start crying on the way to the doctor's appointment or the trip to the store.

And forget about ever having time to write in a journal or return a call. Any time I even thought about reaching for the pen or the phone, CJ could sense I was about to be productive and would cry to be held and coddled. And exercising? What new mom has the energy? Lifting the baby in and out of his bassinet 10 times a night should count for something.

Now we're working on week No. 3, and I've wised up just a bit and developed a whole new plan. My schedule and to-do list now reads only, "Love and provide for my baby, sleep when I can." I figure if I can accomplish anything else between diapers, feedings, playtime and snuggles, that will just have to be an added bonus. Besides, after almost three weeks, I've realized that spending time with little Connor is the most rewarding task of anything I could place on my list, anyway.

BEHIND THE BLUE-STAR BANNER

Until They Come Home
April 28, 2006

With my husband back in Iraq and my parents back at home after a weeklong grandparents visit to Fairbanks, I have now been left to raise our little boy alone for the next three months of his life. For all practical purposes, that temporarily makes me a single parent. But more importantly than that, perhaps, it makes me a manic multi-tasker.

As a woman, multi-tasking has always been one of my more developed skills. I could cook dinner, talk on the phone, finish the laundry, load the dishwasher and make up my weekly to-do list all at the same time, without really breaking my concentration on the other tasks at hand.

But raising a newborn by yourself requires a few more skills than I'd been prepared to master.

How, for example, do you breastfeed the hungry crying baby at the same time you scavenge for missing objects taken by the jealous puppy who has very bad only child syndrome and is chewing up pacifiers under the dining room table to get your attention, while the phone is ringing, the dishwasher is buzzing and the clock says you were supposed to be at work five minutes ago?

And even once you do get that situation under control, how then, do you get yourself showered and dressed when you haven't done laundry in weeks, you're out of shampoo and you really just dread dragging the baby to the store because it never fails that he starts screaming the second you walk through the door, and then your shower starts leaking and you have to call maintenance to come fix it, which puts the entire thing out of commission for two days?

Yes, it's been a crazy week. But I'm slowly learning that with a child, these kinds of crazy days are actually now the standard. No longer do I get to consider a bad hair day an awful day. Heck, a bad hair day would mean I actually got the chance to do my hair at all, which would make it a really great day in my new book.

In order to get our lives together — not attempt to tackle my idealistic Mommy-baby schedule, but simply just survive from day to day — I decided I needed to learn a few more skills.

I started with the big one: mobile breastfeeding.

If you can't move around when the baby's on the boob, you're not going to get much accomplished, because the baby feeds exactly 23.99 out of 24 hours of every single day, and it's pretty difficult to complete any meaningful task in .01 hours. I can't even wash my hair that fast.

So with my new home weight training program — lifting the baby 5 million times each day — I've been able to build up the strength to hold Connor in my right arm for long periods of time while walking throughout the house, picking up the floor and even (very slowly) loading the dishwasher while he happily feeds away.

I have to admit, I'm getting pretty good. And not just around the house, either.

Tuesday, my pastor entered the church office where I work, only to find me with a feeding baby in my arms and a binder of work by my side as I furiously typed a 36-page document and simultaneously prepared inserts for the monthly church newsletter.

He seemed pretty interested in finding out how I was doing it all at once, until he asked what "that tent-like thing" was around my neck covering little Connor and I told him it was my brand new Hooter Hider. That's when he stopped asking questions and simply acknowledged the fact that women were amazing.

When your husband is in Iraq and you have to do it all yourself, somehow you've got to learn to be.

CHAPTER TEN

CHAOS

The life of a brand new single mother trying to pave her own road through motherhood with only a faded road map and a half-eaten ham sandwich can only be described using one word: chaotic.

Before Matt's R and R, I was dealing with deployment with the baby inside my body with nine months of husbandless interaction. Now, I was dealing with deployment with the baby on the outside after an amazing three weeks with a husband I once again abhorred living without.

That little baby changed a lot of things, one of them being the length of my e-mails. I had exactly 31 minutes before Connor woke up from his nap, wet his onesie, pooped his atomic feces through his diaper and onto my pants and fed for about 45 minutes before spitting about half of it back up on my shirt, at which point I proceeded to change and bathe him, change and bathe myself, celebrate a short tummy time and then put him back down for a nap so we could repeat the cycle again an hour later.

I continued e-mailing my Top 5 compilations, but they quickly became Cliff Notes versions of my former lengthy lists.

May 2006

Top 5 Things Michelle Has Learned Post-Connor

1. Schedule — what schedule? Oh, you mean the one where we get up every two hours all night long, poop all day and eat all night. Right.

2. Mobile breastfeeding is key to multi-tasking Mommy success. And just for the record, breastfeeding is the best decision we ever made with our little boy and one of the most rewarding and satisfying things I get to do with CJ each day. And for the most part, I totally take advantage of that time and find myself just mesmerized by my love for him as I stare at his tiny face nearly all 45 minutes of every feeding. But with Matt in Iraq and no help at home, there is a need to keep up on the essentials — like dishes

CHAOS

and laundry — and because Connor is the biggest oinker ever, that requires me to multi-task during a couple feedings each day. But I promise I don't go tromping around the house with a baby hanging off my boob all the time! I make sure to make time to enjoy this precious bonding experience that I'm learning to love so much, too.

3. Cute Connor equals Mostly Invisible Michelle. Especially to grandparents. Much like she did when she said goodbye to my dog at Christmastime (my dog!), my mother bawled when she had to say goodbye to Connor at the airport after a week here in Fairbanks, then turned to me and patted me on the back and said, "Well, we'll see you in a few weeks!" No more tears get wasted on the daughter. I'm basically next to dirt now that there's a grand-baby around.

And she's not the only one.

I walked into the office yesterday after a very long weekend of sleepless nights and gassy, fussy days, really looking forward to some adult encouragement and interaction. Too bad the first words out of the hilarious and cherished Joyce Gardella, our kids' church coordinator, were, "Oh, look! Connor's here!... Oh, and hi Michelle."

4. Babies make great scapegoats when you need to pass gas in public. Like when I was in the store the other day and really let out a loud one. It's so easy to just stare at Connor in the carrier, shake my head, hold my nose and say in my cutest little baby voice, "P.U., Connor, that stinks!" I never have to take credit for my rotten-egg-smelling stinkers ever again!

5. Babies are the most precious gift in the world. It is absolutely amazing to me how you can love something so much from the very second you meet it without any other basis for friendship or love than the fact that this is indeed your child. There is nothing like it. And I honestly can't imagine anything more precious or rewarding. You know I mean that when I'm only four weeks out of a long, hard labor and I've already forgotten the pain it took to bring such an amazing creature into the world and am already hoping God gives us the chance to do it again.

I was able to laugh about motherhood only because I loved it so much. Nothing in my life had been as precious or rewarding as delivering a baby of my own, except, perhaps, for marrying the man who helped me create the baby of my own. He just embodied all my hopes and dreams and laughter and love. He was this tangible piece of Matt that kept me going, kept me smiling and kept me positive from day to day.

Especially on those long, strenuous days.

Before CJ was born, I resigned from my reporting job for Channel 11 and took a month off from my church job to spend time with Matt and do the whole having a child thing. Two weeks after he redeployed, I went back to work — with CJ by my side. My pastor and our church staff allowed CJ to come to work with me full time for the rest of our stay in Fairbanks.

At times, it was stressful trying to calm and nurse a screaming baby in between church member phone calls and Monday staff meetings, but the staff were incredible and held CJ, hugged CJ and helped me raise him while his father wasn't able to be physically present in his life.

Of course, when you have a baby and your husband is in Iraq, everyone wants to be part of the "making sure baby is emotionally provided for" process. That means not just the office staff where you work, but family, too.

When my parents found out in the fall that I was supposed to be a bridesmaid in the wedding of a friend in May, they thought it would be a great idea to plan a family vacation around it. My sister lived in Bozeman, Montana, where she was attending college, and my friend's wedding was only about 10 hours away in Colorado. When you live in Alaska, 10 hours is a day trip. So we made the arrangements — my mom, dad, brother, sister and all. On Thursday, May 4, I set out on my first big travel adventure with a baby.

Until They Come Home
May 12, 2006

Six months ago, when my family suggested a spring family reunion at my sister's place in Bozeman, Montana, I was pretty pumped.

Still pregnant and living in a world of utter ignorance, I thought it would be a brilliant idea to travel by myself while my husband was in Iraq with a 4-week-old infant across the United States. All newborns do is sleep, cry and poop, anyway, and I figured I could handle the three of those by myself with no problem.

CHAOS

And then I woke up.

As I spent three hours packing for my little week-long Montana adventure last Wednesday night, it hit me that this whole traveling alone with a baby thing was not going to be as easy as I had hoped. Whereas I was positive I could get away with two carry-on bags and a car seat for Connor, I discovered that packing for a baby takes a little more than one small suitcase. You have to fit in the diapers, the wipes, the toys, the books and about 500 extra outfits because you know from experience that he'll spit up and poop on the first 499. Add all this to the clothes and books I packed for myself, and Connor and I were trudging into the Fairbanks airport like homeless people carrying around our life's supply of materials.

By the time I got to the plane, I told myself that the worst was over. I was packed, checked in — all I had to do now was make it through 12 more hours of travel with a baby.

The travel part was easy. It was the in-between stuff that stunk.

Boarding a plane with an infant strapped to your chest is a bigger adventure than most people realize. Though you do have an advantage, getting to board the plane early, it's very difficult to raise your hands far enough above your head to place your carry-on bag in the luggage compartment when a 9-pound baby is weighing you down in the front. And when you actually get the darned thing into place, you no sooner sit down than the baby starts crying and needs items x and y from his diaper bag. And because you have no one to grab those items for you, you have to figure out how to politely crawl over the passenger next to you, remove those items from the bag while balancing a baby in your other hand, and then get the child to stop crying before the other passengers vote you off the plane.

If it's the Hooter Hider that you're reaching for, you then face a whole second set of challenges.

On our third flight, the poor guy sitting next to me freaked out when I had to feed Connor and spent the entire flight trying to hold a conversation with me with his head turned in the opposite direction.

But I have to say that maybe the most exciting adventure of all was trying to figure out how to use the restroom while carrying an infant without any help from a second party.

I'd checked Connor's car seat in Fairbanks, and the only thing I had to hold him in was his carrier. I wasn't going to ask a *stranger to hold him while I peed, and I sure as heck wasn't going to set him down on the germy bathroom floors. So, trying to be as efficient and creative as possible, I popped him in his front-loading carrier and braved the bathroom alone.*

Twelve hours later, Connor and I arrived safely in Bozeman — a little crazier, but also a little wiser. And when we head back to Fairbanks today, at least now I'll know to pack lighter, feed faster and this time, pee before we go.

Our time in both Montana and Colorado was absolutely precious. Connor met my family, my sister offered me a couple nights' sleep by diapering and walking the baby in the middle of those late night attacks, and my family was all together again.

But it made me miss Matt. A lot.

Ever since we'd been married two years before, he'd never been able to really get in on any of the family trips or adventures. If it wasn't a deployment to Iraq, it was the six-week-long training that came before the deployment, or the Officer Basic Course that prepared him to be an officer during deployment.

That trip would have been our first as a real three-person family, and we were missing out with Matt not there. Again, like I had so many times throughout this deployment, I reminded myself of the important service my husband was performing for our country. Freedom, I had to tell myself, did not come free. For anyone.

Until They Come Home
May 19, 2006

Over the years, Memorial Day weekend has meant many things to me.

As a kid, it marked the absolute coolest event in the world of children's outdoor activities — the unveiling of the community pool. And then when I got a little bit older, it signaled the opening of the sweetest place in 16-year-old dating land — the drive-in movie theater. In college, it denoted the day I busted out my favorite white platform shoes, and in my young professional life, it designated the day I tore the cover off the grill.

But in all those years, Memorial Day never really meant any kind of memorializing for me. That is, until now.

It's amazing how your perspective changes when you marry a military man and send him off to war. All of a sudden, all those old veterans you always thought took things like the flag and the National Anthem too seriously make so much sense, and you, too, start finding yourself frustrated by the people who think Memorial Day is just another day away from the office. Rather than marking it on your calendar as a day to plan fun cookouts and parties, you start marking it in your mind as a day to really remember the sacrifice of so many in this nation throughout the years — the kinds of sacrifices that your husband and his friends make even now.

I'm pretty sure my 16-year-old self would have rolled her eyes at my 23-year-old self had she seen me e-mailing Joseph Fields, coordinator of the Alaska Moving Wall project, who is helping to bring the famous Moving Wall to honor Vietnam veterans to Fairbanks from May 24-30 this year.

She probably would have sighed, had she heard that I was skipping out on the pool and the parties to visit this wall and help this gracious Vietnam veteran find volunteers to help read the names of those who died not only in Vietnam, but also in Afghanistan and Iraq.

And she may even have voted me out of the lunch table if she knew that I was planning on volunteering myself to read the names of these brave fallen soldiers, dressed not in my fashionable post-Memorial Day white shoes, but in something red, white and blue to display my American pride. The 16-year-old Memorial Day celebrator would have never been caught dead in American flag decor on a patriotic holiday — not in a million years.

The thing is, not in a million years did that 16-year-old girl ever expect to marry a military man. Never once did she think that the person she would grow to love the most would serve for a cause and a country that might ask him to make the ultimate sacrifice. Not for a second did she think before that it could someday be that man or his peers or even his very good friends whose names might appear on some memorial wall on some Memorial Day that she chose to spend meaninglessly blackening a burger and playing in a pool.

Memorial Day is too important to dismiss as simply a day just for fun, or a day just for play. We only have these fun traditions because someone, many "someones," died on our behalf. We have that day because someone stood up and said, "Choose me. I volunteer to serve." We have that day because someone laid down his

BEHIND THE BLUE-STAR BANNER

life so that he could protect mine.

This Memorial Day, with our Stryker brigade deployed and many years of American-involved wars like Vietnam behind us, make it a point to remember those sacrifices. Volunteer to read the names of the fallen. Visit this breathtaking Moving Wall. For five minutes, tuck away the teenager's urge to party and play, and embrace the compassionate calling to respect and remember these brave Americans. Then maybe, just maybe, the 16-year-old self can put aside the white shoes, too, and learn a little lesson about true patriotism and sacrifice.

Until They Come Home
May 26, 2006

After reading one of my columns last week, a friend came to me and asked what she could do to make Memorial Day more meaningful.

"I know I can volunteer at that Moving Wall," she said, "but what else can I do to honor those who have served and sacrificed?"

At the time, I didn't have many answers. Other than those big, huge things, like volunteering, I hadn't thought a lot about what I or anyone else could do to help honor those who have sacrificed so much for our country on this important holiday.

I spent the week really dwelling on the concept of Memorial Day, and what it should mean for me and for us as Americans.

After much thought, I came to the conclusion that Memorial Day is just one day in the year we set aside to remember those who have served. But it's just one day. If we want to really honor these soldiers, both those who have sacrificed with their lives and those who have sacrificed with their energy, their time and their months spent away from family and friends, we need to remember them in the little ways all year round.

For some of us, that's a new concept, and something that just doesn't come naturally. That's a culture, and one that needs to be groomed. But celebrating Memorial Day itself is a start.

If you've never taken the time to honor those who have sacrificed so much for our country, use this precious holiday to begin.

Some ways you can start honoring those who have served this Memorial Day Monday:

CHAOS

- *Visit cemeteries and place flags or flowers on the graves of our fallen heroes. Take the time to actually read their names and their epitaphs, and remember that they are real people, too.*
- *Fly the flag at half-staff until noon.*
- *Participate in a National Day of Remembrance to pause and think upon the true meaning of the day. Listen for the sacred taps.*
- *Attend or volunteer for the Vietnam Moving Wall showing downtown.*
- *Learn more about organizations like the National Fallen Heroes Foundation (www.NFHF.org) and the Veterans of Foreign Wars posts (www.vfw.org). Donate to their local chapters.*
- *Book your travel on www.americasaysthanks.org. Part of the commission from bookings on this site goes to NFHF and the families of fallen soldiers who need financial assistance.*
- *If you know of someone who has died serving our country, write a letter to his or her family remembering that person and all his or her best qualities.*
- *Write a letter to an active duty soldier, especially one serving right now in Iraq. Call the rear chaplains at Fort Wainwright or Eielson to get names of soldiers who don't receive much mail. If you can't find the address of a soldier, e-mail me and I will find one for you.*
- *Write a thank you note to a veteran.*
- *Pray for the safety of all those serving currently, the continued health of all those who have served and the families of those who have lost loved ones.*
- *Take a soldier or a veteran out to lunch.*

This Monday, take the time to actually execute one of these tasks. And then next Monday, wake up and complete a second all over again. Let's ensure that the "memorial" in Memorial Day isn't forgotten by those of us who are beneficiaries of those who have sacrificed so much. And let's make sure we truly remember those sacrifices all year long.

BEHIND THE BLUE-STAR BANNER

That Memorial Day, Connor and I made it a point to celebrate. We volunteered to read names at the Vietnam Memorial Moving Wall, we attended the Salmon Bake for NFHF, we even gathered with the other medics' wives whose husbands were deployed to celebrate the sacrifices our husbands make every single day for our country. At the time, I thought all that was enough.

That night around 2 a.m., I happened to check my e-mail after a late-night Connor feeding, only to find an e-mail from the wife of one of my husband's soldiers.

Melissa Loveless had written to tell me that her husband was killed in combat. On Memorial Day. And she just wanted to let me know.

I was shocked. Completely shocked. I wasn't sure if the e-mail was a joke, or something real. I had just talked to Matt a couple days earlier, and with only two months of this deployment left to go, he had told me that all his guys were in good spirits and staying safe. Though some of them had sustained minor injuries, none of the medics had been seriously injured or killed during this deployment. They were medics — they were supposed to be the ones doing the saving! I didn't know what to do, didn't know what to say, so I wrote Melissa back and asked her what I could do.

As I waited for her response, I just sat up in bed, completely numb to the world.

I had met Jeremy the day before the guys deployed, and I had spoken to his wife via e-mail throughout the entire deployment. It wasn't just some soldier — it was someone I knew, someone I had talked to. And the widow was someone I would consider more than an acquaintance — a friend.

Dear Jesus, please be with this woman.

The depth of her three-sentence e-mail began to set in, and at once, my mind raced to the platoon. There were only 30-something guys in their group, and all of them were very close. How were they dealing? What were they doing? How was Matt doing?

Before he deployed, Matt had told me that he didn't think he could forgive himself if he came home without all his men. And now, one had been taken away. I hadn't heard from him at all. I knew I wouldn't, either, for at least 24 more hours, since the Army turned off all the phones and Internet when someone was seriously injured or killed until 24 hours after the next of kin were notified.

CHAOS

This kept the rumors down, and allowed the next of kin to hear the news directly from the Army and not some secondhand source. I prayed for him and just hoped he was surviving.

My mind was a complete jumble, and I tried to stand up, to go do something productive to keep my mind off the news I had just read, but I couldn't move. My body was in as much shock as my heart, so I just sat, and I just waited — waited to hear more from this woman who was now a young widow.

The Real Meaning of Memorial Day…
May 31, 2006

To all our closest family and friends,

For the past two weeks, I've been thinking a lot about Memorial Day — about what it means, what it should mean and how it should be celebrated. It's really sad that, until my husband was sent to a war zone, I never took the time to really contemplate the meaning of this very important day. And now I can't fathom not taking the time to celebrate it appropriately.

Monday, on the holiday we celebrate as Memorial Day, one of Matt's soldiers was killed by gunfire in Iraq. His name was CPL Jeremy Loveless, and besides being one of the great combat medics in Matt's medical platoon, he was also a husband and father to a beautiful 4-year-old girl.

I met Jeremy the day before he left for Iraq at the medical platoon barbecue. He sat down at our table, and we chatted throughout dinner. The last thing he said to me was that he would really love for me to include his wife (who was staying back in Oregon) on my regular e-mail to the medical platoon wives. And then he gave me a hug, and said, "Please take care of my wife while I'm gone." That was the last thing I ever heard from Jeremy Loveless.

I've spent a lot of time on the phone with his wife both yesterday and today, and I asked her to send me some pictures. This Memorial Day, and for every Memorial Day to come, I want you to remember Jeremy Loveless. I want you to remember that this day isn't just a day for barbecues and burgers, for pool parties and play dates. This day is a day to memorialize and remember all those who have died while serving under the American flag. Please, remember the sacrifices of so many — of the soldiers like Jeremy

BEHIND THE BLUE-STAR BANNER

who have served so courageously, and of the families, like Melissa and Chloe, who will forever live without a father and a husband. These people need our prayers not just on Memorial Day, but all year round.

Please, pray for them, remember them and never forget to honor them. It's the least we can do for their great sacrifices for us.

Love, Matt and Michelle

CHAPTER ELEVEN
COPING

When one of your soldiers dies in combat, it's unlike surviving the death of any other person. Other people die from old age, from disease, from natural disasters or natural causes. This man died at the hand of a bullet. This man died serving his country. And he died serving his country under your care.

Even though I was just a spouse, and it was technically one of my husband's guys who had died, I felt the same pain as my husband. I felt pain *for* him. Although my first instinct was to contact Melissa and to love on her and pray for her and be there for her in every way possible, every thought after that was of the platoon — of Jeremy's closest friends and comrades — and of my husband, and how he would be handling this tragedy.

I worried about Matt — a lot. Jeremy was a man my husband supervised, a man he was in charge of. I worried how he would deal with the fact that this man he was responsible for had been killed in action. Though he sounded like he was coping well on the phone, I worried about the days to come.

When you're in Iraq and you're working 19- and 20-hour days, you don't have time to cope with death. You don't even have time to cope with life. You just focus on the mission and accomplish what needs to get done, trying to be as cautious as possible so that yet another life isn't lost. But you don't have time to deal, I mean really deal, with the fact that someone you know and love is now gone. There just aren't enough hours in the day.

On June 6, I attended a briefing held by the Army Community Services department on post. There, the spouses of the Stryker soldiers learned about the stressors of the returning soldier. And it confirmed all my fears.

ACS asked several soldiers who had already returned from a tour in Iraq to speak to this group of concerned spouses. Each of them noted the fact that the depression, the stress and all the coping with death happened 30 to 90 days after their return. The first days — they were all parties and welcome home events. They were a second honeymoon, a second date, a second chance to start over again with the family.

But after that, once things returned to routine and it was back to the morning PT and the job back on post, they were suddenly confronted with the fact that someone they loved was gone. They were confronted with the harsh reality that someone who was there by their side training with them for this conflict in Iraq just one year ago had given his life to the cause. He wasn't running in the front of the line anymore. He wasn't practicing combat medic duties with the other companies. He was gone. And they were here. And it was a lot to deal with at one time. And I couldn't help but wonder how my husband, an introvert and an emotionally private person, would handle it all.

Until They Come Home
June 2, 2006

My husband and I had just taken a seat at Big Daddy's Barbecue for one last medical platoon get-together when I met him.

As I played with the straw in my water glass and pretended not to hear the crude jokes being told at the next table, Jeremy Loveless approached me and grabbed a chair nearby.

"How are you doing? I'm Jeremy," he said as he offered his hand. "I'm new to the platoon."

I remember noticing his eyes. They were beautiful and blue and the kind that actually smiled when they met yours, as if to say, "No, really, I mean it when I say it is nice to meet you."

He sat down at our table, and we chatted with the other guys throughout dinner as I got to know a little about Jeremy — about where he lived in Oregon, about his passion as a volunteer firefighter, about his short two months in Fairbanks thus far. He told me about his wife and little girl, and asked me to add them to my e-mail list so that they could remain in the loop even from Oregon, where they were staying throughout the deployment. And when it was time to say goodbye, that man gave me a hug and asked me just one thing: "Please take care of my wife."

Those were the last words I ever heard from him.

Jeremy Loveless was killed by small arms fire in Iraq on Memorial Day Monday. He was only 25.

When my husband entered his room at the forward operating base to inventory his belongings, he found exactly what I would expect from this man who so touched me back in August: a large picture of his wife, Melissa, and little girl, Chloe, blown up and hanging on his wall.

As I promised I would so many months before, I called Melissa Wednesday morning, expecting to find a woman falling apart and completely beside herself after losing the most important man in her life. But the woman who picked up the phone on the other end was one with incredible God-given strength and poise, one completely comforted by the lifetime of love her husband left her.

She told me how, even after six years of marriage and in the middle of a large pile of dishes, Jeremy would ask her to drop the chores and sit on the couch and let him hold her. "The dishes can wait," he would tell her as he grabbed her hand.

She shared stories about Jeremy's adventurous side — how he would spontaneously grab Chloe and tell her to jump in the car and whisk the two of them off bowling or to the beach, or to some other exciting location, if only for the day.

She told me about how Jeremy would graciously satisfy her addiction for pictures by regularly dressing up and heading to the family portrait studio without a complaint or a frown, and how he'd make it a point to kiss her and Chloe and tell them he loved them before he ever left the house on a firefighter call.

Three days before he was killed, he told Melissa that he didn't want to have to settle for talking on the phone anymore, that he wanted to hold her and talk to her in person instead. She told him she needed him to keep calling. And he did — all three days in a row before he died. His last words to her were "I love you."

Forever, I will remember Jeremy by these three trademark words. And when I want to honor him, to truly remember the sacrifice he made, I will simply love others the way he loved his family. Like Jeremy himself, that kind of love leaves a legacy that can never be forgotten.

Until They Come Home
June 9, 2006

The week before CPL Jeremy Loveless died, I hit a wall.
After enduring nine months of deployment, spending an entire pregnancy by myself and raising a newborn baby without any help from a second party, you'd think the hardest part of deploy-

ment would have been behind me. After all, all I had to do now was keep busy with the baby for three more months and my hubby would be home and we'd be one big happy family again. These last 12 weeks of deployment? A piece of cake, I told myself.

Wrong.

On May 22, the day of our two-year anniversary, I not only hit a wall; I fell apart. I was at the same time completely depressed and totally bitter that once again this year, I was spending my anniversary munching on mac and cheese and catching up on The Apprentice *while my husband worked thousands of miles away performing a job that, though I knew was important, was taking him away from me. (He spent last May training for Iraq at an exercise in Fort Polk, Louisiana.)*

I quickly grew resentful. When Matt called, I was short with him. When he e-mailed, I replied with one-sentence answers. All of a sudden, I was just so angry that he'd been gone for nine months and would continue to be for three more.

People often think that knowing the value and importance of your husband's work is supposed to make things okay when that significant work calls him away from his family. And most of the time, it really does. I know that my husband is serving selflessly and sacrificing important things, like time with his family, in order to serve a cause and a country we both truly believe in. But knowing that fact doesn't make it any easier when he's missing birthdays and Valentine's Days and Christmases and Thanksgivings. It doesn't make it easier when your son smiles for the first time and your husband isn't there to share it with you. And it doesn't make it any easier when you spend one more wedding anniversary all alone on the couch.

I was just about to share some not-so-nice words with my husband in an e-mail about what he was putting me through and just how I felt about being alone all the time when I received an e-mail from Melissa Loveless. She told me that her husband had died in Iraq just 12 hours earlier.

When I asked her later on the phone if there was anything I could do, she only had a few requests. But one of them was for me and for others to remember just how precious life is, and to savor every moment you get the privilege to share it with your significant other. Treasure every phone call, revel in every e-mail. Don't let a day pass that you don't say I love you, and don't let a moment go by that you allow yourself to become bitter that you can't spend that day together.

Tears streamed down my face as I hung up the phone with this incredible woman, and all of a sudden, all I wanted to do was talk to Matt. I wanted to hold Matt, to tell him I was so sorry for being so short and rude the previous week, and to let him know I just loved him with all my heart and that he meant everything to me. And that I would gladly celebrate a million more anniversaries alone if it meant I could still hear his voice once a week on the telephone.

That was the conversation we enjoyed the very next day.

Even in Jeremy's death, he and his wife taught me a lesson that will live on in my marriage, and in my life as a military wife, forever.

When you're dealing with death, it seems the best thing you can do is move on with your life. And so that's what Connor and I tried to do.

We went back to work. We went back to play. We went back to all the things we did on a daily basis before CPL Loveless was killed. It's just that we had a fresh perspective this time, and we chose to treasure the moments we may have let slip by in days past.

Until They Come Home
June 16, 2006

Sometimes, you just can't get a screaming baby to stop.

I had tried everything. I'd placed Connor in the portable swing we keep near my desk in the church office. I'd executed about 50 deep squats with the baby in my arms. I'd even turned him sideways and placed him in nursing position, only to pop a pacifier in his mouth. (Some tell me this act introduces deception into our mother-son relationship. I tell them it introduces sanity.) Nothing worked.

After a week of sleepless nights, I was at the end of my rope.

That's when Floyd, a male member of our pastoral staff, scooped up my son. Connor — the same baby who had been uncontrollably screaming for minutes on end — stared Floyd straight in the eyes, laid his head on his chest and fell asleep almost instantly.

BEHIND THE BLUE-STAR BANNER

At first, I was completely shocked. I mean, Floyd's a sweet guy, but not exactly the kind of man you might picture cooing at babies and cradling them in his arms. And definitely not the kind of guy you might expect to put them to sleep. He's more the guy you might approach if you wanted your kids to learn some discipline, or get their bottoms kicked on the soccer field. But not fall asleep.

I was beginning to wonder about the magic of Floyd, when I noticed that the incident with this member of the male race wasn't an isolated one.

A couple days after the Floyd-calming mystery, my dad and I traveled with Connor to Colorado to be in a wedding. As I attended to bridesmaid duties, Dad attended to Connor. And before we boarded the plane that next day, Connor offered my dad his very first smile. And his second. And his third. And after almost no interaction with him at all, he offered my baby brother smile No. 4.

It took three more days before I ever got smile No. 5.

Connor loves boys. They're often the only ones he'll make eye contact with, the only ones who can calm him down. They're the ones he pays attention to, the ones he likes to hear. And during deployment, they are the one thing that he can't always have.

As a geographically single mom, I have to go out of my way to ensure that Connor gets the kind of male attention he craves and the kind of male attention he developmentally needs.

Kyle Pruett, a clinical professor of psychiatry at the Yale University Child Study Center, reports in his studies that father-baby interaction is important because it not only helps build higher self-esteem in children, but also creativity and empathy, among other things.

But unlike many children, Connor can't just hang out with Daddy when he gets home from work at night to receive that kind of love and interaction, and he can't just cuddle up next to him when he needs to feel that kind of male security. He can't even hear his voice from day to day.

That leaves me to find men — not as Daddy replacements, but as Daddy assistants — who are willing to hold my baby, to play with him and to love on him, so that he gets the kind of male attention he needs to be a healthy, secure little boy. And that's not always easy — especially when boys find out that yes, babies do indeed poop, and that sometimes, they do indeed poop on you.

COPING

Fortunately, I've been blessed by awesome male family, awesome male pastors and awesome male friends who make time in their day for my son and ensure that he receives the kind of male support I just can't provide. Those simple gifts — those baby holds and those Connor cuddles — are the most meaningful ones anyone could ever offer to a geographically single mom during deployment.

My pastors were seriously amazing during that time, and it was amazing just how much Connor took to both of them. So many times I'd be jiggling poor CJ around the office, trying everything to get him to stop fussing, and all it took was a hug from Pastor Jeff or a soothing phrase or two from Floyd to calm him, quiet him and lull him off to sleep.

Those were the most precious gifts I might have received the entire deployment. They weren't just from guys, either.

One Wednesday afternoon, my friend Karol called me up at work.

"Michelle, I have some extra time this evening. Can I come over and watch Connor so you can take a nap?"

Sure, I'd had babysitting offers before — almost the entire deployment long — but I'd never had someone make herself so available to me — and make it so easy for me to say yes to her generous offer without feeling guilty about burdening her.

Karol came over that night and, just like she promised, grabbed CJ and played with him in my family room while I took my first daytime nap in more than two months. Even though it was only an hour long, that nap rejuvenated me, refreshed me and gave me the energy to love on Connor all the more that night and many afternoons to come.

That night, I prayed that other spouses of deployed soldiers had friends as great as mine.

Two Months Old and a Full Night of Sleep!
June 2006

What do you do when your nearly 2-month-old baby starts sleeping through the night? You write a mass e-mail to 300 of your closest friends, of course! Happy Connor Now Sleeps Through the Night day!

BEHIND THE BLUE-STAR BANNER

So it's been two very long months since I last wrote — two months of poopy diapers, sleepless nights and more precious cuddling and playing time than I've had in my entire life. I have to admit, raising a child alone is just a little bit tougher than I first anticipated. I imagined having a baby would be a lot like, say, playing house. I'd feed him, change him, dress him in cute clothes, and then when I got bored, I'd go play some other game. Except that the changing part takes place 10 times a day, and there's no one to run interference when you get tired. Or when you need to sleep at night.

This week marks the first time in three whole months that Michelle has slept more than four to five hours in one night! Since I tried out this new stricter scheduling idea and started regulating play and nap time during the day (it's amazing what happens when you actually keep the child awake instead of letting him sleep any time he wants all day long!), CJ has slept 8.5 hours each of the last three nights! And I'm like a whole new person!

Of course, even without the sleep, Connor has given me quite a bit of love and laughter to keep me going even on those long days between those even longer sleepless nights. He's now smiling almost all the time and just beginning to coo. He sits up with assistance and is really starting to pay more attention to the world around him.

One of my favorite new developments is that, when he's feeding, rather than closing his eyes and going to his little sleepy "happy place" (which, by the way, looks a lot like complete and utter alcohol intoxication), CJ now looks up at me every two or three minutes, stares into my eyes and then smiles.

Part of you knows you need to keep him feeding so he gets the nutrients he needs and learns how to feed for a good, solid session, but the other part of you is just so tickled and melted when he looks up and smiles at you that you just don't care.

I mean, there's not a whole lot of things that could get me to leave myself exposed to cold Alaska air for long periods of time without protest, but having your son smiling at you definitely makes the cut. So needless to say, our feeding sessions now take twice as long. But are also twice as enjoyable for me, too.

I suppose these new smiling sessions might begin to make up for the fact that Connor's very first smile went not to his hardworking mother, but to her visiting dad. Cue story.

COPING

In May, I had the amazing privilege of being a part of my friend Becca's wedding in Colorado. Dad traveled with me because, frankly, I had no idea how I was going to spend time with my awesome bride friend and attend to bridesmaid duties and take care of an infant while walking down the aisle and carrying a rose at the same time. Not without a husband there to help out. So Dad came with me to care for Connor.

Mind you, up until this point, Connor had spent exactly one week with my dad, and that was the second week of his life. I mean, he couldn't even see more than 12 inches past his face at that point, not to mention emotionally bond with his granddad. Nevertheless, after just one day hanging out with my dad, as I was kissing him goodbye to go get ready for the wedding with the other girls, Connor turned his head and offered my dad his very first smile.

I was positive it was a gas-motivated smile, so I picked him up, turned him toward me and said, "Connor, did you just smile at Granddad?" He then turned his head to my father, who was sitting next to me, and smiled again! At that point, I was basically just in shock and utterly desperate to get a smile out of my son, and so I threw my head in front of his face and smiled real big and yelped, "Connor! Mommy wants a smile! Smile at Mommy!" At which point Connor turned his head, looked all the way around me to my father and smiled again!

Okay, so let's summarize. Michelle spends four weeks with baby boy all alone. She feeds him. She changes him. She stays up with him all night. She plays with him every day, reads him stories every night and attends to his every need and loves him like no one else on earth could even fathom, and after only one week and two days of being with my dad, he gives him not just one, but three smiles.

Slightly bitter.

I kind of felt cheated on. I mean, my son gave away his virgin smile to someone else! I secretly wanted to run into my room and throw a tantrum. But my dad, always knowing what to say and reading me like a book, put his hand on my shoulder and said, "Oh, Michelle, it's just gas. He didn't really smile."

Gas! I thought. Maybe it was just gas! But when I stuck my nose on his bottom, no gas was coming out and there were no *burps on the north end, either. That was it. Dad had officially received the first smile.*

Dad was modest, though, and didn't rub it in my face. I'd get the next one, he told me, the "real" one.

After an amazing time with Becca and Caleb and several of my awesome Ithaca friends there in Grand Junction, Dad and I headed back to Montana to spend some more time with the family before scattering across the country.

There, my baby brother, who had spent exactly 24 hours with Connor at that time, received Connor's very second smile ever.

Of course, he wasn't quite as humble about the experience and took joy in pointing out that, while I danced in circles and made goofy faces and tried everything in the entire book of Ways to Make Your Child Smile and Look Like an Idiot, Besides, *he simply bent down to Connor's carrier and received smile No. 2.*

He also took joy in pointing out that he, unlike me, could get my child to stop crying at the drop of a hat.

"Michelle," he kept saying, "I don't know why you think being a mom is so hard! All you gotta do is shake his car seat and he stops crying! I could even raise this child!"

Of course, he had no desire to shake his car seat at 2 a.m. when my sister and I were trying all the other tricks to get the poor baby back to sleep in his laundry basket (laundry basket, crib — eh, they both have four sides).

But I do have to give him credit — he was a pretty decent uncle when Mandy and I went shopping (hello, no mall in Fairbanks). And it was a blast to shop with my very trendy sister, too, even though my purchases were limited to one cheap pair of pants and a cute summer top on sale. Next out-of-state trip: welcome home Matt outfit.

I should note here that before I left Montana, I did get a smile out of my son — but it was a weak one. Totally lame. But at that point, I was so desperate, I would have taken a stinker-, spit- or even spicy-food-inspired half-grin, just some form of acknowledgement from this guy I called my child that he did indeed think I was worth crooking his mouth at.

You win some, you lose some.

Make sure to tell someone you love him today,
Michelle

COPING

One of the most physically noticeable changes about Fort Wainwright when the Stryker brigade deployed last August were the signs.

As drivers entered the front gate and traveled down Gaffney Road, they couldn't help but notice the hundreds of painted, printed, sewn and signed banners that hung from the gates of the sports field to the train tracks, and almost everywhere in between. They displayed words of support, messages of encouragement, and most of all, symbols of love.

Now, those signs are slowly reappearing, but this time, the "we'll miss you" messages have been replaced by the phrase so many of us have been counting down the days to utter: "Welcome home."

As the community welcomes home the brigade advance party this week and prepares for the main body to return in July and August, we as civilians have an awesome opportunity to support and thank our hometown heroes by offering not just yellow ribbons on our cars and American flags on our front porches, but also action.

Some ways you can support soldiers returning home:

- *Make thank you and welcome home banners. Even if you don't personally know any soldiers. Hang them outside your home or office, or even in the window of your car.*
- *Attend redeployment ceremonies. It makes a difference at these Fort Wainwright events when soldiers see not just their families, but also community members sitting in the bleachers thanking them for their last 12 months of sacrifice.*
- *Make goody bags for returning single soldiers. While married soldiers return to families and freezers stocked with ice cream and candy bars, single soldiers often return to the chaos of checking back into the barracks without as much as a gallon of milk or a tube of toothpaste. Starter and goody bags can make all the difference for these soldiers settling back into Fairbanks alone.*
- *Volunteer to babysit. These couples haven't been together*

for 12 months, and though they will definitely want time with their entire families, they will also need time alone. But don't just offer to babysit "someday." Be specific. Tell them you have nothing to do this Saturday, and you'd love to come over and watch the kids so they can catch a movie. Or just show up on their doorstep and "kidnap" the children so they can enjoy a quiet night alone. They will be more likely to take you up on your offer if they don't have to face the awkwardness of calling you up and asking you to make good on it.

- *Take a soldier to lunch. After 12 months of chow hall food, I promise, he'll love you forever. Or take part in the local "Pick it Up" campaign by anonymously picking up the tab for a soldier's meal when you see him or her in public.*
- *Offer rides. Many soldiers placed their cars in storage or drove them home before deployment and may not have immediate access to transportation. Providing rides to church, to town or even to the grocery store can be a bigger help than you might realize.*
- *Help pack. Many of the soldiers will be moving within three or four months of redeploying. Hauling boxes and sorting socks can make their move less stressful.*
- *Go out of your way to say "thank you." And don't be afraid to do it in public and even when it's not convenient. A few years ago, Matt and I were enjoying dinner at a fancy restaurant when an older couple interrupted us, shook Matt's hand and said, "We just wanted to thank you for your service. We appreciate you." Matt was smiling for hours, and he said it made all the difference.*

For soldiers who have made the big sacrifices for us, executing these little things is the least we can do.

While I was home figuring out ways to support my husband and his friends, it turned out that my husband was at war trying to figure out new ways to support me. And after our whole Valentine's Day rendezvous, he was making an extra special effort around those major holiday times of the year.

COPING

My birthday was on June 28, but almost two weeks before my big day, I received a letter in the mail from my husband. It wasn't unusual for Matt to send handwritten cards and letters from Iraq — he did it two or three times a month, sometimes even four — but this one was bigger, and the envelope was glittery and pink, so I knew it was for some more precious occasion than Flag Day.

As I set down my car keys and carefully tore open the card inside, I smiled. I just knew my husband had remembered my birthday, and he had remembered two weeks early this year instead of two weeks late.

I gently pulled out the card with the beautiful mauve ribbon and read the note he had written inside.

Dear Michelle,

Baby , you are getting so old! Just kidding. I just want you to know how much I love you, how much I adore you and how much you mean to me. Happy birthday! Please take the day to yourself and enjoy every last minute of it. I just wish I could be there to share it with you. I love you, Michelle Suzanne. I cannot wait to share so many more birthdays with you. I love you.

Matt

But that wasn't all.

Inside the card was a creased sheet of cream stationary. At the top were the words "Contract for Services Due," and scribbled below were a list of 10 promises my husband was making on this, my 24th birthday.

Contract for Services Due

I, Matthew David Cuthrell, will pay in full to Michelle Suzanne Cuthrell, all of the below services with no complaints, restraints or ill will. There is no expiration date to the following list. All must be paid prior to our 50th anniversary.

1. Back massage with all the fixings. Foot massage not optional.

2. A ride in a limo to your favorite restaurant.

3. A military ball.

4. At least one night per month to dress up and do whatever you want to do until our 50th. (Dancing is unfortunately included in this offer.)

5. A romantic getaway to Hawaii.

6. A new car! This is subject to available funds. Must be paid prior to 25th anniversary and no earlier than our 10th anniversary.

7. A trip to Indonesia or any exotic place you would like to go.

8. At least one night per month that you get to choose any movie you want and I will watch with no ill will.

9. A new house! Note: House may be previously owned.

10. You are the owner of my heart. It is yours and cannot be transferred to any other person or persons. It is delicate so do with it as you choose.

I, the undersigned, agree to all terms. There are no possibilities of escaping the terms of this contract. Not even death. All terms must be met in full no later than our 50th anniversary or no later than the timeline dictated in each subparagraph.

Signed, Matthew David Cuthrell

I definitely had the best husband in the entire world.

Until They Come Home
June 30, 2006

Okay, I confess. I'm a birthday junkie. Between the riverboat cruises, birthday banners and surprise parties, my husband and my family have always made really big deals out of birthdays, and I seriously live for them.

Even though he almost forgot about my birthday last year until halfway through the day (fortunately, a surprise CD player installed in my car one month earlier served as his saving grace), the year before that, Matt arranged a special dinner at my favorite restaurant in Washington, D.C., followed by a surprise shopping trip at Bed, Bath and Beyond for our brand new place.

And the year before that, he surprised me on my 21st with balloons and streamers all over his parents' house, a dozen roses, a bottle of wine, a dressy dinner out and even some candlelight dancing. Both years, he called me on my cell phone about once every hour, all day long, just to sing "Happy Birthday."

But with Matt in Iraq this year and my family thousands of miles away, I was trying to prepare myself for a laidback, no-glitz day. I didn't know if anyone in Fairbanks even knew it was my birthday, and I told myself that this year would be a good year for me to learn how to grow up and not need a million surprises to feel special. I had to learn how to be a real adult someday, anyway.

I arrived in the office at 10 a.m. Wednesday, and Brenda, our church's financial secretary, was the first to wish me a very happy birthday. At 11, the flower shop delivered a beautiful Hawaiian-themed bouquet — from the entire church staff. At 11:30, Christina, our facilities coordinator, arrived with a caramel white chocolate cake, and at noon, Barb, the caterer who works out of our church, appeared in the office with my very favorite meal ever: Cornish game hens, strawberries and beer bread.

As the entire staff sang "Happy Birthday" and I blew out the candles on my hen — which is a lot easier than blowing them out on a cake, I might add — I gazed at these people I had only known for less than a year, and how incredible they were to go out of their way to celebrate my special day when everyone else so dear to me was so far away.

I left work that afternoon with a smile on my face and a hen in my heart, thinking my birthday couldn't get much better, and headed to my dear friend Laurie's house. I arrived expecting a quiet dinner at home with her and her little daughter, Paige, only to find a surprise gathering of military wives and their young children there to greet me.

I guess growing up will just have to wait until next year.

When your husband is deployed, it's amazing how quickly great friends step in to fill that void in your life.

They take care of you. They celebrate with you. They assume the role of husband for a year. And they make you feel special, even when your husband isn't there in person to do that.

There are very few friends I feel more connected with than the ones I've made during this difficult year. They are the ones who have been there for me when I was pregnant and alone and just couldn't handle morning sickness anymore, the ones who bought me meals when I was a brand new mother and had no idea what on earth to do with a child, and the ones who, without even telling them it was my birthday, made it one of the most special I have celebrated in all my years.

These people have not just been my friends this difficult year; they have been my family.

Until They Come Home
July 7, 2006

As I was cleaning out my garage this week — one of the many endless tasks I'm trying to complete before my husband comes home from Iraq next month — I stumbled across a box from 1 LT Devin Hammond.

Besides being a great friend of ours, Devin is also a single soldier. That means, among other things, that he has no one to ship his boxes home to, no one to maintain his car.

So throughout this deployment, I've tried to pick up the slack and make things easier on him. He mails his extra Army gear home to my house, his car sits in the front of my driveway. I start the vehicle and maintain it as best I can so that storage and car maintenance are two less things this soldier has to worry about when he returns home from a yearlong deployment.

As I moved the pile of boxes he's shipped to my house over the course of the year into his car and washed off his windshield, it hit me that I might be the only one to do anything for this awesome single soldier. And what I did was next to nothing.

Though Devin is very close to his family, they live thousands of miles away back in the Lower 48. He doesn't have a wife, he doesn't have any children. And most of his friends are military personnel who will be returning on that plane with him in August — many who will be coming home to spouses who have been preparing for their return for months.

"We've all seen the movies and commercials where the soldier returns from deployment and is greeted by his family or loved ones with a big welcome home sign or a 'run, jump and hug' maneuver, as I like to call it," Devin wrote me in an e-mail this week. "The part that's left out in that scene is the single soldier who comes off the plane, looks out, sees the married soldiers being greeted, readjusts his bag on his shoulders, puts his head down and goes back to the barracks, just like after a field problem. Yeah, it's depressing, that's why you never see it."

COPING

*In all my plotting and planning for my husband's return —
polishing the furniture, preparing the house, picking out the perfect outfit — I'd forgotten that there would be incredible soldiers
like Devin who would return to nothing more than a new landlord
or a barracks reassignment.*

*These soldiers worked just as hard over the course of this deployment. They've made just as many sacrifices, fought just as
hard for a cause and a country we try to support back here at
home. And they've done it all without the constant letters and e-mails from a wife or children back in Alaska.*

*And yet a missing ring on that left fourth finger sometimes
means that they might not be appreciated, welcomed or loved
upon as much when they return from a completely selfless and
stressful year away.*

*After receiving Devin's e-mail, I wrote some of my other single
soldier friends, asking what we as a community and we as an Army
family could do to make their homecoming just as special as those
of the married soldiers.*

*CPL Juan Gomez said he'd love to share lunch or dinner with
local families — or nice single girls, he joked — upon his return to
share his experiences and pass along stories from this past year.
Coming home to an empty room is not the highlight of redeployment, he said, and he'd love to spend some time in fellowship with
others.*

*CPL Matthew Hall said he'd love to attend some kind of
homecoming party and music concert in Fairbanks — something
fun single soldiers could look forward to and participate in to help
relax after this stressful year away.*

*Devin simply wrote, "When you see that soldier, congratulate
him and welcome him home. It will do wonders for his morale."*

That's the least we can do.

CHAPTER TWELVE
DEVASTATION

Until They Come Home
July 14, 2006

Every Army wife dreams about the big day.

Her husband marches down that plank from his plane, home after a yearlong Iraqi tour, and she — 30 pounds lighter and with abs of steel — runs to meet her man as he drops his jaw, throws his arms around her and tells her that she's never looked so beautiful in her whole life.

Riiight.

I had good intentions of getting into shape before my husband returned from Iraq. I really did!

I drew up a workout schedule. I temporarily cut soda pop from my diet. I even created a fitness contest between my husband and myself. (Mental note: Don't compete with a cheater who "forgets" to record his beginning measurements and claims half-way through the contest that he's lost at least 15 pounds and gained several inches of muscle and is sure to win the little no-guilt cash spending spree we set aside as an incentive for the winner who made the most drastic changes.)

It's just that the brownies in the office and the black leather couch in my living room — not to mention the baby in my nursery — kind of made me forget about that whole health thing until about two weeks ago.

Like many spouses of deployed soldiers, I am now trying to cram 11 months of fitness programs into five short weeks of exercise before my hubby returns to the States.

So for the past two weeks, I have been utilizing my free hours of respite care at the Child Development Center on post and dropping CJ off for one hour at a time so that I, the harried lady who forgot that her husband didn't want to be married to a huffing, puffing stair climber forever, can hit the gym.

For a girl who met her spouse at a gym in Dayton, Ohio, it's kind of ironic that I don't know how to use one. In fact, they kind of scare me.

DEVASTATION

I mean, big, huge sweaty men pumping iron and grunting like they're constipated really don't present the most welcoming image to terrified, un-athletic office rats like me. And super-fit Army women who run marathons and teach 8 million spinning classes each week just make me look bad. Because I was involved in much cooler activities in high school — like band, drama club and speech contests — I had no reason to even enter such a facility. Until the day I became a telemarketer at World Gym.

That's when I fell in love with one of those sweaty, grunting fitness trainers, and, well, the rest is history.

But just because I married a gym junkie doesn't mean I know how to be one.

That was pretty obvious my first trip back to the Physical Fitness Center this month.

I'm not sure what gave my novice status away — my beat up, too-small Wal-Mart tennis shoes or the fact that I was staring at the machine for five minutes before a trainer working with another client in the room came to assist me — but apparently, I kind of looked like an idiot.

I felt like one, too, when I put my legs through the leg curl machine the wrong way and tried to pump them upward like a leg extension. And I felt even cooler when my starting arm curl weight was 5 pounds. And I couldn't finish all 10 repetitions.

I'm super buff, what can I say.

But even two weeks into my five-week workout program, I am starting to notice a difference.

I mean, my new appetite allows me to scarf double the desserts after dinner and bunches more beer bread at lunch — without even feeling guilty about it!

Oh well.

At least when my husband steps off that plane and we execute the run-leap-hug maneuver in three short weeks, I can tell him that I fit half of the "hot mama" description he was hoping for. And Connor James will be there to prove it.

Until They Come Home
July 21, 2006

With two weeks until the Stryker soldiers return home, it's crunch time.

BEHIND THE BLUE-STAR BANNER

In the last week, most of the military wives I know (myself included) have hit up the gym and kicked that deployment fitness plan into high gear. We've scheduled manicures and pedicures and waxed in areas where the sun doesn't shine. We're tanning, we're exfoliating and we're highlighting and dying those roots like crazy. And of course, we're searching for that all-important welcome home outfit.

And I've had lots of help.

I realize that Fairbanks is indeed the fashion capital of America, with its massive malls and scores of trendy stores. Even so, I chose to shop for my homecoming outfit in a city with two major malls, several lone department stores and more trendy strip malls than I can count within a 15-minute drive.

It's a rough life.

So while I was in Ohio for a wedding last weekend, the entire family decided it would be a good idea to help me find the perfect outfit to wear when my husband returns from a year in the desert. Really, they provided the ride, so I couldn't exactly turn away their input.

And with a mother who picked her hot pink mother-of-the-bride dress in the prom section, a father who is still dressed by his wife, an aunt and uncle who really don't enjoy shopping, a baby who had no idea what to think of a real, live mall and a mother-in-law who I was constantly conscious would be seeing exactly what I chose to wear the day I reunited with her son, my trip was interesting to say the least.

First my aunt picked out this sexy red dress that covered maybe two whole inches of my bottom and almost none of my chest and looked like something straight out of the Victoria Secret catalogue. But after trying it on, I decided perhaps the mistress motif wasn't exactly what I was looking for upon Matt's return. At least not for the public part of it. And so we put that one back.

Then my mom chose a dress I could have worn to next month's military ball. And though I tried the fancy frock on to appease her, I had to explain that I had no idea what time Matt would be arriving, or even what day, and wouldn't know until 24 hours before. And if he did indeed arrive at 6 a.m. versus 10 p.m., I might not want to show up like I was about to take him to Prom 2006 in a stretch limousine.

I tried on several dresses that day — fancy dresses, frilly

DEVASTATION

dresses, fashionable dresses, fun dresses — and after an entire afternoon of shopping, finally settled on one that my dad, of all people, spotted on the rack…

A couple hours and one awkward afternoon later, I finally owned a dress to don for my honey. And my dad liked it so much that he even paid for it, which means that no matter how good or bad it really looks, Matt will think I'm a super star.

Now if I can just get my house and my body in as good of shape as my closet and my wallet, I'll be all set for that big homecoming event. Two weeks and counting…

Or so I thought at the time.

One phone call five days later changed everything.

I had just returned home from a dinner at a fellow military wife friend's house. A group of us gathered there every Wednesday night with our small children for the HAIRCUT club (Husbands Abroad in Iraq, Children Under Three), and like all the recent gatherings, we spent most of the night gabbing over our preparations for our husbands. We compared pedicures and poster plans, welcome home outfits and waxing costs. And when we left, all of us retreated with visions of homecomings dancing in our heads.

But when I listened to my answering machine around 7:30 that night, I knew something was wrong.

A reporter from the *Fairbanks Daily News-Miner*, where I worked, had left a few messages and also sent an e-mail.

Golly gee! I thought to myself. *My column isn't due for another 12 hours! I promise I'll get it to you! Really!*

When I called Mary Beth back, though, she didn't want to discuss this week's column.

"Michelle," she said, "our reporter in D.C. just told us that the Stryker brigade is being extended in Iraq. Can you confirm this information for us?"

My heart stopped. Dead stopped. I literally gasped for breath as I shook my head back and forth, violently almost, and practically screamed into the phone, "No. No, that can't be right. I haven't heard anything about it."

A million thoughts raced through my mind as I reached for a nearby countertop to steady myself. I was beginning to feel physically ill.

"I'm so sorry, Michelle, but I'm afraid it's true. Governor

BEHIND THE BLUE-STAR BANNER

Murkowski confirmed it for us this afternoon."

My throat swelled up as I fought back the tears. *I was a profes-sional,* I told myself, *I am a professional! I will not cry simply be-cause another reporter found out some information that I can't even verify is true.*

But as Mary Beth read me the article she downloaded from the AP Wire, I realized that it was. That it had to be.

Just days before he would return home from a year that was nearly unbearable as it was, Matt was being extended and sent to Baghdad. He wasn't coming home. My baby wasn't coming home.

Matt
July 27, 2006

Dearest friends,

I found out tonight that Matt will not be coming home this week from Iraq as originally planned. Yesterday, Secretary of De-fense Rumsfeld officially extended his unit in Iraq for an indefinite period of time. The 172nd Stryker brigade will be traveling to Baghdad to quell violence in the area. Though we know nothing for sure, the soldiers who returned home to their families yesterday will likely be returning to Iraq this week.

Though I have no official information, we are unofficially hearing that three months is the standard extension. One high-ranking official told me to shoot for Thanksgiving or Christmas-time for my husband's return. That would put CJ at 7 or 8 months of age and our deployment at 15 months long. This also obviously changes all our plans for moving. Everything is up in the air now.

I haven't talked to Matt yet, but I am sure he is as devastated as I am. We were counting down the days until we could be a family again, and now that number is indefinite. Please pray for Matt and the soldiers, that they can stay focused on the mission and not burn out. And please pray for the families. We are all heartbroken and in total shock. And to be honest, we are all doing horribly and can't fathom going three more months without our loved ones. I need Matt home, and I know he needs us, and it's really, really, really difficult to look on the bright side through tears and sobs. I honestly have never been so sad and disappointed in my entire life. This is heartbreaking for us as a family. And I just want to be there

162

DEVASTATION

for Matt, and at this time, I just really don't know how. Please pray hard.

Love,
Michelle

After sobbing hysterically and just rocking my precious baby back and forth to comfort myself, a friend from my coffee group called.

"Michelle," Carolyn asked, so gently on the phone, "please come over here. There's others of us here. We can commiserate together."

Wailing, hysterical and driving like a maniac, I rushed to post and stumbled into a house that I had been to so many times on happier occasions — for baby showers, birthday parties, wedding scrapbook nights — and completely fell apart.

"Why us?" I bellowed into Carolyn's shoulder through snot and sobs. "They were coming home. He was supposed to be here next week. He can't be staying there. He can't! I can't take it anymore!"

Together, five of us cried, commiserated and caught pieces of the story that would now become our lives on the evening news. We shared tears, we shared rage, we shared hugs, we shared hard ciders. And at 1 a.m., we disbanded and left to confront and comfort the husbands who didn't even know where they'd be in one week.

Until They Come Home
July 28, 2006

When I received the phone call, my wall countdown read "344 days down, 10 more to go."

That's 344 days that I have slept in my bed alone at night.

Three hundred and forty-four days that I have cooked dinner for one, eaten at a table for one and felt the loneliness of one.

And 344 days that I have enthusiastically anticipated the safe return of my husband, my lover, my very best friend.

Wednesday night, in tears and in rage, I chucked that countdown to the laundry room floor and angrily scribbled over the hot pink writing that has adorned my wall for 344 days with the words

BEHIND THE BLUE-STAR BANNER

"? and counting."

I received official word late Wednesday night that my husband would no longer be returning home next week. After a year in Iraq — 12 months of 24/7 service and sleepless nights with no weekends or days off to recuperate — the Department of Defense has extended his unit overseas for "an indefinite period of time."

And my heart sank.

I feel like a hot air balloon that has been inflated and inflated and inflated to nearly bursting with happy coming-home moments — with fantasies of reunions and family dinners and afternoon walks and military balls, of moments so close within my reach that I could actually smell them. Only someone thought it would be funny to break out the needle, and now what's left of my once near-bursting balloon lies utterly deflated on the floor of disappointment and denial.

I'm heartbroken. I'm heartbroken that the man I love more than anyone else on this planet can't be with me when I need him the most. I'm heartbroken that his son may be 8 or 9 months old now before he ever gets to see him again. And I'm heartbroken that my overworked husband will have to face many more of those sleepless nights and stressful days before he ever gets to return to normal life.

I'm angry. I'm angry that our soldiers were told not months in advance that they will not be returning home to family, but rather days — and in some cases, hours — before their anticipated return to loved ones. I'm angry that there are guys at home who may have to return to war, and guys at war who no longer possess the comforts of home, since they already shipped their personal belongings to family members waiting patiently with "welcome home daddy" signs and Hawaii vacations in the books for September block leave.

And I'm scared. I'm scared for my husband, and all these soldiers, who will likely be deploying to a more dangerous area in the region. I'm scared for my son, who now won't get to know his father until he is old enough to experience stranger anxiety. And I'm scared for myself — that I won't be able to conjure up the strength to emotionally support my husband the way he is going to need it after hearing this news.

Even though my heart and my head are in pieces right now, God has somehow stepped in and let me know that He is going to help reassemble them. With supportive friends and Christ by my

DEVASTATION

side, I'll make it through. And I'll deliberately do it in a way that honors my husband.

It doesn't mean I'll wave my little car flag and sing "God Bless America" in the streets. And it doesn't mean that I'll put on my happy face and pretend that an extended deployment is A-okay with me. Extending troops longer than one year one week before they return to families who've already hung banners and told their children Daddy is coming home is not kosher in my book.

But it does mean that I will put aside my own selfish complaints long enough to encourage my husband. No matter how much it takes, I will tell him over and over again just how much I love him, and how proud his work makes me, until he can find in those words the strength he needs to press onward toward the goal.

He, after all, is the one enduring more days and weeks in a battle zone and more physical and mental trials than I can ever imagine. I'm just the one sitting behind the blue-star banner, waiting not so patiently for my "someday" to come.

CHAPTER THIRTEEN
LEMONADE

It took me 24 hours to process everything, and in those 24 hours, I found myself transferring from tears to tantrums in 5.2 seconds. I was devastated, hysterical and completely unstable.

But after 24 hours, I realized that there was nothing I could do about this extension. My husband was being called to serve, and as a military wife, that meant that I was, too. And if I'd learned anything over the last year of dealing with deployment, I learned that attitude made the difference between survival and insanity. And I had no plans of going insane four months shy of reuniting with my husband. So I cried out to Christ, begged Him for strength and, the next day, put on the full God-given armor that would keep me fighting for four months to come.

Until They Come Home
August 4, 2006

I didn't think I would need my armor this quickly.

After 12 months of deployment, I had already tucked it away in my storage closet, right next to the blue-star banner and the "Half My Heart is in Iraq" magnet that used to grace my car.

But when I received the news last Wednesday that my husband's unit would be extended in Iraq for an additional four months, I realized that the cutesy white welcome home dress and the dainty little tissue I'd stuffed in my purse just weren't going to cut it. If I was going to survive, I'd have to shift gears. And I'd have to do it fast.

One week later, I'm back in my armor and ready to go. Bring on the extension. The warrior has returned.

But not without a few fresh battle wounds.

First, I fought with the cruise line with which we had booked our September Hawaii vacation. They offered a partial refund and made me file an insurance claim to collect the rest. Only the insurance company told me that they were pretty sure they didn't cover military extensions and deployments, even though three different customer service representatives told me they did when I pur-

LEMONADE

chased the insurance in June. I told the man on the phone that that wasn't very nice of him, and then, like any mature wife, called my daddy and told on him.

Then, I had to break the news to my husband's best friend that no, Matt would now not be home in time to be the best man in his October wedding, even though CJ had already moved the date of his wedding once to accommodate my husband's deployment schedule. But that's okay. We only named our child after this man. I'm sure he'll get over it someday.

I spent the rest of Friday afternoon transforming my August calendar into a grid of scratches and scribbles as I marked off all the events I had so anticipated in August — from the military ball (and my first hair up-do appointment in years!) to the medical platoon's welcome home barbecue.

Of course, after dealing with the really big items, I then had to tackle the minor situations that had arisen from this new extension. Like the fact that I'd already given my pastor two weeks' notice at my church job and now had to figure out the best way to go groveling back. And the fact that I now was completely unprepared to tackle another Alaskan winter.

Mental note: Don't sell your car extension cords, winter coats or emergency gas cans at a garage sale the weekend before your husband is supposed to return from Iraq simply because the Army tells you you should be changing stations by October. You might just want them back when you realize that, despite any begging, pleading or bribing you might do, you are indeed going to be spending an entire third winter in freezing Fairbanks. By yourself. Without anyone to go start your car when it's 40 degrees below zero.

Check.

The little prom princess in the white welcome home dress just wasn't able to handle all these little issues and concerns. But the new warrior has definitely got it covered.

You don't marry a fighter without a soldier somewhere inside yourself. It's just that we spouses wage war on a different battlefield. We are soldiers in our homes, fighting forward as single parents and geographical bachelorettes. We are soldiers in our faith, leaning on God completely because we don't have the strength to do this alone. And we are soldiers in our marriage, carrying on, battle after battle, until we get the victory of uniting with our loved *ones once again.*

We do it with a passion, and we do it with persistence, for the spouses we love and the country we, too, serve.

We're fighters. We're survivors. We are military wives.

Until They Come Home
August 11, 2006

I have three coping mechanisms in life: taking showers, downing brownies and dressing up. After two weeks of wrinkly (but squeaky clean!) skin and several afternoon Sam's Club brownie bite runs, I moved on to coping mechanism No. 3: pretending like it's prom and playing at the Pump House.

Hey, when your husband is extended in Iraq for four more months, people pretty much give you permission to do whatever you want. And because they're worried that you're so fragile you might break if they ask even a single question, they pretty much grant consent without a word. You only get the funny looks when you draw 16 other ladies into your night of indulgence and drag them around Wal-Mart in prom dresses for an hour.

Prom at the Pump House sounded like a sane idea when the notion first popped into my head.

I was eating lunch at the Chowder House with a dear military wife friend, and Laurie and I were discussing the sad state of our now closet-bound military ball gowns.

When all of a sudden it donned on me that our ball gowns didn't need to stay banished to our bedrooms forever. We could bust them out — and we could do it this weekend!

It was one of those crazy, spur-of-the-moment ideas. You know the kind — the type where your mind believes you're brilliant while your friend thinks you're nuts as she just politely smiles and says, "Oh, sure, that would be a swell idea," but inside just keeps saying, "You've got to be kidding me. Please don't ever associate with me again, and never tell anyone else you even thought of this."

You know, one of those ideas.

So as Laurie just smiled and lovingly said, "Sure, Michelle, you do that," I proceeded to plan a Prom at the Pump House. For my entire coffee group. For the following Saturday.

I'm one of the youngest in our battalion coffee group, and I

LEMONADE

think everyone just kind of thinks of me as "that crazy Michelle girl" anyway, so I didn't have much to lose. If they thought I was weird, at least it wouldn't be a new revelation.

So, when I returned home from lunch, I e-mailed all the ladies in the group and invited them to an evening at our favorite restaurant with their military ball gowns as an entrance ticket.

I contacted the facilities coordinator at my church. She booked the nursery and toddler rooms to hold children. And then my small group and some Young Life volunteers stepped up to provide free childcare.

One friend offered to take professional-looking photographs, and another from Channel 11 offered to shoot video messages of all the ladies in their ball gowns for their husbands.

But video messages and family photographs in prom gowns just didn't seem outrageous enough. We needed something more.

So I called up the portrait studio at Wal-Mart and made a reservation for 15-20 ladies to shoot their portrait together before the big meal Saturday night.

I'm sure we looked very posh prancing around Wal-Mart in sexy dresses with sparkly purses...

But people keep telling us to make lemonade. And when you're a military spouse, you don't do anything halfway. You don't do deployment that way, you don't do life that way. And you certainly don't do optimism that way.

When you tell a military spouse to make some lemonade, expect a couple kegs full. Or at least enough to feed an entire coffee group of husbandless women in silver and stilettos on a Saturday night.

I was trying.

I was trying so hard to make the most of this extension — to look on the bright side, to make "promenade," to do whatever it took to maintain a positive outlook and bring others on that happy journey with me.

But after the prom column ran in the paper, I received some negative feedback —two letters to the editor that really stung. One complained that I was flaunting my life of leisure by prancing around Wal-Mart in a ball gown while my husband was deployed, and the other complained that I was not responding to my husband's deployment and extension with enough gravity.

BEHIND THE BLUE-STAR BANNER

I admit I'm an HSP anyway (that's a Hyper Sensitive Person). You look at me the wrong way and I may just bust out in tears. But with all the stress of the extension and deployment, I was an extreme HSP. And when I opened the paper the week after the prom column to find two not-so-happy people commenting about my prom charades, I was really upset. And hurt. I just felt like I'd been kicked when I was down, and I just couldn't get any lower than that. On top of a husband in Iraq and an extended deployment besides, now I was being criticized not just in the privacy of my home, but in a public forum where others could see. I was embarrassed. I was hurt. And the completely irrational part of me just wanted to pack up and leave town. This was not what I needed right now.

Then I took a moment and thought things through.

If I was going to be a journalist, and a columnist, besides, I had to expect feedback. I tried to analyze the situation and came to the conclusion that any feedback meant that people were at least reading my columns. And they were exercising their right to free speech — something my husband and I defend to the death — to tell me what they didn't like about them. Thank God they can do that in this country.

After some prayer and quiet time, I was able to read these letters with a much more level head. I was able to ask, "What can I learn from this, God?" and even respond to the issues one presented in a rational way.

Until They Come Home
August 18, 2006

I've never been a great gymnast. I possess no coordination, and I have even less balance. Even so, the circus called. They need some talent for their big Army show.

I am now a tightrope walker, and coping with this deployment extension is my great public balancing act.

In the left bucket of my balancing pole, I place all my grief, all my hurt. I place all the mornings I wake up and stare at my son and wish more than anything that he had a father physically in his life to hold him and to love him. This bucket holds my sad sleepless nights, this bucket holds my stressful single mom days, and this bucket holds all my deepest fears that something could happen

LEMONADE

to my husband in Baghdad that would keep him from coming home to me.

In the right bucket, I place all my optimism. I place all my laughter, I place all my crazy ideas. This bucket holds my brownies, my bonding times with best friends and every ridiculous joke I've ever told, thought of telling or wished I could tell. It holds the humor that keeps me looking on the bright side of life, even when my husband is extended in Iraq.

When I place only one bucket on my balancing pole, I find I can't walk the wire. The load is too heavy for me alone to compensate for. I just can't pull one bucket on one side and stand on something so thin and have any confidence that I'll make it to my destination.

But when I place both buckets on my pole, somehow, I begin to walk.

The grief and the pain that wrench my heart every single day in my husband's absence are suddenly balanced by the fact that I have been blessed in my life by a man I adore, and one who is still alive. And that's something to thank God for.

The truth is that when you deal with something as grave as your husband's deployment to Iraq, you absolutely have to be able to look on the bright side and find joy in the little things in life. If you don't, you waste away your days on this earth — days you could spend encouraging your husband and making him laugh when he has very little else to smile about — being miserable, and making others miserable with you.

Your outspoken misery then affects your spouse, because it takes the focus off his job, which then compromises his physical safety, because he then becomes concerned with your mental state and the way you're handling this deployment.

Maintaining that sacred balance, however, is not an easy task, especially when even the slightest wind can throw it off. Like when you find yourself in tears because your husband will never see the flowers you didn't kill this summer, or when you experience a complete meltdown because you accidentally clip your dog's toe nails too short and make him bleed and toenail clipping falls into the category of Matt responsibilities.

But like any tightrope walker, I know that the only way I can make it in a straight line is if I keep my eye on the prize — my eye on the end — and just keep moving forward. I can't look below *me, I can't look beside me, I can't cram an uneven amount of weight into either bucket, or I'll fall. I simply must carry my pole and press onward, one step at a time, until I'm safely on solid ground on the other side.*

And when I'm finally there, I'll take a deep breath, pitch my pole and tackle my husband with the biggest hug known to man. He's more than worth crossing rocky valleys and raging rivers on razor-thin rope to see. He is my best friend, my confidant, and he is my prize on the other side.

Two weeks after my balancing act commenced, Matt moved safely from FOB Courage in Mosul to FOB Taji in Baghdad. From what Army officials explained to us, the extension was events-driven, which meant that whenever the soldiers accomplished everything on their op-sec top secret list of things set forth by commanding generals and Secretary of Defense Rumsfeld, General Casey (the commander in Iraq) would send them home.

From what everyone told me, however, there was still a lot of work to be done, and we weren't really to expect the soldiers home before Christmas.

A few weeks after that, I shared lunch with the commanding general of U.S. Army Alaska (all the Army posts in Alaska) and the commanding colonel of Fort Wainwright.

I tapped my pointer finger on CJ's car carrier as we walked into the restaurant for lunch. My mind wasn't nervous, but my stomach filled with tingles. Matt had grilled me a hundred times via e-mail over what I was supposed to say and not say and do and not do in front of a commanding general, and I was just so worried that I was going to make my husband look like an idiot in front of his high-ranking officers. But the second I walked in, both men just made me feel so at home. It probably didn't hurt that the general's aide was the husband of a friend of mine, either. The three of them were almost like father figures that day, making sure I was doing okay and asking me all about my life. I'd never talked to a general before about my marriage. He was charming and his manner was truly endearing.

Of course, we also discussed business, too. There was no way I was going to get the opportunity to sit in a room with the general and colonel in charge of my husband and not ask questions about when my baby was coming home.

LEMONADE

Both of them seemed to think, based only on opinion and not on any kind of other evidence, that Army commanders would send the soldiers home before Christmas. They believed that keeping soldiers overseas for two Christmases in a row could be a media and public relations nightmare for the U.S. Army. And besides that, it was an election year, and elected officials wanted to look good to their constituents and show that they were making progress in bringing our troops home and cutting back the number of troops in Iraq. So we did have a couple positive things working in our favor.

After a wonderful lunch with some of the most sincere and caring Army officials I'd had the privilege to meet, I grabbed CJ, loaded up the car and started thanking God for election season.

With a rough timeline set in my head, I was able to move slowly forward toward the goal in a more effective and emotionally stable manner. In order to help inspire other spouses to do the same, I created one of my famous lists. Only this time, I shared it with my fellow military spouses instead of my hometown friends.

August 2006

Top 10 Positive Aspects of the Stryker Brigade Extension

1. We receive more pay. Equals we can actually pay off all those clothes and comfort items we've been buying under the table while we've been in charge of the finances.

2. We have more time to grow out or restyle our hair. So if Tina Turner called and asked for her hairstyle back last time you got your hair cut for that big homecoming, you still have time to mend the situation.

3. We have more time to get buff. And get flexible!

4. We don't have to worry about contraceptives.

5. We still get to anticipate that big run-leap-hug maneuver all of us have been dreaming about. Hey, we could all even take time now to practice in the mirror. Or with each other. We could rent fake families even. You know, just to make sure we're leaping beautifully for the welcome home camera. You only get one leap, you know. And that picture lasts a lifetime, so you don't want to look all awkward in the leap part of your maneuver. Perfection is key.

6. We still get to maintain those romanticized versions of perfect husbands who always stop to ask for directions and never leave the toilet seat up. You know, the ones who look better than Brad Pitt and are smarter than Bill Gates, even though someone once mistook them for Steve Urkel and they can't spell the word "brigade" in their e-mails home. Those ones.

7. We have more time to clean out all those closets full of husband junk that you've been dying to throw away for 40 years but just have never had the opportunity while he was out of the house. Garbage day is Thursday...

8. We can buy a brand new homecoming dress!

9. We can stop mowing the lawn and watering the flowers and trying to impress our husbands with our great yard skills so that when they come home, they can compliment us on just how great we did with that summer weed killer. They'll never know under the snow.

10. We have more time with each other... even the smelly ones you were really hoping would hurry up and PCS.

And then some friends responded and added their own positive aspects to the list:

11. We now don't have to worry about all those relatives who wanted to fly up and see our men the day our husbands came home. No one will want to visit when it's -50 degrees outside!

12. We don't have to worry about how we'll look in a bathing suit anymore. The pool's not open in January.

13. We can continue to maintain complete control of the television remote. The History Channel and ESPN can wait four more months.

14. Ice cream and chocolate chips can continue to count as dinner for the next 120 days.

And then I added some more of my own to my own personal list:

15. Generals and colonels start feeling really bad for you and take you out one-on-one to expensive lunches and even give you their general's coin (engraved with your name on it, even!).

LEMONADE

The general's aide (who is also an old coworker of Matt's and a friend of mine) told me to throw my coin down on a bar somewhere when Matt returns and make him buy me a beer. I told him I didn't drink beer, and he said, "Well, have him buy you a wine. A cocktail. A Coke, whatever. Just show him how cool you are." Apparently, generals' coins are good for free drinks anytime. Hit me on the smoothies and chocolate shakes, baby! Free for life!

16. You make lots of media contacts when something this major happens to your husband's unit. And that's a good thing, when you're a journalist.

I told all the media outlets that contacted me that I wanted them to try talking to others first, because I didn't want to become the voice of the 172nd spouses simply because I was an easy contact. But very few people to none would talk on the record. And because I feel strongly as a journalist that you have to be able to put a face to a story or the people in your story simply become numbers — and because I didn't want my husband to be "some soldier" overseas, or some guy that's being extended for a year that no one cares about — I spoke.

I know it's a little weird for a journalist to be on the other end of an interview, but I can't expect others to listen to my spiel about the importance of putting a face and a life and a name to a story if I wasn't willing to do that myself.

So in the period of two weeks, I was quoted in the Army Times, the Fairbanks Daily News-Miner, and I was interviewed on the NBC affiliate here in Fairbanks and also on CBS Radio News (which apparently aired nationally three days ago, because I received an e-mail from someone who reads my column from his home in Minnesota telling me that he heard me on the radio at home the other day).

17. You get the opportunity to meet important people.

The Secretary of the Army, one of two state senators and every government official in a 60-mile radius all showed up for the Military Appreciation Day held downtown that was originally intended to be a Military Welcome Home celebration.

Conveniently, Donald Rumsfeld is also coming to town next week, as well, supposedly to dedicate a war memorial. But I'm pretty confident that, while he's here, he'll take the time to speak to Stryker spouses.

BEHIND THE BLUE-STAR BANNER

CJ was my other positive motivator.

People always told me "kids grow so fast!" — but I always just thought that was something you said to a baby who had just outgrown the cute newborn stage and now wasn't very attractive. That, or, "He's getting so big." But suddenly everyone began saying it to me, and I began praying that they meant it literally — not in the ugly kid kind of way. Because he really was.

At his 4-month checkup (which actually fell closer to 5 months), the doctor told me he was in the 25th percentile for weight and height measurements, and that he could start eating solid foods between 4 and 6 months. We tried our first round of rice cereal around 5 months; it didn't exactly go over very well.

It's very difficult to operate a video camera and shoot that picture-perfect first-scoop moment when you are the photographer, the feeder, the scene setter and the excitement causer, all in one person. I'd always pictured Matt there operating the camera as I bent down to scoop that very first bite of rice cereal into our baby's mouth. It just wasn't the same feeding him those first bites by myself with only a camera to ooo and awww with me. And when Connor torpedo spit the nasty cereal out of his mouth and onto my face, I had no one there to laugh with. Or clean me up.

September 2006

Top 5 Things I've Learned from my Baby Boy

1. Fast is never fast enough when it comes to food. We are now experiencing solid foods, and even though the rice cereal didn't go over very well the first time, once we got the whole spoon and swallow act down, it's become a CJ favorite. Of course, he is constantly pulling my hand that holds the spoon toward his mouth, trying to make me feed him faster. Mental note: If you want to model chewing to your child, maybe you should try it yourself instead of gulping down your meal in 5.2 seconds in order to feed him his before the situation turns into meal-time meltdown.

2. Boys can indeed be drama queens. Everything is a drama with Connor. If I leave the room when he's crying to go grab a blankie or a spoon, he screams like he's dying until I return three seconds later. I find myself saying, "Oh my gosh, CJ, I'm so glad I saved your life!" at least once a day as I pick him up from his crib and he instantly turns off the show. Drama, drama, drama. Really, I have no idea where he got it from... those must be Matt's genes.

3. Pain is funny. Especially if it involves Mommy getting hurt. We were playing around on the ground today, and I was trying to be silly and make him laugh. I jumped around, danced around, sang songs, played with his feet. But it wasn't until I accidentally banged my teeth on the necklace that was swinging around my neck while I was dancing like a moron and screamed in pain (because it hit those brand-new braces) that he laughed. Maybe I should teach my son how to not be a warped sicko and think pain is funny sometime in this lifetime. But, hey, the laughter made my ouchie all better real fast, so I'll take it, even if it means I have to lose a few pints of blood in the process.

4. Despite common misconceptions, dogs make the best baby toys. Connor adores Ranger. More than he likes me and Matt, actually. As Matt and I have used the Web cam for Connor to see his daddy, Connor has been constantly distracted by little Ranger, who hears Matt's voice and runs around the area below my feet at the computer, which, then, makes Connor squeal with joy and become even more distracted and completely ignore his daddy on the other end of the computer. Oh well. I mean, it's not like Matt is in Iraq and only gets to see CJ on a Web cam or via video one out of every seven days or anything. So it's totally cool that the entire time he gets to talk to him, CJ pretty much ignores him. And me. Alas, I sense this is a preview into the teenage years where we once again utterly do not exist...

5. Always cover the spewing fountain. Always. Because when you're changing the baby's diaper in the office and you take more than those allotted three seconds to get the new diaper over the pee pee that the old diaper covered, you're going to see a fountain of urine not just on you, but all over the office carpet. And then you're going to have a blast begging the office assistant to steam clean the carpets while you find some sort of suitable clothes to change into.

By month four and a half, CJ found his feet. They quickly became the greatest toys known to man; he had to be touching them and holding them up in the air constantly.

BEHIND THE BLUE-STAR BANNER

One night, I put him down on a blanket on the floor in the family room with some toys he'd just recently taken an interest in. I was only about 20 feet away washing dishes in the kitchen, when all of a sudden I heard a piercing scream. I dropped my dishes and went sprinting into the family room to see what was wrong, and Connor had his arm caught under the back of his knee and his foot up almost behind his ear and his head and he couldn't figure out how to get it down. For two seconds, I debated running for the camera, but the bloodcurdling screams changed my mind and I fixed my son first.

It was ironic; hilarious parenting moments like those kept me laughing and kept me missing Matt, all at the same time.

Apparently, Connor picked up on that.

During what I thought were the last weeks of deployment, I dropped CJ off at the Child Development Center on post for one hour four times a week so that I could work out down the road at the gym on post and get big and buff for Daddy's homecoming. The childcare was free while Matt was deployed, and the workers in the hourly baby room were so fantastic with Connor.

One day, when I drove back to the CDC to pick him up, the lead teacher asked me if I was lonely.

"Am I lonely?" I replied, really confused.

"Yes, ma'am. As long as we're talking to Connor, he's great. He's happy. But as soon as we stop talking, he bursts into tears. We have to be talking to him constantly to keep him happy. Do you have anyone to talk to at home?"

Oops.

Until They Come Home
August 25, 2006

If there's anything positive about the fact that my husband is missing out on our son's life, it's the fact that Connor is only 4 months old.

I can't remember anything from when I was that young, and I keep praying that he won't, either. Or at least, he won't remember the part about not having a father around to hold him and play with him for the first several months of his life.

But the way this deployment and extension will affect him and his development, even years down the road, concerns me. I think about it all the time — about how not having a father in his life during that first year might cause emotional issues for him later. And about the fact that, by the time Matt comes home in three or four months, Connor will already know who Mommy is, and will have absolutely no idea what a daddy is or what he does in a person's life.

At times, that revelation is overwhelming. And sometimes, it brings me to tears.

Thankfully, I have support.

Many of my friends have children Connor's age and deal with the same issues and concerns as me. I lean on them heavily to offer advice, provide encouragement and especially lend creative ideas about how they keep Daddy in their children's lives, even at this young age.

Julia Wozniak, for example, keeps lots of pictures of her husband around the house and provides toys for her 9-month-old daughter that hold pictures of her husband inside them. That way, Alana becomes familiar with Daddy's face. And when her husband, Devin, calls, Julia holds the phone up to Alana's ear so she can learn his voice, too.

Brenda Sharp actually regularly plays a video of Daddy for her 5-month-old and 2-year-old sons. It's a DVD of her husband, Kevin, reading stories and talking to their sons. She also reads her older son the book My Daddy is a Soldier.

"I tell him his daddy is just like the little boy's daddy in the story," she said, "taking care of the bad guys and making the world a safe place to live and when he comes home, we get lots of hugs and kisses, too."

And Shelly Huhtanen and her 2-year-old son talk to Daddy on a tape recorder every night before bed. Hayden kisses the recorder and talks about everything he did that day, so that his daddy can hear his voice. Shelly catches her 5-month-old boy making noises on the tape for Daddy to hear, as well. When the tape is full, she mails it to her husband, Mark, so that he can feel like a daily part of their lives, and the kids, a part of his.

But dealing with an extension with older children — children who understand what it means that Dad not only missed the fourth grade, but will now be missing half the fifth grade, too — can be a little more difficult.

Carolyn Brewster said her children, ages 4, 6 and 8, take their cues from her, and with a positive attitude herself, are actually dealing very well.

"I have been very careful with my words and attitude regarding the extension because I believe firmly that I set the tone for how they will react," she said. "I was very upbeat about how well all the daddies did in Iraq and that there were more families in a different city (Baghdad) which really, really needed their help."

They also pray for Daddy at all meals, and make sure to include him in all the decisions they make as a family. The Brewster children have even changed their Daddy mantra to "kick butt and come home soon," taken from one of the signs posted on the fence on base.

With a video recorder in one hand and a picture of Daddy in the other, Connor and I are adopting that mantra today.

When the Stryker brigade was extended, a friend from my small group wanted to do something about it. He thought up the idea to put together an inspirational tea party for all the spouses of the brigade and bring up a motivational speaker from the Lower 48. The catch — he wanted to do it in three weeks.

Convinced he would never be able to book a speaker who could make it to Alaska with three weeks of notice, I offered to help. I told him if he got the speaker, I'd do the rest.

He called me the next day at work with the name of the speaker he'd booked and her bio. And that's how I became the organizer of a tea party and motivational speaker event for an anticipated 400 Stryker spouses that utilized more than 100 volunteers and 10 corporate sponsors and handed out more than 30 door prizes and was executed in a grand total of three weeks.

With a new baby in the house (and me unwilling to compromise my Connor playtime), my planning and plotting was limited to naptime and bedtime, which meant that I basically didn't sleep for three weeks straight.

Ellie Kay was amazing. She was an author, speaker, media personality and military wife. She'd written 10 books, hosted her own radio talk show called "Saving Tips with Ellie Kay," appeared regularly on MSNBC and toured the world speaking about her two areas of interest: finances and the military. Oprah produced an entire series based around her book *The Debt Diet.*

LEMONADE

She was exactly what the Stryker spouses (and I) needed to hear at that very moment, at that very place in time. She was a gift from God, and though I was the one who was supposed to be helping give this gift of Ellie Kay to the military community, in the end, I felt like I had been the one who had received the gift.

That night, a member of my old college newspaper contacted me. She asked if I would be willing to write a commentary for the opinion page of *The Ithacan* about dealing with this deployment and extension and living as a military wife just two years after graduation.

As I sat down with my computer — an item that had become my personal therapist as of late — I tried to keep the lessons I'd learned so powerfully that day at the front of my mind. My husband was extended in Iraq because my country said, "We need help here." That's an honorable duty. And if I wanted to support Matt in this endeavor — one he had no choice to endure or not — I needed to change my attitude and stop playing the blame game. And I needed to do it fast.

Alumna Reflects on Responsibilities as a Military Wife
The Ithacan
August 31, 2006

I was 23, nine months out of Ithaca College and 11 weeks pregnant with our first child when my husband deployed to Iraq last August 16.

This month, he was supposed to come home.

I'd already completed everything you do when your husband is returning from a yearlong deployment. I'd cleaned the house and hung the banners, serviced the vehicles and purchased the pretty dress.

I'd decorated a welcome-home onesie for our 4-month-old son, and I'd replayed over and over in my head just how that whole run-leap-hug maneuver I'd seen on all the war movies I'd ever watched would play out the second I saw my best friend enter that Fort Wainwright holding area.

But on July 26, just 10 days shy of that much-anticipated reunion, those dreams of heartfelt hugs and family dinners were crushed. Secretary of Defense Donald Rumsfeld announced that, though more than 350 of the soldiers from the 172nd Stryker Bri-

BEHIND THE BLUE-STAR BANNER

gade Combat Team were already home in Alaska in the arms of loved ones, he was extending our brigade in Iraq for up to 120 more days. An unprecedented four more months. And most of the soldiers now home would have to return to war.

My heart broke in half. All those days of preparation and anticipation, all those months I'd endured as a geographical bachelorette and a single mother, all of them were now not coming to an end. I wasn't going to see my husband. Even after a year, Matt wasn't coming home from war.

I was devastated.

For 12 months, I'd rationed my energy, my patience, my perseverance and my strength. I'd rationed my stressful single mom days and my lonely TV dinner nights, and every emotionally unbearable day in between. And after 12 months, I had no more left to give. I was depleted. Spent. And for 24 hours, I honestly didn't know how I was going to march on.

And then I took a peek at our wedding album, and I remembered how.

I remembered that I am a member of the Army, too. I may not have been commissioned, and I definitely didn't enlist, but when I recited my wedding vows, I took an oath of office far more important than any other promise I've ever made. I agreed that day not just to be some woman married to a military man, but to be a military wife. And a supportive one, at that.

Of course it's not easy. Every day is a battle. Every day I wake up and make a deliberate choice to live out this day to the best of my ability, with as much hope and optimism as possible, and use this day to serve others while my husband does the same. Every day I force myself out of bed, buck up and remember that I am sacrificing for a cause much greater than myself.

It doesn't matter that I am raising our first and only child alone. It doesn't matter that I stare at little Connor every day, wishing more than anything that his daddy could know what a joy his little boy is. And it doesn't matter that I do it all alone, without the most important man in my life there to help me, support me or comfort me when I feel like I'm doing it all wrong.

Like my husband, I have a call. I have a duty. And rather than wallow in the grief that that responsibility sometimes entails, I choose to make that sacrifice willingly, and serve to the best of my ability, so that my husband can, too.

CHAPTER FOURTEEN
BLESSINGS

Until They Come Home
September 1, 2006

I don't remember my exact first thought the day the Army told my husband and me that we were moving to Fort Wainwright, Alaska, but I'm pretty sure it was something along the lines of, "We can't move to Alaska! I don't think they believe in pink cowgirl hats there — I'll never feel at home!"

What can I say? I was born and bred an Ohio girl, and that comes with country music and cowboy hats, competitive football and corn on the cob.

Don't get me wrong — I attended school in New York and spent a semester studying in Singapore, and so I was well aware that there were indeed people in the world who didn't live for Friday night football and count down the days until the Country Music Awards. I just never thought those people and those places could make me feel at home the way my buckeyes and cornfields did for the first 18 years of my life.

Until now.

Never in my wildest dreams did I think that a place that sees temperatures of 50 degrees below zero could make me feel warm and fuzzy inside.

But this community — even in the crazy state that it is — has made me feel more welcome, loved and supported than any other community I've ever been a part of. And that includes the city I've called home for 18 years.

This community has reached out to me during the hardest days and moments of my life thus far, and offered me more than just a welcome sign and a packet of road maps. This community has offered me incredible love and support, and a continued source of strength and encouragement that just keeps calling me forward, no matter how tough those steps become during this deployment and extension.

This community put together one of the nicest military appreciation events I've ever had the privilege of attending at Pioneer

BEHIND THE BLUE-STAR BANNER

Park on August 17th. With a plate of Big Daddy's pork in one hand and a fresh Pike's dessert in the other, I had the honor of listening to several of our state's government officials, and even the Secretary of the Army, as they encouraged the Fairbanks military community to keep on keeping on.

Last Saturday, this community helped sponsor the Ellie Kay Tea Party at Friends Church. With their financial and volunteer support, the members of this community offered a wonderful opportunity for Stryker brigade spouses to be encouraged by a motivational speaker during a really discouraging time in our lives.

This community has offered free video conferences from the University of Alaska Fairbanks to Iraq, free childcare at Zion Lutheran Church, free Mom's Days Out at Door of Hope Church and a million other pick-me-ups that have blessed us all during this rough period of time. In this way, Fairbanks has reached out to all of us on a very personal level, and let us know that we can make it through this deployment. And they'll be right by our side as we do.

They tell me this with the signs and banners they hang in their office windows. They tell me this with the yellow "Support Our Troops" ribbons they stick to the bumpers of their cars. And they tell me this with the way so many of them, when they find out I'm a Stryker spouse, offer that sympathetic smile, hug or handshake, look me in the eye and let me know from the bottom of their hearts that I'm in their thoughts and prayers, and that if anyone can make it, I, as a military spouse, can.

That kind of overwhelming love and support doesn't just make Fairbanks a place I have to live for a little while. It makes it my new home.

If any month, September was the month for extra blessings. The "Tiger Team" from Washington, D.C. had arrived to make our lives as Stryker spouses more bearable. They brought with them an emergency childcare team, plans to provide free childcare every Tuesday and Thursday night, extended respite care hours and a whole slew of professionals who made our post a better place to be while we dealt with extensions.

The post arranged for free car winterization checks and free Stryker spouse events. Friends offered meals at night and warm wishes and calls throughout the day. Family sent cards and gifts and uplifting messages that blessed me at a time I could have just

BLESSINGS

jumped back into bed and said to heck with the world.

People made the extended deployment of my husband bearable.

The ability to laugh at myself didn't hurt, either.

Until They Come Home
September 8, 2006

Before my husband deployed to Iraq last August, we engaged in a long conversation about self-defense.

I was (and am) afraid of the dark, and he was afraid of the techniques I might use to ward off perpetrators. I guess Matt wasn't convinced that singing "You Are My Sunshine" over and over again would change a burglar's mind and transform him into a happy, helpful person full of sunshine and flowers who didn't want to take my money and beat me up.

Matt wanted to buy me a gun. I refused to keep one in our nightstand. Really, I had no idea how to shoot one and was pretty sure that if someone broke into my house, I would probably have to ask him how to pull the trigger in order to fire it, and I figured at that point, the whole gun scare tactic thing would be pretty useless. Besides that, I was pregnant and unable to take shooting classes, and so I found my out and happily rejected my husband's kind offer.

That's when my neighbor bought me a can of Mace to plop in my nightstand drawer instead.

And oh the fun Mace and I have had together.

It's amazing the things you think you hear at 1 a.m. when your husband is in Iraq and you live in a house all by yourself.

I had just fallen asleep one night last October when my beagle bolted from the bed and began barking boisterously — something Ranger doesn't often do in the middle of the night. And all of a sudden, I thought I heard footsteps, too. Then voices.

My heart raced, and for a moment, I fell into complete panic. And then I remembered my Mace — my precious can of Mace that had guarded my nightstand for two whole months. Yes, tonight Mace would be my saving grace.

But just as I whisked it from its place in my bedside drawer and stood back from the door, ready to spray, it hit me. I had no idea how to spray Mace! I'd never even opened the can before! If I was going to cause any kind of irritation that would even give me close to enough time to escape, I'd have to know how and where to spray the stinking bottle!

So, convinced I was brilliant and quick on my feet, I performed a little test spray. Directly into my eyes.

Of course, at that moment, my nose inflamed, my sight blurred and I began puking all over my bedroom carpet. And then Ranger did, too.

Blind, itchy and gagging, I felt my way to the bathroom attached to my bedroom, threw Ranger in the shower and then jumped in half-clothed myself — continuing to hold the stupid can of Mace in my left hand just in case my attacker was the persistent type — and rinsed furiously until we could both calmly breathe again.

If there ever was anyone in my house, he probably laughed so hard at the sight of a pregnant lady and her dog crying, screaming and choking together in the shower with a can of Mace hanging out the curtain that he took pity on us and found some other more proficient person to burgle.

Needless to say, I banished Mace from the bedroom for a bit. The midnight sun was enough protection for me all summer long anyway, and I figured that Matt would be home by the time I saw nighttime skies again.

But now with the extension, without a husband home and with darker days ahead, Mace and I are getting reacquainted.

The difference is that this fall, I have a sticker showing me which way to point the stinking can, just in case my imaginary friends go boom again in the night.

I was driving on post one day a week after the Mace column appeared in the paper. As always, I stopped at the front gate for the military police to check my ID and car tags. But the man who checked my ID this time looked concerned. He glanced at my name to confirm the curious look in his eyes, and then looked up at me.

"Ma'am," he said, quite disturbed and a little sternly, "I read your column in the newspaper last week about the pepper spray. We teach self-defense classes here on post. You need to take them."

His tone told me that he was disappointed that I would let myself get in a scary situation like that in the first place. With self-defense classes on post, I'm sure he thought there was no excuse for me to spray Mace into my eyes. He was probably right. But in the moment, I felt defensive, shook my head and told him I would do that.

When my husband comes home, I thought silently to myself.

Until They Come Home
September 22, 2006

I saw him for the first time Saturday night.

He was there. He was real. He was alive. And I could hardly contain myself.

Tears welled in the corners of my eyes and my heart fluttered as I stared at my husband through a pixilated picture on a computer screen for the first time ever and whispered to myself, "God bless technology."

Although it seems every spouse of a deployed soldier in the world (and all their second cousins' best friends' sisters) has used a Web camera to video conference with her spouse overseas, for one reason or another, we were never able to.

First there wasn't a Web cam where he worked. Then his Internet was too slow. Then I didn't have a Web camera that worked properly. Then he couldn't download the instant messenger program I used to chat.

After all our crazy attempts and with no fruit to show for it, I was feeling a little left out of the whole cyberspace phenomenon.

I mean, Web camming has actually become a verb in the military community, and being a journalist, I don't take nouns-turned-verbs lightly. Women and men actually leave Family Readiness Group meetings and nightly potlucks by the drove to go video conference with their spouses.

Now I know why.

I can't even explain what it's like to see your husband moving, breathing and laughing in real time. I hadn't seen Matt's face or even a picture of his face since he was home in person for his R and R in April, and seeing him on the other end of that video conference sent chills down my spine. I immediately turned into the giddy high school girl on a first date with the guy she always dreamed of marrying.

BEHIND THE BLUE-STAR BANNER

I made him do stupid things like show me his biggest smile, and look straight into the camera so I could see his beautiful hazel eyes. I got butterflies. And it was the perfect medicine for a stressful eight weeks.

For the last few months, I've felt so disconnected from my husband. We'd talked on the phone only three or four times in two months, and he'd e-mailed much less frequently than he could when he was back in Mosul. I found myself flipping through old photo albums and watching home videos to remind myself how he looked, how he smiled and how he joked when he was in an ornery mood.

Part of me felt like I was losing him — losing the intense and intimate connection we've consistently shared over the last five and a half years we've been together. It's hard to maintain depth and intimacy in your relationship when your communication is limited to what he can read in an e-mail in the 30 minutes he has to spend on the computer and what he can spit out in the 30 minutes he has to call once every two weeks. And it's easy to feel like you don't know each other as well as you did — that your lives have gone from completely intertwined to completely independent with only the love you have for one another to tie the two together.

But the Web camera bridged that gap and gave me a gift that no other person or object could have provided: the gift of closeness and reconnection. Seeing and hearing the words "I love you, Michelle" come out of his mouth on a computer screen were an instant fix to my detachment. It didn't matter that the image was pixilated. It didn't matter that there was a time gap between the audible words and the visual ones. It was Matt. It was his love. And it was perfect.

The Web cam was a saving grace in our marriage. It wasn't that our marriage was bad. Far from it. I fell more in love with my husband every single day, and I was continually reminded of the blessing God provided in this special man.

But it is very difficult to move forward in a marriage when the only communication you have is for 30 minutes once every two weeks on a telephone. Or an e-mail every day to hold you over. Marriage maintenance becomes your only goal, and growth is something you figure you'll work on when he returns home.

The Web cam, however, provided that opportunity for growth.

BLESSINGS

By seeing Matt's face, hearing his words and having the time to actually discuss "in person" what was going on in our lives, we were able to delve deeper into our relationship. That one device made all the difference in the world to make me feel reconnected to the most important man in my life again.

Of course, I'm not sure what exactly he thought when he saw me on the other end.

At the end of August, my friend Chris and his orthodontic staff placed braces on my teeth. Mental note: Don't join a small group led by an orthodontist, because when you complain about constant jaw popping and frequent headaches, he is going to make you go to the dentist, who is going to refer you to the orthodontist, who, in a small town in Alaska, is going to be your small group member. And then he is going to call you after work one day and ask you to come "pick up the Bible study packets" for that night and you are going to walk out of his office with x-rays and spacers and an appointment for braces the following Monday with promises that those braces will realign your teeth and fix that jaw before you get arthritis or joint problems later in life.

I was the only person over the age of 13 in the office the day my braces were installed. Except, of course, for the mothers of all the little kids getting braces. The best part is that I looked 13 again and talked with a lisp, which was great, because I already looked 13 without the dang things.

And, of course, I was just thrilled for my husband to come home from a 16-month deployment in Iraq to a metal mouth. I was afraid people were going to see us holding hands in public and file a pedophile report. But, hey, at the rate the Army was moving, I thought perhaps the dang things would be off by the time he saw me!

That was the first question I asked CSM Jeff Mellinger the day I met him, anyway.

Excuse me, sir, will my husband be home in time to see my fabulous, fashionable braces?

CSM Mellinger was General Casey's sergeant major. He was the guy with the big guns and the big calls and the one who was working with Casey to orchestrate and execute the plan in Iraq. Basically, he was one of the top highest-ranking NCOs in the entire U.S. Army. And he dropped by my house in September to chat like it was totally normal.

BEHIND THE BLUE-STAR BANNER

Of course, when he called and left a message on my machine, I was pretty skeptical. I'm just glad that when I returned his call, I didn't say, "Shut up, is this Dennis (my brother-in-law)? Dennis, I told you to stop pranking me while Matt was in Iraq. And no, my refrigerator is not running, thank you very much."

I just wish he would have left a more detailed message, like, perhaps, "Hello, Michelle. My name is CSM Mellinger. I am the most important military dude you will probably ever meet in this decade. I am constantly interviewed about the progress of the war in Iraq since, you know, I am practically in charge of the whole dang thing. Donald Rumsfeld and George Bush come to me for advice, and I could basically squash your husband like a bug if I wanted to. Oh, and by the way, my wife reads your columns in the *Fairbanks Daily News-Miner*, and I would really like to meet you. Can I come over for lunch tomorrow?"

Maybe then I could have started cleaning my house and baking the chili before the morning he stopped by my place.

I had run into his wife at a military appreciation day downtown to help encourage the spouses affected by the deployment extension in August. I was walking with Connor to my car, and she recognized me and stopped to talk. We chatted for a bit, and then she told me that her husband, too, was deployed. But she wasn't from Fort Wainwright. I then proceeded to ask her what her husband did, and then, completely casually, she responded, "Oh, he's just the Commanding Sergeant Major of Multi-National Forces Iraq." At which point I stopped, re-evaluated everything I'd said in the conversation until that point because I was simply the wife of a 1 LT, and I'd been in the Army exactly 2.5 years and knew practically nothing next to this veteran of 36 years, and just prayed that I hadn't said anything too dumb.

She then went on to explain that the Army told her she could live wherever she wanted, since her husband would be in Iraq for two to three years (equaled Michelle no longer has a license to complain). And for some strange reason, she picked Fairbanks, and therefore, began reading my column.

Our meeting was enjoyable, and the CSM was an incredible guy. I totally trusted him with my husband's life. He answered all my tough questions, was as honest as possible, gave me his sergeant major's coin (quite an honor in the military community), his e-mail address and a big smile as he went on his way. He e-mailed me a few times after that to see how I was doing and to let me know that they were going to get our soldiers home as soon as possible. And that when he knew anything he could tell me, he'd be sure to relay the information. And I felt super cool receiving his e-mails, because on the top of each one was the word "unclassified." I was a rock star.

As CSM Mellinger would occasionally e-mail me from Iraq, Matt actually wouldn't talk a lot about what was going on in Baghdad, or with his unit. He would have rather spent the short time we got to communicate talking about Connor, us or all the positive things we had to look forward to when he returned home. But I could tell in his tone and through his e-mails that he was burnt out, emotionally and physically, and just ready to come home.

We still didn't know when that might be. They were supposed to return home in December, but that was just an estimated date. It could have been earlier, it could have been later. From the talk around town, it was a real possibility that the unit may have been extended again — especially since the violence in Baghdad hadn't seemed to subside. If that happened, I just didn't know how the spouses and children back home were going to survive. There were more divorces and more broken-down spouses on Fort Wainwright than anyone should see in one lifetime. Dealing with this extension was so stressful and so difficult. If I hadn't had the strength of Christ, I honestly don't know how I would have made it through it.

Until They Come Home
September 30, 2006

The thing I love most about trials is that they change us.

Unless you are an emotionless android, you absolutely cannot endure a real trial and come out on the other side the same person you once were.

The great part is that you get to choose — choose to become bitter, choose to become bolder, choose to become stronger, choose to become better. The resulting outcome depends on you and the decision you make to respond to that crisis in your life.

With the official word Wednesday from my Family Readiness Group leader that a Fort Bliss unit will be leaving in October to replace our soldiers, and that they will in fact be home before the

BEHIND THE BLUE-STAR BANNER

120-day extension ends, I'm able now to see some light at the end of the tunnel. With that light comes a lot of reflection about how I've reacted to this tunnel, and how I've traveled this road. Who am I, now, on the far side of the tracks?

It's been a long tunnel, that's for sure. And probably the greatest trial I've ever had to endure. I've been incensed, I've been distressed, I've been bitter, I've been battered. There were days I threw my shoes at walls and nights I sobbed myself to sleep, mornings I just couldn't get out of bed and evenings that I didn't think I could physically miss my husband any more.

But I think in the end, I've learned much more than exactly how many hours I can cry without losing my voice for work the next day, and how many days I can go without hearing from my husband before I have a complete emotional breakdown.

These 13 and a half months, for example, have taught me compassion. I now not only sympathize with single moms and lonely friends — I can empathize. I understand what it's like to watch the joy in your child's eyes as he discovers the world, and not have anyone to share that moment with. I understand what it's like to come home to an empty house, day after day. And I understand what it's like to be alone. Every night. All the time.

This year has taught me the value of friendship. Not shallow, surface-level friendship. The real support. The kind that means I can call you at 1 a.m. when I think there's a burglar in my house and I just sprayed myself with Mace. The kind that means that you hear how sick I am on the other end of the phone and instead of sending a get well soon card, you drop everything, run me to the hospital and stay up with me all night long. The kind that means that you show up at my house because you have an extra hour in your day and you just want me to be able to take a nap while you watch my child for 60 minutes. The people who have supported me this year have loved me in practical ways, and taught me by example to love others.

And this year has taught me the value of true to the core, unabashed, unashamed, toughing-it-out, I-will-be-there-for-you-no-matter-what, diehard marriage love. It's tested me in the promise I made when I recited "for better or worse" two and a half years ago, and it's strengthened my marriage in ways I would have never believed. Matt and I are a stronger and healthier couple today for having endured the trial of deployment this year. And though we *may not have loved every minute apart, we've chosen to grow every minute, and that makes this moment in our marriage a success.*

When I look down the tunnel from the far end, I realize that there's not just light at the end of the tunnel, but all through it. I just have to be willing to see it, and to choose it.

CHAPTER FIFTEEN
GRATITUDE

When your husband is deployed, your 6-month-old baby is sick and your 24-year-old body is sick and tired of enduring deployment with a 6-month-old baby in the frozen tundra of Fairbanks, Alaska, it's hard to remember to choose to see light throughout the tunnel *all the time.*

October brought the season's first snowfall and the romantic days of early Alaskan winter where cute couples dressed in their matching scarves and hats and set out on their snow machines for intimate dates in log cabins with hot chocolate by the fire.

Meanwhile, I was dressing a baby in a snowsuit the size of Egypt (first-time mother syndrome — paranoia takes over your life) while slipping on the ice of my driveway and trying to manage shoveling dates between nursing sessions, a 30-hour work week and maintaining my sanity.

In the midst of it all, it was at times difficult to remain positive. All I wanted was my husband there to enjoy this beautiful new life we created together. My expectations weren't high — you know, just long nights of intimate conversations by fireplaces we didn't own while the snow fell gently at our window and we stared passionately into each other's eyes while our beautiful baby boy slept in our arms.

"I need to keep positive," I told myself, time and time again. "See the light, choose joy!"

Many times, I turned to my *Chicken Soup for the Soul for Military Wives* book for some inspiration and encouragement, but most often, I turned to my Bible.

Before I became a Christian, I viewed the Bible as a fairytale book. The world was bad, Prince Jesus was good, he came along and saved the world and everyone lived happily ever after in heaven. I didn't think, at the time, there was much more to the story, and I certainly didn't think that anything else in that book could have directed my path 10 years later as a military wife.

When I made the decision to accept Jesus Christ as my personal Savior and live a life that I hoped would be pleasing to Him, I opened that Bible again. All the "good Christians" I knew read

GRATITUDE

their Bibles, and I figured if I wanted to look as cool and holy as them that I should probably pretend to start reading mine, too. I even started highlighting verses and underlining words in my Bible, because then when I went to Sunday school and we looked up Bible verses in class, everyone saw my highlighted verses and thought I was a good little holy Bible reader.

I believe that was actually my official title — "good little holy Bible reader."

It wasn't until later in life that I actually *really* started reading the Bible. It was there that I discovered the magic of those powerful, powerful words.

Every time I opened up that book, something inside me just felt fulfilled. No matter the stresses I'd endured or the mishaps I'd experienced, those words just seemed to melt those away and provide me with a peace and a guidance that I'd never experienced in my life before I started reading.

All of a sudden, I discovered advice — real life advice — that applied to me, more than 2,000 years later. God spoke to me through those words, and I felt my life coming under the control of something much greater than myself.

I needed those words during deployment more than at any other time in my life. I needed the reassurance that I could make it through this hard and costly adventure — that I could be strong, that I could be supportive, that I could come out on the other side a more mature, caring and loving person. I wanted to know how God wanted me to view the situation, because my life experience told me that when I adopted God's point of view, my life just ran more smoothly, and my trials just didn't seem so bad.

As I flipped through my Bible, literally looking up in my index "ways to stay positive" (my concordance didn't have "ways to not kill yourself and fall into a deep depression when you experience a deployment extension in Fairbanks, Alaska, and you miss your husband more than anything in the world and it's kind of depressing to raise a beautiful baby boy by yourself"), I came across verses that spoke to me, but not in a "stay positive, go, team, go!" kind of way. Instead, those verses revealed to me my fatal error:

"Rejoice evermore. Pray without ceasing. In everything give thanks, for this is the will of God." (1 Thessalonians 5:16-18)

Give thanks. In everything. Even deployment extensions.

It didn't say "stay positive" — staying positive is a set of decisions to not think things are all that bad — it said to "give thanks," which meant not just to endure the trial while not hating it, but to give thanks for the trial in the process.

What a counter-cultural approach.

In this case, gratitude meant not just offering a lighthearted "thank you" when I got something I wanted, or nodding in appreciation when served by another person. It meant more than sending thank you notes after a great party and more than recognizing people for the awesome work they performed in my and many other people's lives.

The choice of gratitude meant a different lifestyle.

Gratitude was an attitude. It was the way I decided to wake up every morning and face the day's stresses and temptations and thank God that He trusted me enough to face those temptations and stressors and come out on the other side kicking, well and alive. It was facing hard times with joy, knowing that, through these difficult times, I had an opportunity to further develop my character — that I could grow closer to the character of Christ by enduring trials that molded me, built me and refined me.

In practical application, that meant that I gave thanks when it was the hardest. That meant that I found ways to be thankful that my husband was gone and thankful that I had some obstacles to overcome.

Largely, I found ways to be thankful through humor and by appreciating the people God had placed in my life to help confront those difficult issues.

Everywhere I went, I was blessed by amazing people, amazing coworkers and amazing friends who just uplifted me and encouraged me in ways that few people do in this lifetime. The community was amazing, the Army was great and I just couldn't get over the ways all of them were reaching out to someone as insignificant as me.

Their choices made my choice to be grateful incredibly easy.

Until They Come Home
October 6, 2006

When the Stryker brigade first deployed to Iraq, I experienced an outpouring of support.
There was my family, who called about every five minutes

GRATITUDE

from places like Ann Arbor, Michigan; Dayton, Ohio; and Bozeman, Montana, just to make sure I hadn't overloaded on brownies and showers and buried myself in my featherbed for the next 365 (or so they thought at the time) days.

There were my hometown friends, who sent about 5.2 million cards and letters the first two weeks my husband was gone.

And there were my Fairbanks friends, who made more leftovers and lasagna and dinners and desserts than I could ever imagine eating all by myself, even if I was pregnant for the first eight months of deployment.

But these days, my encouragers come in slightly different packages — the kind that hold 50, 60 and 70-year-old men in matching hats with special pins who hang out at American Legion posts on weekend nights.

Oh, how I love my veterans.

This year, they have become some of my very best cheerleaders.

There's something very special that happens when a person in the world of the current deployed soldier interacts with a person in the world of the former deployed soldier. No matter the age, no matter the gender, no matter the war, no matter the experience, there's an instant connection there, and one I've really come to treasure as I've chatted with the wonderful veterans who have formed a special place in my heart this year.

Billy Smith of American Legion Post 11 is one of them. And this month, he made that special place even warmer.

Earlier in the month, Mr. Smith visited me at my work place. He wanted to know what I thought he and his fellow veterans and Women's Auxiliary Team at Post 11 could do to help encourage military spouses, especially the ones dealing with the deployment extension. When he mentioned a ladies' day out, I was absolutely all about it.

Two weeks later, he walked back into my office with a poster advertising a military spouse's day out that included Mary Kay, facials, pedicures, glamour, hors d'oeuvres, live jazz, phone card giveaways, free daycare at Zion Lutheran Church and even free limo rides from Top of the World limo.

That's what I love about veterans — they just don't fool around.

So Saturday, I and any other interested spouses will have the *opportunity to be pampered by wonderful men and women who have already been there and done that. For four hours, we will be able to sit down, relax, and for 240 minutes, put aside the fact that our spouses are serving in a dangerous war where people die every single day.*

That isn't a gift we receive lightly.

And coming from such brave souls who all of us in the active military community admire so much, it's a humbling thing.

It is humbling to be served by those who served before you.

It is humbling to be treated by those who have opened the doors for such blessings in your life.

And it is humbling to be honored and sacrificed for by people who have already honored and sacrificed for you on many occasions before.

But it's something you allow, and something you enjoy, because you know that someday — when your spouse is home and warm in your arms — you, too, will be called to give back.

I only hope my husband and I can return in support, graciousness, pampering and love the kind of blessings we have received from people like the veterans at Post 11 this year.

Until They Come Home
October 20, 2006

As an unofficial member of the U.S. Army, I'm used to standing in lines.

Hurry up and wait is just one of those realities in the military — and one I usually confront with a tap in my toe and frustration on my face.

But Wednesday night was a totally different story.

For the first time in my life as a military spouse, I stood in a line on a military post excited, smiling and completely content to wait on my feet for an hour and 15 minutes while the line crept slowly forward to the front of Murray Hall. I would even call the experience pleasant, if line standing can be classified as such.

Hey, I'll sing a song backwards while standing on my head and writing love notes to the Army if it means that at the end of that line are tickets for my son and myself to fly to Anchorage for a weekend. For free.

For all the complaining I occasionally do about the military

GRATITUDE

("the Army stole my husband," "I hate deployment" and "Matt brought a third party into our marriage and I'm telling!" have all been household phrases in my home at one time or another), the commanders, rear detachment and post organizations at Fort Wainwright sure have reached out to Stryker families this year — and not just in a "we'll do the least we can and scrape by at bare minimum" kind of way.

They've applied for grants that have given each family eight hours of free respite childcare each week, plus five hours of free care every Tuesday and Thursday night. They've set up a Family Assistance Center with staffed personnel nearly any time of day, and brought in teams of counselors (Family Life Consultants) to consult with anyone at any time.

They've set up free bowling nights for Stryker families, set up free humor and motivation-inspiring events for spouses. They've even turned the Last Frontier Club into a family-friendly place where burnt out single parents can bring their kids to play laser tag and crawl through play land tubes when they just can't take another round of "who can beat Mommy the hardest with his He-Man, just-like-Daddy's sword" anymore.

Some people tell me that that's the least the Army can do for keeping our spouses overseas for an additional four months, or for deploying them overseas at all. But my husband signed up to serve, and he considers his job an honor, and that means that everything the Army does for us beyond providing a paycheck, some healthcare and a form of communication is just icing on the cake.

The Army does not owe it to me to provide free childcare nearly any day of the week. They do not owe it to me to send their rear detachment team out to hang up my Christmas lights because my husband isn't here to do it for me. And they certainly do not owe it to me to arrange an incredible all-expenses-paid trip to Anchorage for a weekend of shopping and fun with a plane ride down and a train ride back to cheer me up in the middle of an extension.

But the team at Fort Wainwright does it anyway. Because they want to. Because they choose to. Because that's a gift they can give us during a stressful time for our families. It's just that, in the middle of that heartbreak and chaos, I haven't always been able to view it as one.

I'm done "surviving" the Army. Today, I am going to start appreciating not only the roof the Army puts over my head, but

BEHIND THE BLUE-STAR BANNER

the hard work and sacrifices the Army's home-front personnel make every single day so that I can live a more comfortable life while my husband serves overseas. And I'll do it one joyful line standing at a time.

Until They Come Home
October 27, 2006

I've always made a deliberate choice in my life to surround myself by people who remind me to look and reach outward.

Now, in the middle of a 15-month deployment and extension and when the whole world is telling me it's all about me, I've found those connections even more important, and those examples, even more vital.

In the midst of my sad deployment soirees, these role models grant me the courage to close the pity party, and the confidence to cater to the community. And they remind me that loving others, especially when I feel I need love the most, is one of life's greatest callings.

Of those role models, there are few that have lived out that kind of example for me this year in ways as clearly or as humbly as fellow military spouse Christina Grice.

Christina started out as my key caller for my Fort Wainwright Family Readiness Group, but she quickly became a friend.

The first time she stopped by my house for dinner, she shared with me her ambitions of becoming a foster parent, and possibly adopting children in the future.

Immediately, I was blown away. Here was a woman whose husband was deployed to Iraq, who was left alone for a year at a time, and who, nonetheless, was choosing to pursue a certification to become an official foster parent so that she could serve someone else in a meaningful way, despite her own hardships.

She and her husband didn't care that he might return home to a strange child in the house. They didn't care that they could be placed with a child who might need extra grace and attention. They didn't care that there would probably be many stressors involved, and in the end, they might not even be able to call the child legally theirs. They wanted to become foster parents, because they wanted to make a difference.

I was completely inspired.

GRATITUDE

For nearly a year, Christina waited for a foster child. But she didn't just wait. In the meantime, she became a Big Sister with Big Brothers Big Sisters, took and continues to take Hospice training to become a certified Hospice volunteer and actively worked with the local CASA program to become a court-appointed advocate for children, all while her husband served in Iraq.

Finally this month, after nearly a year, she received her first foster child — a baby born eight weeks early with exposure to alcohol and cocaine. With only two days' notice, Christina embraced the opportunity to welcome the tiny infant into her home, and a newborn baby into her life.

Like any mother, she's been up with the baby in the middle of the night, woken up for those every two- and three-hour feedings. She's scoured Value Village and Salvation Army for preemie clothes, she's searched Wal-Mart and Fred Meyer's for the best bottle nipples around town. And she's done it all alone, with only two days to prepare for the kind of responsibility raising a child — and raising one as a temporary single parent — entails.

Her efforts are already paying off.

The baby responds to Christina's cuddles and care, and her diligent feeding and nurturing have caused half a pound of weight gain in an infant who weighed less than a gallon of milk when she entered Christina's home.

Not knowing if she and her husband will have the opportunity to adopt this child, Christina is emotionally cautious with her new foster daughter, but nevertheless, dedicated to loving and providing for this child as if it were always hers.

"If I have her for two months or two weeks or two more days, all I can do is give her the best start that I can," she's told me more than once.

She reminds the rest of us that, despite our own adversity, we, too, have an opportunity to make a difference in the world, one heart and one pound at a time.

As I submitted my third column on gratitude in a row, I looked to the stars and closed my eyes.

"Thank you, God, for people like this in my life."

CHAPTER SIXTEEN
PATRIOTISM

Until They Come Home
November 3, 2006

Between the sugar high of Halloween and the turkey gobbling of Thanksgiving, Americans often forget about Veteran's Day.

It quickly becomes this holiday smashed into the "holiday season," but one that, because it is a part of that October-November-December holiday rush, often times gets neglected.

"I don't have time to celebrate Veteran's Day," "I don't really understand Veteran's Day" and "I really just don't feel like celebrating one more holiday right now" are some of the excuses I've heard for not taking time out on November 11 to honor the veterans of this country who have served overseas and on the home front to ensure the safety and security of our country.

And as people tell me that they "just don't feel like" celebrating another holiday that they don't really understand that celebrates people that they sometimes can't make much sense of, I can't help but wonder the kinds of qualities they value if selfless sacrifice and duty to country don't make their Top 10 list of important traits to honor and respect.

I'm sure the veterans we celebrate on that special day "felt like" serving every day they fought wars overseas. I'm sure their missions made sense to them 100 percent of the time, every single day. I'm sure they woke up every morning and said to themselves, "What a great day to put my life on the line. I really feel like getting up today and making a huge sacrifice for my country. Can I please stay in this tent one week longer with no sleep and only a couple Meals Ready to Eat to keep me going? Oh, and could you please shoot at me in the process? That would really make my day, and make a lot of sense, too."

Thanking and honoring veterans needs to be something we do even when we don't feel like it. Even when we don't quite understand them. Even when we don't understand their mission, or why they love their country so much.

Veterans serve when they feel like it and when they don't.

PATRIOTISM

They serve when they understand the mission and they serve when they just don't get it. Every day, they lay down their Isaacs — all the things they don't want to sacrifice the most, including their families, their comforts and their life's safety — because they want to follow some mission handed down to them from on high to serve country, and serve it well. Whether that call is from the president, the military or from God himself, they follow that voice and they serve, because they believe so much in what they do and what they have.

The least we can do for these selfless servants is take one day out of the year to honor them and their faithfulness to serving our country.

Here are some practical ways to honor these heroes this Veteran's Day:

- *Write a veteran a thank you note. Or send a letter to an entire VFW or American Legion post.*
- *Write a letter to a soldier currently serving in Iraq or Afghanistan.*
- *Talk to your children about who veterans are, what they do and what their service means to our country.*
- *Attend local programs put on by VFW and American Legion posts.*

Don't let the "I don't understand" and "I don't feel like it" excuses get in the way of honoring the people who have served and sacrificed when they didn't understand and they didn't feel like it. That kind of service is too important to ignore.

In so many ways, and through so many November events — Veteran's Day, the elections — the values my husband treasured so much that he put his life on the line every day for them — patriotism and freedom — just finally clicked for me. And not in the shallow, go-tell-people-to-wave-their-flags-in-the-streets kind of way, or the way it had in so many instances throughout my columns over the last year. This time, it was different. This time, it was genuine.

As an Army wife, people just assume service and patriotism are traits you understand, and that you understand immediately.

They expect that the moment you slide on that wedding ring

from the soldier across the way, you know what service means, you know what sacrifice means and you know what love of country means.

But that's not always the way it works.

Though I have always admired and appreciated my husband's deep commitment to service and country, I've never quite felt it in my heart the way that he has. I've never loved the United States so much that I would be willing to serve under its flag and surrender my life for a cause it deemed worthy. I've never cried at the Pledge of Allegiance, or choked up during the National Anthem. Maybe I'm not that patriotic, or maybe I'm just not that brave.

Watching your husband serve a country and a people he doesn't know while you wait for him on the home front changes a lot of things. Attending the funerals of people he works with, sharing tears with the loved ones they'll miss, voting in elections because of the type of men that they are — all of them ingrain this much deeper sense of gratitude for country in your heart than the kind they sell in red, white and blue packages at Wal-Mart in July.

For the first time in my life, I began to catch a glimpse of the kind of passion my husband has experienced his whole life for this United States of America. One month shy of his much-anticipated return, I finally began to get it — and catch it with a fire.

Until They Come Home
November 10, 2006

I still remember the first time I saw his eyes.

Dark, deep, but full of pride, staring straight at my husband in his Stryker vehicle as if he were a soldier himself, lifting his pointer finger in the middle of the Mosul streets and proudly displaying the black ink on the pad of that finger.

For the first time, that Iraqi man voted. You could read the freedom all over his face.

I don't often take time to look at that picture my husband sent me of the Iraqi referendum he was a part of last October 15. But I don't have to look to remember. The image is burned in my brain, I hope, forever.

It's the image I recall when people tell me that my husband has done not one bit of good there in that country of Iraq.

It's the image I recall when people tell me that the time he's sacrificing with his family and his newborn son are meaningless, and that the lives he's touching are lives that could care less about the sacrifices he's making to be there.

And it's the image I recall when people tell me that they forgot to vote, didn't take time to vote, or didn't make it a priority to vote here in this country on election day.

If only they realized how precious that privilege really was.

Not that I haven't ever been there. I've been of voting age for six years, and shamefully, have only voted in three elections that I can remember.

Somewhere in between my first presidential election at age 18 and last Tuesday afternoon, I got lost in the excuses.

Oh, I'm living in New York right now to attend college, I'd tell myself. And so is it really fair for me to send in an Ohio absentee ballot when I won't even be living there to experience the effects of my vote? (Of course, I did submit my Ohio absentee vote for the 2004 presidential election — and was pretty darn tickled when it seemed that absentee voting in the state of Ohio actually mattered that year.)

But ever since my husband served in Iraq to provide a safe election environment for an entire country of people who had no idea what democracy, voting or choice were all about, I've taken my right to vote a lot more seriously.

Voting is this incredibly special opportunity we have in this country, and when we fail to take advantage of it, we spit in the face of all those who fought and died to ensure the kind of freedom and choice we enjoy here in the United States.

When we fail to vote, we take for granted the sacrifices of so many who paid with their blood for us to wake up on election day and cast a vote, not because our religious organization made us do so, not because our cultural organization made us do so, but because our country allows us to make decisions about its future.

That kind of freedom is the kind of freedom I catch glimpses of in the eyes of the man in my husband's picture — the kind of freedom that I imagine he waited in many long lines to experience that first election day. The kind of freedom I'm sure he appreciated all however many hours he stood in line to ink his finger. The kind of freedom I'm sure he'll enjoy and be grateful for many elections and referendums to come.

As I stood in line to vote for my own officials on Tuesday af-

BEHIND THE BLUE-STAR BANNER

ternoon, it was that kind of freedom that I remembered, I cherished and I treasured. And as I proudly placed my "I Voted Today" sticker on the chest of my black pea coat, I thanked God that people like my husband make that feeling possible every day.

Until They Come Home
November 18, 2006

I used to think that patriotism was a show.

Patriotism was something you wore on July 4. It was the way you decorated your house, or the way you talked about your country. At least those were the ways I always expressed my own patriotism — through the material, and through the obvious.

Enduring a deployment on the home front this year, with a husband serving under the American flag because of his own personal commitment to country, my ideas of patriotism, and of expressing that patriotism have changed just a bit — a fact that became obvious to me Wednesday afternoon.

That's when I attended a Veteran's Day play put on by Bob Marok's Weller Elementary class at the downtown VFW, and found my eyes glassy and my cheeks damp after events like the signing of the Pledge of Allegiance and the singing of the National Anthem.

Never before in my life have I cried while staring at the grand 'ole flag. But something about watching a room full of children proudly displaying their flags — the same flags sewn to the arm of my husband's uniform — marching around the room and singing their hearts out for a country they were so proud of just moved me.

Children are so amazing. They fly American flags fervently, and sing our nation's anthem with enthusiasm and joy. They don't debate the politics of flying a flag and ask a million questions about what that flag flying suggests, and whether that implies that you're blindly following your country's leadership or ignorantly throwing your support behind one party or another. They're passionate, they're nonpartisan, and they're just proud to be Americans. Watching them Wednesday afternoon, I've realized that they are some of the most patriotic people I know.

They, like I've seen only soldiers and veterans do in my lifetime, love their country, and don't hesitate to shout it in the streets. They reflect the kind of love for country that my husband

PATRIOTISM

has always displayed for me in the six years we've been together — but something that, until this Veteran's Day, I didn't quite understand.

I didn't understand the way Matt always removed his hat for the singing of the National Anthem, or the way he stood at attention anytime a flag passed by. I didn't understand the look in his eyes when Lee Greenwood sang "God Bless the U.S.A.," and I didn't understand the tone in his voice when he talked about this nation, and his love for serving it.

The children I saw singing so proudly on Wednesday afternoon are the closest thing I've seen to it. They, along with soldiers and veterans, have taught me that patriotism isn't an act. It isn't a song, it isn't a dance. It's not the colors of your clothing, or the way you pretend to be all about America when you run for office or become a public figure. It's not the flag pin you place on your coat, or the way you tell others over and over again that you are indeed patriotic.

Patriotism is a lifestyle. It is a lifestyle that includes constant gratitude to the people and events that have earned us the freedoms we enjoy today. It's a life of appreciation for the melding and the molding of a country that, granted, is far from perfect, but sure offers a lot of opportunities for people to try to get it close. And it's a constant recognition that we are blessed to be Americans. It's enthusiasm, it's passion, and it's a love of country that goes far beyond the surface level.

And it's thankfulness.

After a 16-month deployment to Iraq, that thankfulness for our great country is something I experience every day as I intentionally remember that we are the land of the free, because of the brave.

Until They Come Home
November 25, 2006

As I drove onto Fort Wainwright Monday afternoon, I couldn't help but notice all the welcome home signs that once again adorned the fences down Gaffney Road.

There were the signs that had been taken down at the word of the extension back in August and the signs that had been newly created now in November. There were the signs that had hung on

BEHIND THE BLUE-STAR BANNER

those fences for nearly four months, and the signs that even groups like the Daughters of the Revolution now hung to welcome home soldiers extended in Iraq.

I love those signs. They energize me, and they make me feel like my husband is really coming home this time. They take away that cautious excitement I hold in my heart and replace it with utter and outgoing wild anticipation of my husband's return from Iraq in just 10 short days.

As I maneuvered down and around the back side of post singing, "My husband's coming home! My husband's coming home! My husband's coming home, hey, hey, hey, hey!" and finally parked in the Northern Lights Chapel parking lot, those signs were the visions dancing in my head.

Until I walked through the front doors.

There in the chapel were soldiers — many of them — dressed in uniform, and silent and staunch, handing out programs and offering that somber greeting that I've become familiar with at so many of these events. There was an air of seriousness, and an ambience that told me, "Now is not the time to sing."

That's when I realized in a cruel paradox that these soldiers, more than anyone else, know that there will be no "welcome home" sign hanging on that fence for Kraig Foyteck.

SGT Foyteck died on October 30 while performing clearing operations in Iraq. He was only 26.

Though I've attended memorial services for fallen soldiers in my husband's unit before, this one hit me in a way that few others have.

This man was two short weeks away from returning home to his mother in Illinois and his friends at Fort Wainwright. After nearly 15 months, he was on the very doorstep of a return flight home. And not after an easy deployment, either.

Before the Army extended his unit and moved them to Baghdad, SGT Foyteck had earned a Purple Heart award for breaking four bones in his back. Though he could have taken time off for healing and returned to the States, he decided to stay in Iraq and be with his men — even for four months more. Four months that eventually cost him his life.

As I sat in that chapel pew and listened to story after story about how SGT Foyteck loved water, loved diving and loved his mother, I couldn't help but shed a tear for a man who, ironically,

PATRIOTISM

should have been home.

He is one of the men I will always consider a true hero, and one of the men I will always thank in prayer for selfless sacrifice to country.

There may not be a welcome home sign on the fence for Kraig Foyteck, but I know he'll be remembered by many in our community, anyway. Because that is our duty. That is our responsibility. That is our privilege.

As the soldiers of the 172nd Stryker brigade begin returning home this week, please, take the time to love on them and honor them. Hang signs for them and jump on and attack them.

Just make sure that as soon as you do, you then make it a point to honor and love on the families who will never hang that welcome home sign on the fence, and those friends who will never experience that welcome home hug.

Call them. Hold them. Cook for them. Love on them. And if you think about it, hang a sign for them: We will never forget.

I will never forget.

CHAPTER SEVENTEEN
REUNION

Until They Come Home
December 1, 2006

With four days left until my husband returns from Iraq, I'm a little on edge, to say the least.

People keep asking, "You mean you only have four more days until Matt comes home?" and everything in me just wants to bark back, "You mean I have four whole more days until Matt comes home?"

Days feel like mini-eternities when you're anticipating something as big, important and thrilling as your very best friend's return from a 16-month deployment to Iraq. And after 483 days of single motherhood and stress, apprehension and anxiety, four more days really does make a difference.

Especially when you see happily reunited military couples everywhere you go. Practically every other spouse I know has her soldier home, and not-so-secretly, I'm a little sad mine isn't here, too. But that's the reality. Not every soldier can fit on the first flight home. But, hey, at least Matt's coming home, and that's something I can thank God for.

Looking on the bright side, that extra time does give me four more days than my other Task Force 2-1 friends to prepare for the big welcome home event — preparations, that I've come to realize, are basically going to overtake my life for the next four days anyway.

My to-do list is actually now three pages typed and single-spaced and includes such major responsibilities as shaving my legs — a job that, at this point, is going to take a weed whacker to complete — and stocking Matt's favorite dill pickles in the pantry. (Task No. 1: Stop being so anal retentive before my husband comes home and checks himself into the loony bin on account of an obsessive compulsive list maker of a wife who assigns herself 500 tasks to complete before the return of her husband. Check.)

Though relearning how to cook, grocery shopping for two, hiding all the items I've purchased during retail therapy sessions and deep cleaning the blinds and the guest bathroom toilets I haven't touched in a year are pretty daunting tasks, maybe the most intimidating chore on my list is to complete the famous welcome home signs.

It's no secret I'm no Martha Stewart, and the ladies who've busted out their cute and crafty signs in 5.2 seconds have just hit that fact home for me even more clearly. I mean, it took me two weeks of sign staring just to figure out what the heck they were using to make their signs, not to mention understand how they painted them.

When I went to Wal-Mart Sunday to buy my materials, the employee behind the counter in the outdoors section had to actually gently remind me that outdoor tarps were meant to repel liquids, not hold them, and that using 99 cent acrylic paint would probably not leave a permanent mark on a water-deterring piece of plastic. But hey, I was welcome to try if I wanted to.

So I settled on some cheap fabric in the art department and, six hours later, completed my sign. Of course, that took forever, too, because I felt this huge pressure to write something creative since I am, indeed, a writer. My friend in advertising suggested a sign over our garage door that read, "This driveway isn't going to plow itself. Welcome home, Lt. Cuthrell." But I figured I should at least make Matt feel welcome before I pointed out the driveway that's now caked in ice. So I settled for something a little more welcoming:

"Tan, $30. Hair, $41. Dress, $52. Run-leap-hug, priceless. We love Lt. Cuthrell."

With four days to go, though, that sign is now only half-true, since the dress I originally bought for the big run-leap-hug maneuver is now looking a little chilly and the whole run-leap-hug thing is probably going to look more like a run-slow-down-be-careful-not-to-suffocate-the-baby-in-the-process maneuver than a leap.

But the last line of the sign is still and will always be true. And in four more days, Connor and I can both show our hero just how much.

The week before Matt returned home, I was a harried mess. Besides the welcome home sign and the house cleaning and the personal preparations and the emotional ones, I just felt this innate need to stay busy. Time was passing so slowly, and it seemed everyone in the world had her husband in her arms but me.

BEHIND THE BLUE-STAR BANNER

On two occasions the week before, I volunteered to take pictures of the reunions of friends in our battalion who were arriving home sooner than Matt. I followed them to the Alert Holding Area where the soldiers returned on buses and watched them as they pranced to their husbands and kissed lovingly in their picture-perfect outfits, as I snapped photos with tears glistening in my eyes.

I could hardly wait for those moments to be mine.

The night before Matt's long-awaited arrival, I didn't sleep a wink. I climbed into bed early, hoping to fend off those black-eye-circle blues, but I just couldn't fall asleep. I lay in bed in my pink and blue plaid pajamas, tossing and turning and telling myself that this was the last night I had to sleep alone. Actually, I was really more preoccupied with the thought that this was the last night I would have to wear pajamas to stay warm at night. Well, at least for a month.

I envisioned every possible scenario for our reunion — how it would look if it was sweet and sentimental, how it would feel if it was tear-filled and hysterical, how it would play out if it was jovial and jolly. Would I scream when I saw Matt, or would I become speechless? Would Matt cry when he saw me, or would he smile? Would he become emotional the first time he held CJ, or would he just breathe in the moment and store it for life? I was so impatient, and I just wanted to know. I just wanted to experience it. As I finally faded off around 3 a.m., visions of Army uniforms danced in my head.

But only for a few hours.

I was up bright and early around 6 a.m. the next day. Though my beau wasn't returning until nearly 6 p.m., I had a million tasks on my to-do list I absolutely had to complete before the big moment. I had to work out and shower, bathe CJ and dress him. I had to bake the last-minute goodies to make the house smell homey, and set out the last-minute candles to make me look like a good housewife. I had to complete final sweeps, dusts, trashcan empties and polishes, and most importantly, I had to get myself ready.

You'd think if you hadn't seen your husband in 16 months, you might go meet him in a trash bag, or a sweat suit, or something you couldn't get away with at any other point in your life. I mean, it's not like he would really notice. He wouldn't have seen a woman out of uniform in more than a year, and so besides the fact

REUNION

that you're his wife, you're basically raw meat.

But that's not the way it works in reality.

You spend so much time anticipating that big reunion and the pictures that will spring from that reunion that getting ready the day of becomes something comparable to prom preparations.

I took exactly 90 minutes to style hair that normally takes me 20. I spent 20 minutes shaving legs I'd shaved the night before, and nearly half an hour perfectly applying makeup I'd worn for weeks in three-minute applications. I tried on about 50 different outfits, even though I'd already purchased an outfit for the occasion, and finally called my friend Leah to come help me decide which one to wear.

"Leah," I told her as I ambled nervously down the stairs in my house and into the family room, "I'm just not sure about this one."

Standing up from the place where her 2-year-old girl sat playing on my family room floor, she spun to face me and covered her mouth.

"You have to wear that one! You have to! Sexy mama!" she cried. I stared down at the knee-length black and red dress that clung to my body. It was a throwback to the 70s, and with my black knee-high leather boots, it just screamed, "I'm ready for a husband at home."

I liked the combination for the reaction I knew it would spark in my husband, but hesitated to wear it to the AHA because of the clothing I'd seen on other women during my two visits to other redeployment ceremonies. Alaska is a casual place, and most women at the other ceremonies were wearing jeans and cute sweaters, or a jean skirt at most. Except for the four girls wearing coordinating trench coats, hooker boots and I'm guessing, not much else underneath, non-pant outfits weren't really in style for the big coming-home day. With Leah's forceful recommendation and a big hug and smile, I decided to do it anyway.

Two hours later, CJ and I trotted in my high-heeled boots through the two feet of snow piled up outside the Alert Holding Area and made our way to the front row of the AHA, where a friend of Matt's had saved us a seat. Children cloaked in red, white and blue and waving flags and yellow ribbons scurried about the garage-like building while nervous moms and spouses stood on the sidelines, rechecking lipstick and prepping digital cameras.

BEHIND THE BLUE-STAR BANNER

There we waited, shifting from side to side on cold metal chairs for more than an hour for the moment our hero would arrive.

Until They Come Home
December 8, 2006

After spending 24 hours a day for seven days a week for four weeks a month for 16 months of deployment learning how to wait, you'd think small increments of time like an hour and a half would just fly by. But standing in that Alert Holding Area on Fort Wainwright Tuesday night, 90 minutes felt like an eternity.

I guess patience isn't exactly in large supply when you are anticipating the imminent return of your husband from Iraq.

Standing amidst the other moms and dads and spouses and children who were also impatiently awaiting the arrival of loved ones, I found myself fidgety. I picked up Connor and then put him back down every five minutes, and I must have readjusted the belt and buttons on my black and red welcome home dress at least 50 times.

Every moment felt like another extension, and every minute felt like another deployment. I talked a million miles a minute, and I must have asked my friend at least 20 times if the soldiers had left Eielson Air Force Base yet to head to Fort Wainwright.

I detested the anticipation. I had so many emotions built up inside from 16 months of missing my husband like crazy, and was experiencing this physical longing stronger than anything else I'd ever known to just touch him, hug him and hold him.

Which is maybe why, when the Army band began to play and those three magic garage doors simultaneously began to open, I broke down into tears.

I cried as the nearly 200 soldiers disembarked the buses that transported them from Eielson as the crowd erupted in cheers and the families burst into applause. I wept as the soldiers made their formation on the far side of the room, and I sobbed as they regally marched across that hangar-like area to their place in front of us. And when their commander released them to their families, I broke down.

Soldiers sprinted toward us, frantically searching for their families, and in the crowd, I just couldn't see my husband. He was-

n't in the very front, he wasn't in the very back, he wasn't near his old commander, he wasn't near anyone else I knew.

I was starting to panic, when all of a sudden, two soldiers cleared my path of vision and for the first time, I spotted him. I literally lost my breath. My heart fluttered the way it did the first time I met my husband, and I felt just like that 18-year-old girl again as we made eye contact for the first time. My heart dropped, and my husband beamed.

I've never run so fast with a child in my arms in my entire mommy life. I had tunnel vision as I trotted toward the man of my dreams and flung my one arm around his neck as he embraced the two of us with the biggest smile I've ever seen from a man in uniform.

He held us tight, told me through giant smiling teeth that he loved me and missed me, and then pulled away to look down at his son for the first time since he was 11 days old. And in an act that I'm positive must have been from God, Connor looked up at his daddy and smiled as if Matt had been a physical part of his life for all eight months.

I cried. Then I laughed. Then I smiled. Then I shed another tear.

We hugged, we kissed, we stared at the beautiful life we had created together. And when it was all said and done and our run-leap-hug maneuver was complete, we walked out of that AHA, hand in hand, with our worlds once again connected and our love once again in tangible form.

There's no more counting down the days "until they come home." My hero is home, and my life is once again complete.

There was nothing — and I mean absolutely nothing — more special than driving with my husband home from the AHA to our house. We held hands the whole way, and at every stoplight and stop sign we came to, we took the brief pause to kiss passionately and just stare into longing eyes that hadn't caught glimpses of each other for eight entire months.

Butterflies swarmed my stomach, and I just couldn't stop smiling as my husband squeezed my hand three times and mouthed the words "I love you" across the darkness of our Corolla. Everything felt surreal, and I just couldn't believe that it was really my Matt sitting across the way.

BEHIND THE BLUE-STAR BANNER

When we reached the house, Matt came to my side of the car and opened the door, and then, as I grabbed some of his bags and CJ's diaper bag, he leaned in and picked up his son in his car seat for the first time since he had taken him home from the hospital eight months earlier.

Gently, almost too carefully, Matt carried CJ into the house, and when he pulled back the navy Arctic carrier cover that protected Connor's face from the frost of Fairbanks, CJ instantly peered out and into his daddy's eyes and met them with a smile.

Matt lifted him out of the carrier and together, they played on the family room floor for nearly an hour — laughing, falling, standing, swinging — as I stalked them with both a video camera and digital camera to capture the moment.

You could see it in his eyes — CJ knew who his daddy was.

MY HUBBY IS HOME!
December 10, 2006

To all our closest friends and family,

I know I promised no more mass e-mails, well, ever, but I'm breaking the rules because my husband is home from Iraq!!!

Matt returned from the longest deployment on the face of the earth on Tuesday night, and we have been enjoying the most amazing family time ever! Check out my column about our homecoming at www.news-miner.com. (Side note: Four different people have asked me why I'm ending my column now. Did I somehow forget to mention the title of my column? It's called "Until They Come Home." That means I write until they come home. They're home. I'm done. I'm not starting a column called "Now That He's Back" anytime soon.)

Many of you have sent e-mails asking how Matt is doing, how Connor is doing with Matt and how Matt is doing with Connor. In an act of God, Connor took to Matt instantly, as if he'd always been around. They played together all night his first night home, and they chummed around all day long the following day. Connor is loving having two playmates in the house instead of just one tired Mommy playmate, and he doesn't even flinch when I hand him to Matt. All day yesterday he was even reaching his arms out to Matt when I was holding him. Of course, Daddy cheats and

REUNION

gives him treats to win over his affection, so I don't let my feelings get hurt when Connor wants to go to Daddy. Matt had to buy his love in veggie puffs and afternoon snacks. I earned it in emergency room visits and sleepless nights.

I joke, but Matt is really doing so well with CJ. He's such a natural dad and so good with him. They roughhouse between naps and "walk" through the house. They play patty cake on the floor and airplane in the sky. CJ lets Matt put him down for all his naps, and even smiles when Matt changes his diapers, which, you know, increases Matt's Daddy rating by about 500 points. (Hey, I have changed six to eight diapers a day for more than 240 days, or anywhere between 1,440 and 1,920 diapers. I don't feel bad about handing off the duty for a few days, so don't start pulling out the "Poor Matt, he just came home from Iraq and Michelle is already putting him on diaper duty." After battling insurgents for 483 days, diaper duty is like a privilege! Really, I'm honoring him. I wouldn't want him to feel useless upon returning home!)

And Matt, well, he is the same old Matt — more aware, more outgoing and more adventurous in his food choices (he eats pineapple now! Where was he on that one during pregnancy?!) — but the same fun, adorable, chiding, amazing man I said goodbye to 16 months ago. He's just a little more tired from a 12-hour time zone change and a five-day flight home with little sleep, but I think he's finally starting to get on a regular schedule. He slept until 4 a.m. this morning, which is an improvement over the 2 a.m. "Let's go watch a movie! Come play! Come play!" wakeup calls I've gotten the last three nights in a row.

But really, I don't care. We've had so much fun, and I absolutely love that I can wake up to my husband at 2 a.m. and get dragged out of bed to go watch another episode of CSI or Smallville. My heart is healed, and my family is whole. I really cannot remember a happier week in my entire life.

Thank you so much for all your support, prayers and encouragement over the last 16 months, for both of us. You have been such a source of strength. God bless you, and enjoy your families. You have no idea just how long you will get to enjoy that precious, precious time. Make the most of it.

Much love,
Matt, Michelle and CJ

BEHIND THE BLUE-STAR BANNER

Matt's reintegration with our family actually played out much more smoothly than I had imagined. I'd attended briefs upon briefs that told me that he would be withdrawn, tired and overwhelmed when he came home — and I did see shadows of those things — but for the most part, Matt jumped right back into the everyday routine with pizzazz and style. He didn't miss a beat. And although I tried not to pile everything on him at once, he insisted on changing diapers and being a part of bath time and helping prepare meals again. He even made me attend a girls-night-only function while he watched CJ.

"I need some alone father-son time," he told me. "And you need some time by yourself after 16 months of deployment."

When I walked back into our house after only two hours away, CJ was lying on the floor screeching and giggling as Matt was pretending to bite and tickle his toes. It was the most beautiful sight I'd ever seen.

We had officially become a family again, and everything in my world just felt right.

Until They Come Home
December 15, 2006

As I sit down to write this, my very last deployment column for the Fairbanks Daily News-Miner, *my husband is curled up with our beagle, napping on the living room floor, and my son is soundly sleeping, swaddled safely in his crib. My bedroom is decorated with Army Combat Uniforms, and my closet reeks of sweaty desert boots.*

The only light glows from the Christmas tree we decorated the day after Matt returned from Iraq, and the only sounds spring from the hum of the overloaded washing machine and the drone of the family room television, blaring a program on a channel I haven't checked out for 16-plus months.

And as I collect another camelback and clean another sand-filled carrying case, I can't help but think to myself, "This is the way a home should look at Christmastime."

There are no blue-star banners to decorate my door this Christmas, no "Half my heart is in Iraq" stickers to ornament my car. There are no picture albums poised to peruse during those sessions of holiday blues, no "All I Want for Christmas is You" songs set to resound in my car's CD player.

It's only video cameras and "I'll Be Home for Christmas" this year.

What an incredible gift.

With my husband back home and our precious son in our arms, I can't help but reflect on a year that has tested me, tried me, trounced me and, most of all, taught me.

This year has taught me the value of friendship, the value of faith, the value of family and the value of service. It's taught me that soldiers are selfless heroes, and God — thank God — is in control.

But maybe most of all, this year has taught me the value of pure, inconvenient, until-death-do-us-part real love.

Yes, on the other side of a 16-month deployment, my husband and I are both different people. But our marriage is still very much the same. It's the same wonderful relationship that makes me sing in the shower, smile in the streets and tell anyone who will listen that there is such a thing as a soul mate. Because I've found him.

Matt may eat pineapple and Diet Pepsi now, and he may occasionally swerve off the road to miss pretend IEDs and invisible roadside bombs — I mean, really, can you think of a bigger terrorist target than Fairbanks, Alaska? — but in the end, he's still that same man I married almost three years ago.

He's still the same man who sings songs when I'm sad and makes me dance when I'm down.

He's still the same man who tackles me when I'm busy and tickles me when I'm not.

He's still the man who changes his clothes four times a day and offers to wash the laundry four times a week.

And he's still the man who supports me on the home front every single day. Only now, he's added "amazing father" and "outstanding soldier" to his list of incredibly attractive qualities.

To the community, thank you for your never-ending, diehard support of this awesome man and the entire 172nd Stryker brigade during this deployment. To Fort Wainwright, thank you for your compassionate care for the families left at home. To the returning soldiers, thank you for your incredible work and selfless sacrifices. To your families, thank you for your positive attitudes and constant source of strength.

And to my husband, my best friend and my greatest hero of

all, thank you for your service. Thank you for your sacrifice. And thank you for your love. It is that kind of love that inspires me to be the kind of woman who could ever deserve a man like you.

Welcome home.

ABOUT THE AUTHOR

An experienced writer, columnist, public speaker and editor in chief, *Behind the Blue-Star Banner* is Michelle Cuthrell's first full-length book.

She graduated from Ithaca College in 2004 with a degree in journalism and a penchant for the personal. After working as a part-time reporter at the *Ithaca Journal*, she soon found her heart in writing about her own life experiences. She moved with her husband to Fort Wainwright, Alaska, in January 2005, and immediately began composing bi-weekly travel columns about the Last Frontier for her hometown Ohio newspaper, *The Vandalia Drummer News*.

When her husband deployed to Iraq in August 2005, she used the opportunity to switch her focus from travel to trials. She began working as a cameraperson and then a features reporter at the NBC affiliate television station in Fairbanks, KTVF Channel 11, where she reported, edited and presented feature stories involving the military community.

Between October 2005 and December 2006, Michelle composed a weekly column titled "Until They Come Home" for the *Fairbanks Daily News-Miner* and the military newspaper *The Alaska Post* about her personal experiences as a military wife dealing with deployment on the home front.

Letters to the editor of both papers called her columns "refreshing," "honest" and "authentic." One writer commented, "We need more Michelles during these hard times."

This kind of rapport in her local community opened the doors in 2006 for Michelle to speak publicly. Between January and October, Michelle served as the guest speaker for Fort Wainwright Family Readiness Groups — a support network of military spouses who meet monthly throughout deployment — as the keynote speaker for the Fairbanks chapter of Rotary Club International and on other occasions around town.

She was interviewed on and appeared in such media as the *CBS Radio News*, the *Army Times* and CNN's *Anderson Cooper 360,* as well as various mothering and military Web sites. Motivational speaker and author Ellie Kay even used an excerpt of Mi-

ABOUT THE AUTHOR

chelle's book in her newest edition of her best-selling book, *Heroes at Home*.

Michelle, her husband and their energetic 2-year-old son currently reside in Western Washington, where Michelle serves as the editor in chief of Good Catch Publishing, and Matt continues to serve with the U.S. Army at Fort Lewis.

For more information about bulk ordering
Behind the Blue-Star Banner
or booking Michelle Cuthrell for your next workshop,
motivational event or conference,
please check out www.behindthebluestarbanner.com,
or e-mail behindthebluestarbanner@gmail.com.

GOOD CATCH
PUBLISHING

www.goodcatchpublishing.com